Praise fo

"In this deep dive into obsession, Jeff Smoo~ ~ research and analysis with what motivates him and other solo climb~~ ~ a thought-provoking, compelling book."

—Sharon Wood, author of *Rising* and first
North American woman to summit Everest

"A rare inside view of solo climbing by someone who practiced it and articulates the risks, rewards, and mindset required to succeed at this very dangerous game. Gripping, insightful, highly recommended."

—Nicholas O'Connell, author of *The Storms of Denali*
and founder of www.thewritersworkshop.net

"With insight and compassion, Jeff Smoot has done an exceptional job of capturing the complex psychology behind one of the least understood veins of the climbing experience."

—Geoff Powter, clinical psychologist and author
of *Strange and Dangerous Dreams and Inner Ranges*

"In *All and Nothing*, Jeff Smoot thrillingly follows a clear thread from climbing trees to extreme rock solos to the GoPro generation, delving deeply into the sociology, psychology, and spirituality of free soloing."

—Paul Pritchard, author of *The Mountain Path*

"Jeff Smoot's timely book explores the mystique of free soloing, introducing a fascinating cast of characters across cultures and generations. Weaving in his personal experiences, he analyzes the allure of the pursuit and the psyches of the climbers who cannot resist this dangerous sport. Strikingly honest and intensively researched, *All and Nothing* is a gripping, often disturbing read."

—Maria Coffey, author of *Where the Mountain Casts Its Shadow*

"Meticulously researched and splendidly written, *All and Nothing* is captivating. Read this book, and you'll have a deeper understanding of not just free soloing, but the call of adventure itself."

—Sir Chris Bonington

All and Nothing

Inside Free Soloing

JEFF SMOOT

MOUNTAINEERS
BOOKS

MOUNTAINEERS BOOKS is dedicated to the exploration, preservation, and enjoyment of outdoor and wilderness areas. www.mountaineersbooks.org

1001 SW Klickitat Way, Suite 201, Seattle, WA 98134
800.553.4453, www.mountaineersbooks.org

Mountaineers Books and its colophon are registered trademarks of The Mountaineers organization.

Printed in South Korea
Distributed in the United Kingdom by Cordee, www.cordee.co.uk

25 24 23 22   1 2 3 4 5

Copyeditor: Laura Lancaster
Design and layout: Jen Grable
Cover photograph and frontispiece: *Brad Gobright free soloing* Blues Riff *(5.11c), Tuolumne Meadows, Yosemite National Park* (Photo by Dan Krauss)

Library of Congress Cataloging-in-Publication Data is on file at https://lccn.loc.gov/2022013929. The ebook record is available at https://lccn.loc.gov/2022013930.

Mountaineers Books titles may be purchased for corporate, educational, or other promotional sales, and our authors are available for a wide range of events. For information on special discounts or booking an author, contact our customer service at 800-553-4453 or mbooks@mountaineersbooks.org.

DISCLAIMER: Rock climbing is a dangerous sport that generally should not be attempted without a rope, proper safety gear, and a competent belayer. The author has made every effort to provide an honest and accurate accounting of the people, places, and events related to free soloing and other high-risk sports as researched and experienced by him. This book should not be viewed as a guide to or promotion of those activities. Neither the author nor the publisher are responsible for how readers interpret these accounts.

Printed on FSC®-certified materials

ISBN (paperback): 978-1-68051-332-5
ISBN (ebook): 978-1-68051-333-2

An independent nonprofit publisher since 1960

TO MY DAD—
FOR TRUSTING WHAT I WAS DOING UP THERE
AND NOT MAKING ME COME DOWN

CONTENTS

Hazel Findlay free soloing Diagonal *(5.8), Dinas Mot, Wales* (Photo by Paul Diffley, Hot Aches Productions)

PART III: OVER THE DREAMJUNK WASTELAND

PART IV: UNDER THE INFLUENCE

PART V: WE'LL QUIT WHEN WE'RE DEAD

CONCLUSIVE

Pray heed the tale of John E. Dope,
Who always climbed without a rope;
Over cliff and crag he lithely sped,
He slipped just once—
But still he's dead.

—Bill Cox, *The Mountaineer*, 1939

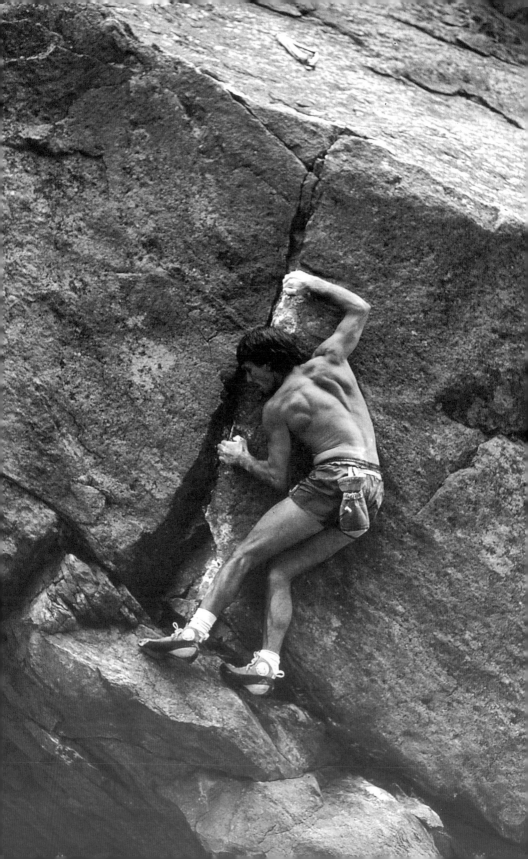

A PIVOTAL MOMENT

The fear sank in as I started toward the wall. *You shouldn't do this,* said an internal voice. *What if you fall?* Ignoring it, I left the trail and scrambled up a talus slope. The shaded block of granite cut like a knife's edge through the sharp afternoon sunlight. I looked down and focused on treading my way through the boulders.

When I reached the base of the wall, my heart was pounding so hard I could hear it. I sat down on a boulder, took several deep breaths, and tried to calm myself. The voice was screaming: *Don't do it!* Inhaling all the negative thoughts racing through my mind, I forcibly exhaled until they dissipated— until my mind was as still as the granite itself.

Negative thoughts always flooded my mind when I free soloed a route that scared me, thoughts about what could go wrong—a hold breaking, a foot slipping, botching a sequence, losing control. I'd fall, hit the ground, and end up in the hospital if I was lucky. Climbers fall all the time. I've hit the ground twice, both times while using a rope and protection. The second fall, from 30 feet, required knee surgery. But such incidents are anomalies for climbers

Bob Horan free soloing Horangutan *(5.12a), Eldorado Canyon* (Photo by Jeff Smoot)

who rope up, place protection, and are belayed by a partner—climbers who play it safe.

Free soloing is different. Falling off means hitting something, whether a ledge or the ground, and likely being seriously injured or killed. Even if I fell and lived, a rescue would be unlikely as I often did not tell anyone where I was going or what I was doing. My only companion was the flood of negative thoughts racing through my mind, eliciting doubt and fear.

On these outings, which were becoming more frequent, mild anxiety would build to near-panic the closer I came to going through with it—a tingling on my skin, shiver down my spine, churning in my gut. Some days I turned around at the base of the cliff. Other days I didn't even get out of the car. Today was not one of those days.

I picked up my rock shoes and inspected them, spitting on the soles and then rubbing them on my shorts until they were perfectly clean and dry. I tied on my chalk bag and approached the wall, looking up at the fingertip-thin crack that shot straight up to the lip of an overhang. I closed my eyes and visualized myself flowing through the sequence, my hands pantomiming every move of the climb. *You can do this,* my inner voice reassured me. *It will be perfect.* I chalked up and started to climb.

I was attempting to solo a 5.12 route—thin, overhanging, and harder than anything I'd ever climbed without a rope. At the time, I was traveling with world-class climbers who were working on some of the hardest rock climbs ever attempted, establishing hard new routes rated 5.13, the top of the scale in the US in the mid-1980s. I was in the best shape of my life, and challenging routes were starting to seem like no big deal. Compared to some of the routes I'd been climbing with ropes, this little 5.12 didn't seem that hard. The challenge was a mental one. I had never soloed anything that hard in my life.

I had started free soloing easy routes years before. At first it was because I lacked a partner, but, as my skills improved, I began purposefully soloing more difficult climbs, higher off the ground. Still, I stuck to routes well within my comfort zone. Nothing bad happened, so I kept upping the game.

Then one day, while climbing with Peter Croft, one of the most accomplished free soloists in the world, something clicked. We were soloing laps on a 600-foot wall near Leavenworth, Washington, when Croft started up behind me, climbing directly below me as I pulled through a 5.10 crux. If I had fallen,

I would have knocked him off the wall. My ego swelled. If Peter Croft had that much confidence in my ability, I must be pretty good.

That afternoon I ran into some friends who were going to try an overhanging crack that seemed to spit everybody off. I'd tried it a few times with a toprope belay and failed miserably. This time, when I fell off, I hung on the rope and played around with the moves until I figured out a sequence. On my next try, I pulled it off.

"Pretty easy for a 5.12," I told my friends, bragging a little.

"You made it look easy," one of them said. "You could solo it."

I wished he hadn't said that, but it was too late—the seed had been planted. That night, I drew a diagram of the crack in my journal and wrote detailed notes describing each jam, each foothold, each sequence of moves. It became an obsession. *You could solo it* became *You will*.

The route was short, but if I fell off at the crux, I'd fall 30 feet and either land on my back and smash my head on the sharp granite blocks below or swing out of control and hit the ground face-first. Young and full of myself, I was willing to take that chance.

I put three fingers into the crack up to the second joint, wrenched them tight to lock them in place, set my feet on tiny edges, and pulled off the ground. After several moves, the crack narrowed and bottomed out, allowing me to slot in only two fingers up to the first joint. Those four fingertips wedged precariously in the shallow crack held my body weight; the meager footholds offered little more than leverage against the pull of gravity. Focusing intently on each move, I made sure my fingers were locked in, my feet placed as securely as possible before making the next move. A thought crossed my mind: *You could climb down from here if you wanted to.* Then another: *Once you make the next move, you can't*, but I dismissed them.

I reached my left hand high and stuck my index and middle fingers as far as I could into a slot, wrenching them tight to lock them in. Then I brought my right hand up to a higher slot that I could jam in using a thumbs-up position, with my ring and little fingers barely in the crack. Hanging off two fingers of my right hand, I pulled my left hand out of the crack and turned it over, stuffing my pinkie and ring finger in as far as possible and wrenching them tight. At precisely that moment, both of my feet slipped off the wall.

My feet were flying away from the rock, my body swinging like a pendulum, threatening to pull me off-balance and wrench my fingers from the crack. Instead of feeling a jolt of adrenaline or fear, I was simply aware that I needed to act quickly. I instinctively torqued harder to keep my fingers locked in, and tightened my arm and core muscles to slow my swing. I looked down, half-expecting to be catapulted into the air and dropped violently onto the rocks below, but my fingers remained firmly wedged in the crack.

As I rocked back toward the wall, I spotted the footholds, each as thin and small as the short edge of a ruler. At the perigee of my swing, feeling a sensation of weightlessness, I pressed the toes of my rock shoes gingerly onto the holds and shifted my weight slightly downward. My feet stuck.

I continued upward as if nothing had happened, letting go briefly with my right hand and inserting my pinkie and ring finger into the slot and wrenching them tight, preparing to reach up to a bomber jam. Then my feet cut loose again.

As I swung outward from the wall, I knew I was probably going to fall. Still, I felt only a sense of calm detachment, as if I were in a dream, a disinterested observer watching to see what would happen. Everything stood out in sharp relief: the red and orange splotches of lichen on the rock, the jagged shadows etched into the talus blocks below me, the smell of sage, dust, and chalk hanging in the air. I felt a bead of sweat running down the side of my face.

As my body rocketed away from the wall, my fingers shifted in the crack, and the sharp edge tore into my pinkie finger like a scalpel, drawing blood. The sudden stab of pain brought my mind sharply into focus. I tightened my grip, fighting to hang on. My feet swung out over the talus and then back toward the rock. I was overgripping, swinging too fast, losing control. *You won't be able to stick your feet on those tiny holds*, the voice told me. *If you don't stick those footholds, you're fucked.*

There was no time to dwell on the situation. I focused exclusively on what I had to do. If I could stick my toes on those footholds, I could hang on, and if I could hang on, I could make the next move. I had one chance. Letting go was not an option.

My feet hit the footholds and stuck. I held on, made the next move, and then pressed myself over the lip of the overhang. I paused briefly on the steep slab to smell the blood on my finger. Then I licked it off, wiped my finger on my shorts, chalked up, and picked my way carefully to the top of the wall.

At the top, I pulled onto the ledge in a daze and sat down. Looking down at the talus blocks, I felt sick. The stark reality of what I had just done overwhelmed me. I had gotten away with something, barely pulled it off. I realized, with absolute clarity, that if I didn't quit free soloing, I was going to end up dead at the bottom of a cliff.

INTRODUCTION

"ARE YOU CRAZY?"

Humans have a primal fear of falling from high places. We are hardwired to avoid situations where we could fall to our deaths—when fear is punctuated with a jolt of adrenaline, it's time to step back. This is why it's such a thrill to ride the elevator to the top of the Empire State Building, walk across the Golden Gate Bridge, or creep up to the brink of Beachy Head. Of course, some people aren't content to stand behind the railing enjoying the view; they want to edge closer, to feel the pull of the void.

In 2012, American skydiver Gary Connery jumped out of an airplane without a parachute and landed safely using a wingsuit. In 2016, Luke Aikins jumped without a parachute or wingsuit from a plane at an altitude of 25,000 feet and landed safely in a specially designed net. That same year, New Zealand free diver William Trubridge dove to a depth of 334 feet without the use of fins or an air tank or regulator, a discipline that requires intense mental focus. And in 2017, American rock climber Alex Honnold climbed the *Freerider* route on El Capitan, an iconic 3000-foot granite wall with a crux pitch rated 5.13a on the Yosemite Decimal Scale, in much the same way—without a rope or protective gear, just his hands, feet, rock shoes, and a chalk bag.

Wolfgang Gullich free soloing Separate Reality *(5.11d), Yosemite Valley* (Photo by Heinz Zak)

Honnold's climb wasn't the first big-wall free solo. Alexander Huber had free soloed the 1700-foot, 5.12a *Brandler-Hasse Direttissima* in the Italian Dolomites in 2002; Austrian climber Hansjörg Auer had free soloed a 2700-foot 5.12c route called *Via Attraverso il Pesce* in the Italian Dolomites in 2007; and, in February 2015, Brette Harrington had free soloed a 2500-foot 5.11a route called *Chiaro di Luna* on Aguja Saint Exupery in Patagonia. It also wasn't the hardest free solo ever done. Huber had free soloed a 5.14a route called *Kommunist* at Austria's Schleierwasserfall in 2004, and in 2008, Scottish climber Dave MacLeod had free soloed a route called *Darwin Dixit* rated 5.14b at Margalef, Spain.

What made Honnold's solo of *Freerider* so noteworthy was the combination of the two—height and difficulty—a 3000-foot wall with continuously difficult climbing and a 5.13 crux 2000 feet off the ground. That, and the fact that it was the subject of an Academy Award–winning documentary, *Free Solo*, allowing everyone to vicariously experience that primal fear: if Honnold slipped just once, he would die.

WHEN SOMEONE FINDS OUT I'M a rock climber, they usually want to know my take on *Free Solo*.

Then they ask: "You don't *do that*, do you?"

"Yes, I do," I reply.

"Why would anybody *do that*?" they wonder. "Are you *crazy*?"

Most free soloists have had similar exchanges, been asked to justify their penchant for climbing without a rope. Some say they love the challenge of pitting themselves against nature; others say it's the adrenaline rush they get while pushing themselves to their limit, or the dopamine high that follows. Still others say it's the quasi-religious, Zen-like quality of pure focus they experience while climbing, of being in "flow," in the "zone," or "one with the rock." Free soloing makes them feel part of a great cosmic unity of man and stone, grooving on the authentic experience realized only in that moment between life and death when all ego disappears, where they gain a fleeting, transcendental insight into some fundamental truth of life, or some such bullshit.

Some climbers don't have a "why," and instead say, "Why not?" or "Because you can't." They won't say it's the only thing that makes them happy, that the mundanity of "normal" life depresses them, or that the impulse to climb rocks without a rope because they *want to, have to,* no matter who might suffer, is the strongest one in their life. Nor will they admit that they are addicted to risk, compulsively putting themselves in perilous situations, lacking the control to stop even when they know better. And they won't tell you they do it because they are self-centered assholes, although some of them may be.

Mark Twight, a prolific free soloist and extreme alpinist, thinks "why" is the wrong question entirely; he says we should be asking "not why, but *how*?" As in, how can we overcome our fear of death and enter a state of mind so focused that we not only survive a life-threatening ordeal but enjoy it?

Others, like John Long, longtime free soloist and editor of *The High Lonesome: Epic Solo Climbing Stories*, question the value of even asking the question. "There is no objective truth to any judgment per soloing, though some pronouncements sound better to our rational mind than others," wrote Long. "But I do think that trying to derive some definitive statement about what soloing is, or should be, or can be, or shouldn't be, is expecting too much of our quantitative skills."

American psychologist Ernest Becker wrote about a professor of medieval history who had confessed that "the more he learned about the period, the less he was prepared to say [anything] about it." Becker felt this sentiment also applied to his writing exploring the general theory of mental illness, especially when he was not himself a psychiatrist. "Why," he asked, "should someone try to rake this area over again, in what can only be a superficial and simple-minded way?" to which he answered:

> What I would like to do in these few pages is to run the risk of simple-mindedness in order to make some dent in the unintended imbecility brought about by specialization and its mountains of fact. Even if I succeed only poorly, it seems like a worthwhile barter . . . someone has to be willing to play the fool in order to relieve the general myopia.

Like Becker, I find myself wondering if I should be taking on the messy subject of free soloing, a practice that is perceived by many as "insane," "suicidal," or "a death wish" but defended by its proponents as a perfectly sane, rational, life-affirming activity, a subject that is so complex, with participants whose motives are so diverse and ineffable, that even one of the reigning experts believes defining it may very well be impossible.

Despite the inevitable criticism that such a work will engender, I am willing to play the fool. This book is my answer to those who ask, "Are you crazy?"

AT THE RISK OF BEING simple-minded—of exceeding my quantitative skills, as Long put it—I will try in these pages to make a dent in our collective understanding of free soloing by exploring the phenomenon through a variety of lenses (sociological, psychological, spiritual, psychotropical, and personal) to discover what drives some climbers to do something most people, including many accomplished climbers, consider unimaginably dangerous. Even writing about free soloing seems dangerous. Because of how films and magazine articles influenced me to take up free soloing, I worry that the film *Free Solo* and other media portrayals, possibly including this book, will inspire impressionable young climbers.

Back when I started climbing in the 1970s, free soloing was a fringe activity; only a few climbers did it, and you didn't hear a lot about it except occasionally around the campfire or perhaps briefly in a climbing magazine. Mainstream media did not generally report on it, and, except for a few films and televised specials, people only saw free soloists in person at rock climbing destinations like Yosemite, Joshua Tree, or Eldorado Canyon. Then in 1981, *Backpacker* magazine published "The Only Blasphemy," an essay recounting John Long's near-death experience while free soloing at Joshua Tree National Monument (now a national park) with John Bachar.

Soon after, free soloing caught the attention of mainstream media. Bachar, the hero of Long's story, was featured in beautifully photographed rock-shoe advertisements, on magazine covers, and soloing difficult routes in Yosemite National Park and Joshua Tree. Articles about Bachar appeared in *Life*, *Newsweek*, *Rolling Stone*, and *People* magazines. He was featured on the TV show *That's Incredible* and starred in a Gillette razor commercial. Free soloing briefly entered the cultural consciousness and, for the most part, people thought it was crazy. Bachar disagreed. "People who say I'm crazy don't have a clue to what's going on," he told *People* magazine. "To me, hanging off my arms at three hundred feet feels normal."

Witnessing Bachar climb hard routes without a rope, seeing him on TV and the covers of magazines, and reading about him inspired me to start free soloing in earnest. A loner by nature with complex inadequacy issues, I was instantly drawn to his style of climbing, and I was not alone. Everywhere I went, people—mostly men in their late teens and early twenties—were free soloing. We believed that, if we had sufficient resolve to train hard, get strong, hone our technique, and condition our minds to shut out all distractions, we could dare to enter Bachar's realm, to experience the same sense of mastery he evoked. We could, if we were sufficiently inspired, travel to Yosemite or Joshua Tree ourselves and solo the same routes he did. We could emulate our hero. We, too, could be like gods.

Bachar, of course, didn't inspire the average reader of *People* magazine to take up unroped rock climbing. To people who did not climb, free soloing remained, at best, an obscure fringe activity. But in 2018, *Free Solo*, the Academy Award–winning documentary filmed and co-directed by Jimmy Chin and Elizabeth Chai Vasarhelyi, was released and Alex Honnold became a household name. You no longer have to explain what free soloing is. It's hip, cool, part of popular culture. It's also dangerous as hell.

Some free soloists will tell you climbing without a rope isn't really that dangerous; that driving on the freeway is statistically more dangerous than free soloing. And while very few free soloists fall, when they do, the results are predictable. Still, it is hard to name more than a handful of climbers who have died while free soloing. Many free soloists have died, sure, but mostly from other causes—a wingsuit accident, a rogue wave, a car crash, falling down the stairs at home—or, quite often, scrambling on easy ground while approaching or descending a route.

Then, in 2019, there was an uptick in deaths attributed to free soloing. As *Rock and Ice* magazine reported that July in "Broken Holds and Lost Lives: How Loose Rock and Free Soloing Ended Two Climbers' Lives," Robert Dergay, a forty-eight-year-old experienced climber, fell and died in May while free soloing an "easy" route in Colorado's Eldorado Canyon. Dergay's death was followed by that of Austin Howell, thirty-one, who regularly soloed difficult routes and was working on a film about his exploits, when he fell off a difficult route on Shortoff Mountain in North Carolina. And then there was Elijah Baldwin, a thirteen-year-old who, while visiting Snow Canyon State Park in Utah with his family, died after falling an estimated 75 to 100 feet climbing alone and unroped on technical terrain. Was this uptick a statistical anomaly, or had the film *Free Solo* and other media representations led to an increase in free soloing fatalities?

I CAN SAY FROM EXPERIENCE that there's nothing like nearly falling to your death to bring your life into sharp focus. The moment where my life hung from four fingertips jammed into a crack led me to reflect deeply on why I free soloed. Within a year, I got married, started a career, had a child, and quit climbing altogether—well, sort of. It's hard to quit. It gnaws at you.

John Bachar once said, "I'm going to give all I've got for climbing, and that's what I'm going to do for the rest of my life." And he was right. In 2009, he fell off a 5.10, a route well within his ability, at Mammoth Lakes, California, and died. His death left his teenage son fatherless.

It wasn't Bachar's first fall while free soloing. In 1976, he was lucky to walk away after falling off a 5.12a in Eldorado Canyon. A few years later, he barely pulled through while on-sight free soloing a 5.11 in Yosemite and later admitted, "I didn't feel good about it, like the rock let me get away with something." Despite those close calls, he kept soloing, going on to solo a 5.13 in Joshua Tree, a difficulty rating that had been the top of the scale only a decade earlier. Even though he never soloed anything that hard again, he kept at it, year after year.

I wondered what drove Bachar to continue soloing after his near-death experiences, even after the birth of his son, Tyrus, in 1996. But then again, I had started soloing once more just a few years after nearly falling off. And I kept at it even though I was married and had kids. I could wonder the same thing about myself: why?

I wonder the same thing about Alex Honnold and every other free solo-ist. What drives us? Fame, fortune, peer pressure, sponsorships? Are we crazy? Do we have a death wish? Or is it something else?

According to Mark Synnott, author of *The Impossible Climb*, Honnold decided soloing was cool after noticing that free-soloists were getting atten-tion from climbing magazines and being featured in popular videos. Honnold decided if he wanted to be a rock star, Synnott suggested, free soloing was the thing to do, but I think it's more complex than that. Yes, Honnold has become a star, but that isn't why he took up free soloing.

Leaving off free soloing for a moment, most climbers have trouble answering the question: Why do you climb? As Anthony Brandt wrote in the introduction to Edward Whymper's book, *Scrambles Amongst the Alps*, climbers "are famously inarticulate about their reasons for climbing."

If justifying climbing itself as a moral pursuit is so difficult for those who do it, what motivates climbers to forego a rope or safety equipment is even more puzzling. "If you have to ask, you'll never know," Brandt wrote. "The public, for the most part, has to ask."

PART I

It's the Ropes That Will Get You Killed

*"I know ways to get it across but it's too risky for me," I said.
"Too risky?" Angel laughed. "Ricardo, listen to yourself!
Look at what you're doing. Look where you're going. You love
risk. There is no other explanation."*
—Richard Grant, *God's Middle Finger*

At age thirteen, I was scrawny and emotionally troubled, not the least bit athletic, certainly not climber material. I could do five pull-ups on a good day and could run a mile without stopping—that was the extent of my athletic prowess. While other boys my age spent their lunch hour sexually harassing girls on the playground, I hid out in the library with the other outcasts, trying to avoid a gang who tormented me verbally when they could find me. The library seemed to be the one place they never looked.

One of my fellow outcasts, Dave, liked to search through *National Geographic* magazines for photos of Indigenous women wearing very little clothing. One day, having nothing better to do, I went along. But I soon lost interest in Dave's quest when I saw a picture of Jim Whittaker

A day's outing on the east face of Tibrogargan, Glasshouse Mountains, Queensland, Australia, August 1935 (Nancy Hodge Collection)

standing atop Mount Everest, posing heroically with his ice axe thrust upward into the gale, adorned by a small American flag. Digging farther through the stacks of *National Geographic* revealed more treasures: "Triumph on Everest," "Americans on Everest," "First Traverse of Everest," "We Climbed Utah's Skyscraper Rock," "Climbing Half Dome the Hard Way." I found books too: *Scrambles Amongst the Alps, The White Spider, Annapurna, The Challenge of Rainier*, thrilling tales of historic climbs in the Alps, life and death on the Eiger north face, early ascents and tragedies in the Himalaya, and the whole history of climbing on Mount Rainier, a glacier-draped mountain I could see from near my house.

Reading those articles and books and seeing the photos of those heroic men climbing lofty peaks and impossible faces filled me with a strange longing. My interest was beyond sparked—it exploded. I wanted, more than anything in the world, with every fiber of my being, to be a climber.

I made the mistake of telling Mark and Eric, two members of the gang, about my newfound desire. They caught up to me in the library and sat down, smirking maleficently.

"Whatcha reading there?" Mark asked.

"Yeah," Eric added, snatching the book away, "what's this?"

"Mount Everest?" Mark snorted. "What's this about?"

"Mountain climbing?" Eric retorted.

"Yeah, so?" I said.

"Are you going to climb Mount Everest?" Mark asked derisively.

"Sure, why not?" I said defensively.

"You can't be a mountain climber," Eric scoffed. "You have to be strong to climb mountains."

"Yeah," said Mark scornfully. "Look at your little arms. You can't even do one pull-up. *Ha, ha!*"

After that, everyone in their tribe would sneer at me when they passed me in the hallway.

"Look, it's the mountain climber. Good luck on Everest, fuck face!"

CHAPTER 1

A Way of Life

Climbing is as old as human history. With our prehensile limbs, humans were built for climbing, hanging, and swinging our way up trees and cliffs—even before we had ropes. So it's no surprise that for thousands of years humans have sought shelter in the mountains, living, hunting, foraging, and playing among cliffs, and burying their dead in seemingly inaccessible caves. And, sometimes, climbing—even unroped climbing on steep, exposed terrain—can be of such importance to a culture that it becomes a part of daily life.

One such place is the Wadi Rum region of southern Jordan, where inhabitants summited nearly all of the towering rock formations hundreds or even thousands of years ago. Names and directions are carved in the sandstone, and there are cairns and rock walls along the routes, often in places accessible only by exposed technical rock climbing. The first hunters to traverse the *Thamudic Route* on Jebel Rum, Kharajat, son of Sa'adan, and Jahfal, brother of Taym, carved their names on the rock more than two thousand years ago, making it the world's oldest-known rock climb.

There are numerous so-called Bedouin routes in the Wadi Rum, climbed by the Thamudic and Nabatean tribes who inhabited the region long before the Bedouins. These ancient hunters and herders usually climbed barefoot—sometimes while carrying an ibex, stray goat, or vessel of water—up or down massive, complex sandstone walls, often without the aid or protection of a rope. Because of their intricacy and difficulty, and the sheer exposure leading up thousand-foot-high cliffs, modern climbers rarely attempt these routes without ropes and equipment.

So it is perhaps not surprising that when European visitor St. John Armitage started following a Bedouin hunter up Jebel Rum in the 1950s, he turned back, describing the ascent as "hair raising . . . poised between heaven and hell. . . . Never again would I set foot upon those ghastly cliffs."

Armitage's wife, Sylvia, apparently had a keener sense of adventure; she and Charmain Longstaff, another Englishwoman who had been on the failed attempt, returned to try again. They persuaded a Bedouin named Sheikh Hamdan Amad al Zalabia to guide them to the summit. "Hamdan climbed with bare feet as surely as a mountain goat," Longstaff wrote in the *Ladies Alpine Club Journal*. She recalled, "It was very easy climbing, but it was very exposed. This made us feel tremednously clever and accomplished." They reached the summit in just two hours, a remarkably fast time, which impressed the guide. "You English women are as strong as men," Hamdan remarked.

English climber Tony Howard also recounted in 2015 in a blog post on *Cicerone* a time in 1984 that he and his partners were directed by locals to the top of Jebel Rum in the Wadi Rum. "That's the way to the top," the locals told them. "It's easy. . . . You won't need ropes." Howard and his climbing partners took a rope anyway, which was a wise decision as the first pitch of rock turned out to be 5.7 in difficulty. "Eventually," Howard recalled, "we continued up through steep, exposed cracks and chimneys, marveling at the Bedouin's ability to climb alone in such wild and exposed surroundings—and climb back down with an ibex on their back!" It was not without risk, though.

Howard later climbed a route on Jebel Khush Khashah where a Bedouin woman had fallen to her death while carrying water down from a cliffside spring.

A CLIMBING CULTURE ALSO EXISTED on St. Kilda, a remote island chain in the Outer Hebrides, nearly 50 miles off the northwest coast of Scotland. One visitor, J. Sands, who was stranded for months in 1877, described the storm-swept islands as "bounded on the north-east and south-west by enormous precipices that rise like walls out of the sea" in *Out of the World, or Life in St. Kilda*. For centuries, a small community of hardy, Gaelic-speaking people fished, herded, farmed, and climbed here. No one knows how they came to inhabit the islands, but how they survived there for so long, given the often-brutal conditions, is simple: they supplemented their diet of fish with the eggs and meat of the birds that frequented the cliffs around their home—especially fulmar, puffin, and northern gannet.

Although the "bird snatchers" (as the St. Kildans have been called) did use horsehair ropes to lower themselves hand over hand to raid the sea-cliff nests, they were well-known for their unroped climbing. As the scholar Martin Martin wrote in *A Late Voyage to St. Kilda* published in 1689 following his visit to St. Kilda, "The inhabitants, I must tell you, run no small danger in the quest of the fowls and eggs, insomuch that I fear it would be thought a hyperbole to relate the inaccessibleness, steepness, and height, of those formidable rocks which they venture to climb." Martin recalled watching two young men who climbed a cliff high above the sea to capture two hawks "in a few minutes, without any assistance at all." That is, without ropes or equipment.

According to Martin, the island's culture revolved around birds and climbing, and the people often discussed the nuances of climbing particular cliffs or the way a person had to contort his body in certain difficult places, as well as "the fatal end of several in the exercise of it." R. M. Barrington, who visited St. Kilda in 1883 to climb for sport, noted in his 1913 *Alpine Journal* article, "There is no part of the world, as far as I am aware, where the practical advantage of being a skilled cragsman was so well recognized. The chief topics of conversation in this out-of-the-way island are climbing and birds."

Climbing was so imbued in the local culture that it was a rite of passage for young men of the island to perform a stunt on the "Mistress Stone," a block spanning a gap near the top of a small sea stack visible from the village. "He is to stand on his left foot, having the one half of his sole over the rock, and then he draws the right foot further out to the left," Martin described it, "and in this posture bowing, he puts both his fists further out to the right foot." By performing these contortions, a young man proved his skill as a climber and his worthiness to take on a wife. One of the inhabitants urged Martin to perform the ritual himself. Martin declined. "I told him this performance would have a quite contrary effect upon me by robbing me both of my life and mistress at the same moment."

Sands, who visited the island nearly two centuries after Martin, was less hesitant, agreeing to join a group of men and boys climbing a sea stack to gather birds and eggs, writing:

All the men but two, who were left to take charge of the boat, ascended the cliff, and I was tempted to go along with them. . . . With the end of a rope round my waist, held by a man who preceded me, I clambered up such paths as one may see in a nightmare. I thought it best not to look too far ahead but to keep my attention fixed on the ground at my feet. Sometimes I was indebted to my guide for a pull-up some difficult bit, and I succeeded in reaching the top. The height was probably eight hundred feet—the highest rocks on this island being over a thousand.

On a trip to the island of Soa to catch fulmar, Sands recalled the island's inhabitants' comfort with the terrain: "An old man called MacRuaridh or the Son of Rory acts as my guide, and although he totters on level ground, he goes up the hill without any difficulty." Upon reaching the top of the cliff, his guide became restless. "He soon grew tired of doing nothing, and began to peer over the edge in search of young fulmars, some of which he saw on a cliff adjacent, and caught." On a later excursion, Sands watched all the inhabitants head down the cliffs to pluck grass for their cattle. "I saw the women lying on the narrow sloping ledges on the face of the rocks," he wrote. "A false step, and they would have fallen into the sea, hundreds of feet below, or been mangled on the projecting crags."

Despite their skill, accidents were not uncommon. Near the end of his stay, Sands encountered one of the island's inhabitants sitting at a cliff edge and looking down grimly.

"Who is below?" Sands asked.

"Neil," the man answered.

"Is he far down?"

"Far—far," the man replied.

As he stood there, Sands could hear the fallen climber's voice calling from far below. "It is a dreadful trade," Sands concluded. But to the St. Kildans, climbing was no leisure sport; it was critical to their survival.

ON THE ISLAND OF RAPA NUI (also known as Easter Island) in the southeastern Pacific Ocean, *Tagata Manu*—leaders known as the "Birdmen"—were selected through a ceremonial competition that included rock climbing. This ritual, which originated sometime after AD 1600, replaced clan warfare as a way to select tribal leaders, perhaps on the assumption that fewer lives would be lost. It was not always so.

Each spring, select clan chiefs appointed one or two *Hopu Manu*, proxy warriors who had trained for years, to compete in the *Tagata Manu* ritual. The ritual began at Orongo, a ceremonial village on the knife-edged rim of the Ranu Kao caldera overlooking three rocky islets. At the signal, the *Hopu Manu* descended a steep cliff of loose volcanic rock to the shore 1000 feet below. Not everyone made it. The warriors who survived then swam across nearly a mile of shark-infested ocean currents to the craggy islet of Motu Nui to await the arrival of the *Manu Tara*, or sooty tern, the sacred bird of the Rapanui. As if the risk of falling off a cliff, drowning in the sea, or being eaten by a shark was not enough, the *Hopu* had to be wary of other competitors who might steal their food or even kill them.

When the *Manu Tara* arrived, sometimes weeks later, the *Hopu* who was the first to gather an egg would race to the top of a cliff and shout, "*Ka varu te puoko!*" or "Shave your head!" His chief would then remove all the hair from his head as the warrior swam back to the island, free soloed up the sea cliff with the egg in a special headband, and presented the intact egg to his chief. The chief would be appointed the new *Tagata Manu*, a sacred person considered the living embodiment of the cult's fertility god. He would live in sage-like isolation for a year, and his clan would rule over the other clans until the next Birdman was selected. Some years, nearly all of the *Hopu* died, either from drowning, shark attacks, or falling off the cliffs.

The *Tagata Manu* ritual died out after ships arrived from Peru in 1862, and the invaders captured thousands of Rapanui, including the king, his son, and the ritual priests, and forced them into slavery. Christian missionaries arrived soon after and put an end to what remained of Rapanui culture.

ON AUGUST 15, 1865, a group of mercenaries brought in by white settlers attacked a Yahi summer village in present-day Northern California and killed every American Indian in sight. The survivors disappeared into the inhospitable, rocky landscape, so fearful for their lives that they left their dead behind.

The Yahi, or Yahi Yana, were one of several tribes that had lived in the region for thousands of years. But when gold was discovered at Sutter's Mill, northeast of present-day Sacramento, in 1848, the number of white settlers in the territory exploded and the Yahi were forced to retreat to less hospitable landscapes. Deprived of their customary resources, the tribe stole from the settlers and raided their stock to survive. Predictably, the settlers responded by trying to exterminate them.

At first, the settlers assumed the 1865 massacre had successfully eradicated the Yahi. But then in 1870, a party tracking a missing cow discovered a small band of Yahi living in a cave in a remote canyon. They killed them all, or so they thought—strangely, the bodies disappeared without a trace.

In the early morning of August 29, 1911, a half-starved, nearly naked American Indian man was found at a slaughterhouse near Oroville, California. He was placed into protective custody at the University of California's museum of anthropology in Berkeley as a sort of living artifact: Ishi, "the last wild Indian in North America, a man of Stone Age culture" according to Theodora Kroeber, author of *Ishi in Two Worlds* and *Ishi: Last of His Tribe*.

According to Ishi, he was three or four years old in 1865 when the first massacre took place and seven or eight when the second attack occurred. He'd survived both massacres, staying hidden in the wilderness for more than forty years with a handful of other survivors.

The Yahi had a climbing culture necessitated by the rocky landscape. According to Ishi, the Yahi used ropes to pass difficult places on cliffs where they traveled frequently. But they also climbed without ropes on less frequently traveled terrain, including on Black Rock, a basaltic plug dome rising 250 vertical feet above what is now called Mill Creek near Mineral, California. Called De'wihaumauna (Yahi for "high up"), Black Rock dominates the landscape and was a sacred object to the Yahi, the central point of their ancestral universe. With steep cliffs on all sides, it was also a convenient place to spy on or hide out from white intruders. Ishi reported he climbed alone to the top of Black Rock for that purpose, clinging to thin holds far above the ground, watching unseen as the white mercenaries searched.

Black Rock was not the only rock formation that Ishi and his tribesmen climbed. They also used a turret-shaped rock formation called He Húi hui lulu as a watchtower, as well as a tall, barrel-shaped pillar called Han mā'wi mā'du (the place where the souls of the deer go, according to Ishi) as both a watchtower and a place of worship and tribal ritual. According to Ishi, Han mā'wi mā'du was bound with ropes that were used to climb it. However, in 1914, Ishi led a team of anthropologists to the summit of the free-standing pinnacle via a cleft up one of the vertical sides of the tower. As Alfred Kroeber noted in his journal, the rock was crossed by horizontal bands of white rock that could have been interpreted as ropes in the Yahi mythology. If there had been ropes in earlier times, they were long gone.

THE ETHNIC MIAO PEOPLE OF Ziyun County, a mountainous region of Guizhou Province in southwest China, have been climbing cliffs without ropes for hundreds of years. The earliest Miao climbers ascended the steep karst cliffs lining the Getu River to collect herbs used in traditional medicines and swallow dung for fertilizer, and to place the coffins of deceased family members in caves. But these days, they mostly climb the cliffs for money.

One such climber is a forty-something Miao woman named Luo Dengping, one of a small group of "spidermen" hired by the local tourist authority to climb up and down a 300-foot cliff to entertain the tourists who flock to the region. Her father, a highly skilled spiderman, passed the centuries-old tradition down to boys in the Miao village but refused to teach his daughter. It was for boys, not girls, Luo knew, but she became obsessed. She watched her father carefully, studying his movements on the cliff. One day when she was fifteen, she went off and climbed the cliff by herself.

After that, her father could not say no. He taught his daughter the skills handed down from earlier generations—not just the movements, but the philosophy. "Climb based on your own physical capabilities," Dengping says, describing what her father taught her. "Be bold yet careful."

Eventually she was hired by the tourist board and became the first "spiderwoman." She's now a professional climber who free solos for a living, earning five thousand to six thousand yuan a month, plus tips (about US$800–900). During peak season, she repeats the climb five or six times a day. "This sport needs courage," she says. "Every time we climb, it's crucial that we assess our surroundings and our own body condition. Our life depends on it."

CHAPTER 2

No Harm Will Befall You

Most historians agree that climbing as a sport began in the 1850s, with the Golden Age of Alpinism, although some may argue it started with the first ascent of Mont Blanc in 1786 by Dr. Michel-Gabriel Paccard and Jacques Balmat, under the pretext of taking scientific measurements. Until then, and even into the mid-1880s, climbing for any reason other than science or exploration was considered, as one early climber put it, "a positive act of egregious folly." The sanity of anyone who climbed a mountain for "fun" or "because it is there"—especially alone and without safety precautions—would have been subject to intense scrutiny and debate.

By the 1850s, British climbers were heading to the Alps without any motive beyond, in some cases, the imperialist drive to be the "first" to conquer a peak. These sport mountaineers generally didn't use ropes, as the hemp ropes of that time period were weak and prone to breaking. Further, their method of roping up (before pitons and running belays were introduced) meant that, if one climber fell, they could easily drag an entire rope team into the void—as tragically happened to Edward Whymper's party in 1865 on the first ascent of the Matterhorn.

Although early mountaineers didn't trust ropes, they were almost always accompanied by other climbers, and usually employed a guide. But sometimes they went out alone, if there were no guides or other climbers available during a spell of good weather, as Whymper did when he ventured high on the Matterhorn by himself in 1862. He remarked in *Scrambles Amongst the Alps* that climbing alone "awakens man's faculties, and makes him observe." He made good progress, but nearing the summit pyramid he found himself in a precarious place, "with arms and legs divergent, fixed as if crucified against the rock," and turned back.

During the descent, Whymper slipped and nearly fell to his death. "I was perfectly conscious of what was happening and felt each blow," he wrote, "but like a patient under chloroform, experienced no pain . . . more remarkable, this bounding through space did not feel disagreeable."

His experience led him to believe that "as improbable as it seems . . . death by a fall from a great height is as painless an end as can be experienced." Even so, Whymper did not venture onto the Matterhorn alone again.

IN 1881, AN OXFORD LAW student named Walter P. Haskett-Smith visited the Lake District, a picturesque region of craggy mountains, deep lakes, and glacier-carved valleys in northwest England (romanticized in William Words-worth's 1807 poem, "I Wandered Lonely as a Cloud"). Haskett-Smith had been introduced to mountain exploration the previous year, during a university reading trip to Wales, and had found it a pleasant, invigorating diversion. His younger brother, Edmund, accompanied him on this trip, and the pair spent two months exploring the fells, scrambling up faces and gullies. They didn't use a rope on this fairly easy terrain, but the pair wouldn't have roped up even if the terrain had been more challenging; the use of ropes and belays for safety was something of a novelty at the time. It would take until 1885 for roped, belayed climbing to be widely adopted by Lake District climbers, and the first pitons did not appear on the scene until many years later. Like his contemporaries, Haskett-Smith viewed climbers who used ropes and equipment as incompetents.

Haskett-Smith returned to the Lake District year after year, eventually setting out to scramble up the Great Gable, a rocky ridge high on Wasdale Head. He then tried for the summit of Napes Needle, a hitherto unclimbed 70-foot-high exposed rock pinnacle. Alone and without a rope, Haskett-Smith made the summit. It was no scramble but rather a technically challenging ascent; his route up the needle is rated Hard Severe on the British rating scale, roughly 5.6 on the Yosemite Decimal System, justifying the use of a rope and protection even by modern standards. A fall would certainly have meant severe injury or death. When word of his ascent went public, it led to a boom in the sport's popularity that kicked off the golden age of Lake District rock climbing. Haskett-Smith, however, acted as if it wasn't a big deal.

In his entry in the Wasdale Hotel book immediately after the climb, he wrote just a few uninspired lines:

> A fine climb of the arête character may be found in Gable Napes. This arête is the right hand bank of the right hand of the two great gullies which are seen from the hotel and is marked by a peculiar pinnacle at the foot of it. The pinnacle may be recognised (till the next gale of wind) by a handkerchief tied to the top.

Haskett-Smith's free solo of the Needle was not the first notable solo climb in the Lake District. During a nine-day outing in 1802, English poet Samuel Taylor Coleridge descended a ridge on 3,209-foot Scafell Pike to evade a storm, unwittingly making what some people have referred to as the first recreational rock climb. He climbed down a series of rock steps and slabs where he felt that if he had lost his grip he would "have fallen backwards & of course killed myself," he wrote to a confidante. He described the experience as transporting him to "a state of almost prophetic Trance & Delight." By modern standards, Broad Strand is considered a scramble, with a few technical moves above large drops with unforgiving landings. Most modern climbers don't bother roping up on it, but a few who experience Coleridge's trepidation may have wished they had.

CLIMBING WITHOUT A ROPE WAS not only a British phenomenon. In the Dolomites—a region of craggy mountains in Austria and northeastern Italy—daring alpinists gamboled about on the limestone cliffs, unburdened by rope or partner, with the skill and indifference of goats. One of these climbers, Georg Winkler, was the son of a wealthy Munich pig butcher. Georg Leuchs, a friend and climbing companion, described him in an article published in the 1935 *German & Austrian Alpine Club* journal (DöAV) as "a tight, but slender, medium-sized fellow, with soft, almost girlish features, an inconspicuous personality who, at first sight, did not suggest the unusual mental and physical powers that were inherent in him." Leuchs also recalled that Winkler's father had "endowed him with a substantial amount of money," which allowed him to go on mountain adventures in the Alps.

Leuchs had met Winkler in 1885, when he was sixteen, at the home of his friend, Karl Schmidt, from which the trio embarked on a two-day hike. Winkler wasted no time displaying his rock-climbing mastery as well as his playfulness. Leuchs wrote:

> *There are a number of mighty boulders along this route, some up to the size of small houses. Their mostly vertical and seemingly smooth walls exerted an irresistible charm on Winkler to try out his climbing skills. . . . There we saw him ascend with cat-like agility and lightness, with astonishing pull-ups and sheer eerie digging positions and overpowering one after the other of these repellent boulders, despite our warnings.*

After their bouldering session, Karl Schmidt parted company, but Leuchs and Winkler continued their adventure, hiking to the Jamtal Hut where they marveled at the peaks rising above the glaciers. When Leuchs got up the next morning to hike down the valley again, Winkler was gone. He had left alone early in the morning for the summit of the Vordere Jamtalfernerspitze.

Leuchs worried that Winkler's attraction to solo climbing was dangerous, and predicted that if he continued to pursue it, he'd end up being killed. His concerns were not unfounded.

On September 17, 1887, Winkler arrived in the Dolomites. Wearing a pair of canvas sailing boots with hemp soles, he began his solo first ascent of the southernmost Vajolet Tower, a 600-foot limestone spire that had long been considered impossible.

From some vantages, the Vajolet Towers resemble bony fingers extended skyward from a broad hand. The easternmost, the Winkler Tower or *Winkler Turm*, stands slightly apart, like a finger pointing off in its own direction. Winkler's route, now called the *Winkler Crack*, follows a line that slices the vertical limestone from the base of the tower's southern face to its rounded summit. With four pitches of steep climbing, it is rated roughly 5.6 by modern standards. At the time of Winkler's ascent, it was close to the limit of the most difficult established climbs and set a new standard for boldness—changing the perception not only of what was possible but also of what was desirable. Even so, Winkler nearly didn't make it down alive. As he rappelled, a falling rock cut part of his rope, leaving him hanging by only a few strands.

Winkler has been credited as the first free-solo climber, but he wasn't a purist by any means. Although he often climbed alone, Winkler made many of his solo ascents using a hook attached to a 40-foot rope as an aid. "Since overhangs are very difficult for him due to his small size, he makes himself a throw anchor," wrote Heinrich Klier in the 1956 DöAV, explaining Winkler's practice. "He fastens it to the rope, hurls it over the blocking point until the sharp prongs cling to something, then he climbs up on the rope."

Some suspect that Winkler's eagerness to expose himself to risk was due to the influence of Eugen Guido Lammer, an idealistic Austrian mountaineer and writer of the era, who argued that climbers should forgo mountain guides and artificial aids. By the age of twenty, Lammer had made a solo ascent of the north face of the Tamischbach Tower in the Ennstal Alps, a range of limestone peaks in eastern Austria, and in the ensuing years made solitary ascents in Switzerland's Pennine Alps, including the Zinalrothorn and Weisshorn in 1887.

Lammer published articles and books that explored the emotional aspects of confronting risk and danger on the peaks—that in fact urged the engagement of risk and peril as vital aspects of climbing. Mountain climbing, he wrote in his book *Jungborn* in 1896, demanded "the conquest of danger through one's own strength, one's own know-how, one's own presence of mind, unceasing stamina and many other aspects of the self." His philosophy would inspire generations of impressionable young climbers, including Winkler, to approach the sport with zealous self-reliance.

Winkler kept a detailed diary in which he wrote about the more than fifty peaks he climbed, including first solo ascents of several difficult routes on the Ackerlspitze from Griesner Kar in 1883 and the Totenkirchl in 1885, and his emotional responses to risk and reward. His diary was eventually published in 1906 under the title *Empor!* (which translates to "Upwards!") and it made Winkler something of a cult figure among young German climbers, who would, in turn, hurl themselves against the "impossible" peaks of the Alps.

On August 14, 1888, Winkler made a solo traverse of the Zinalrothorn, a sharp fin of red gneiss rising to 13,848 feet above the town of Zinal in the Pennine Alps. In his book *Alpenglow*, Ben Tibbetts, an accomplished British alpinist and guide, describes the Zinalrothorn as "one of the most beautiful summits in the Alps" and "possessing ridges with impeccable rock quality."

The spectacularly exposed north ridge of the mountain was described by Leslie Stephens (father of writer Virginia Woolf), a member of the team that first ascended this serrated knife's edge in 1864, as "the nastiest piece of climbing I have ever accomplished."

Winkler's solo traverse of the Zinalrothorn was a worthy achievement, but two days later he set out alone from Zinal to climb the Weisshorn, a pyramid of snow and rock rising to 14,783 feet, without telling anyone the route he planned to climb. He did not return.

"I have long been aware of the danger involved in my climbs," Winkler wrote in his diary, "and soon realized that it is, indeed, seeking out and overcoming this very danger that affords a climber unlimited satisfaction. The union of this danger with the infinite magnificence of the high mountains exerts an irresistible, demonic attraction."

When Winkler did not return from the Weisshorn, a team went to search for him, thinking the Schali Ridge, on the south side of the mountain, was his likely route. An old shepherd had seen Winkler, though, hiking up the meadows toward the west face before disappearing, and the search team looked there. They did not find him, only his hat and a photograph on the glacier below the west face, near a fresh avalanche cone. They surmised Winkler had been swept off the west face and buried by an avalanche. His body was finally recovered on the Weisshorn Glacier in 1956.

Leuchs last met with Winkler during the winter of 1886. When he read of Winkler's death on the Weisshorn the next summer, he wrote:

My prophecy, which was really not meant to be evil, had been cruelly fulfilled. Hardly ever has such a youthful mountain victim been mourned so lively in the broadest range of alpinists as Georg Winkler . . . in alpine literature, even more so in the giant stone monuments of nature to which his name is attached, he lives on in the future.

MANY OF THE EARLIEST RECORDED climbs in North America were made by surveying teams exploring the mountains of the West. One such explorer was David Douglas, an English botanist in his twenties. While collecting specimens, he had spotted an attractive pyramid of rock and snow near Athabasca Pass in the Canadian Rockies, which he would later claim was over 17,000 feet high—a gross exaggeration typical of early explorers. During a trip over the pass, Douglas set off alone and reached the summit after only a few hours' efforts. Besides being one of the earliest recorded solo climbs in North America, Douglas's ascent was also significant because he had summited the mountain, not for a good scientific reason, but simply because he saw the peak and felt compelled to climb it.

Similarly, in 1864, surveyors Clarence King and Dick Cotter attempted to ascend the highest peak of the Sierra Nevada, which they had named Mount Whitney in honor of Josiah Whitney, the leader of their survey team. Unfortunately, they climbed the wrong mountain. Determined to climb Mount Whitney, King set out a few days later to correct his error. Climbing alone up the precipitous west side of the mountain, he came within a few hundred yards of the summit but was forced back by insurmountable cliffs. The 1864 survey party left the area soon after, but King returned in 1871, this time reaching the summit of the highest rocky peak. Unfortunately, he climbed the wrong mountain again, this time a peak now called Mount Langley, which lies just south of Mount Whitney.

King finally succeeded in climbing Mount Whitney in 1873, after finding a more accessible route. He did not claim the first ascent, however, as he discovered a rock cairn and arrow shaft at the top, evidence that American Indians had reached the summit before him.

BORN IN 1838 IN DUNBAR, Scotland, John Muir spent much of his childhood exploring, including once climbing the ruins of Dunbar Castle. "That I did not fall and finish my rock-scrambling in those adventurous boyhood days seems now a reasonable wonder," he later wrote in *Story of My Boyhood and Youth*. Muir's father, Daniel, was a devout fundamentalist who, like many good Scotsmen, believed hard work and piety were the paths to salvation, and that a young boy's spare time should be devoted to reading scripture and not wandering idly about.

After the family emigrated to Wisconsin in 1849, Muir's sense of wonder, youthful restlessness, and active mind led him to study nature with an almost evangelical zeal, perfectly exhibited in a one-thousand-mile walk from Indiana to Florida in 1867, during which he nearly died of malaria. The next year, he traveled to California and discovered the Sierra Nevada. Living at the foot of the Range of Light, Muir saw the mountains to the east as "a circle of friends." As he wrote in *A Thousand-Mile Walk to the Gulf*, they cause you to "lose consciousness of [your] own separate existence: you blend in with the landscape, and become part and parcel of nature."

In the summer of 1869, Muir went to work herding sheep for John Delaney, which allowed him time to freely explore Tuolumne Meadows. One 10,991-foot granite spire, rising like a beacon above the grassy meadows and polished domes, called out to him: Muir knew he would climb it. All season long, the young Scotsman gazed longingly at the peak, and, when his summer's work came to an end, he set off alone to its summit.

He chose a circuitous route that culminated with 400 feet of exposed rock climbing on the peak's west face, an ascent that for Muir was nearly a religious experience. "This I may say is the first time I have been at church in California," he wrote, "led here at last, every door graciously opened for the poor lonely worshiper."

Muir's route up what is now called Cathedral Peak is not especially difficult by modern rock-climbing standards. It is rated Class 4, nothing a beginner couldn't manage, but with some Class 5 moves, including 15 feet of difficult and exposed climbing at the top. If you fell off there, you'd fall a long way.

Muir described Yosemite's peaks and granite walls as irresistible, drawing him to the very edge. "I could not help fearing a little that the rock might split off and let me down, and what a down!" he wrote in *My First Summer in the Sierra* of his experience standing on the rim of Yosemite Valley. "After withdrawing from such places, excited with the view I got, I would say to myself, 'Now don't go out on the verge again.' But in the face of Yosemite scenery cautious remonstrance is vain; under its spell one's body seems to go where it likes with a will over which we seem to have scarce any control."

In 1872, Muir climbed 13,149-foot Mount Ritter, the mountain's first-known ascent, via a route that involved a horrifically exposed rock face a thousand feet above a glacier. Muir had gone off by himself, hiking and scrambling for two days to reach the remote peak, despite having reservations about whether the route was possible and thinking perhaps it was foolhardy to try. However, given his resolve to "guide [his] humbled body over the most nerve-trying places [he] could find," he went for it.

Based on Muir's gripping account of the ascent, he barely pulled it off:

After gaining a point about half-way to the top, I was brought to a dead
stop, with arms outspread, clinging close to the face of the rock, unable to
move hand or foot either up or down. My doom appeared fixed. I must
fall. There would be a moment of bewilderment, and then a lifeless tum-
ble down the once general precipice to the glacier below. When this final
danger flashed in upon me, I became nerve-shaken for the first time since
setting foot on the mountain, and my mind seemed to fill with a stifling
smoke. But the terrible eclipse lasted only a moment, when life burst forth
again with preternatural clearness. I seemed suddenly to become possessed
of a new sense. The other self—the ghost of by-gone experiences, instinct,
or Guardian Angel—call it what you will—came forward and assumed
control. . . . I found a way without effort and soon stood upon the topmost
crag in the blessed light.

Though Muir inspired others to follow his example with his eloquent
rhapsodizing about the freedom of experiencing wild nature on its own
terms, he nearly always climbed alone. "No mountaineer is truly free," he
wrote, "who is trammeled with friend or servant, who has the care of more
than two legs."

Once in Alaska, a missionary named Young insisted on accompanying
Muir on an attempted climb of Glenora Peak, despite Muir's attempts to dis-
suade him. Although Young was able to match Muir's pace, he ran into trouble
when they encountered loose rock near the summit. Predictably, Young fell
and dislocated both arms, which necessitated a difficult retreat. Because of
experiences like this, Muir didn't trust other people; he preferred to climb
alone.

For the most part, though, Muir focused on the sublime nature of solitary
wilderness exploration. "Go quietly, alone," he extolled his readers. "No harm
will befall you." After reading Muir's words, many young men and women—
me included—have gone into the mountains in search of moments when life
could burst forth with preternatural clearness. But, sometimes, when things
go wrong, we experience something quite different: a moment of bewilderment followed by a lifeless tumble down into the void.

CHAPTER 3

Lords of the Abyss

Paul Preuss was born in Altaussee, a picturesque mountain town in Austria, in 1886. At age six, he was afflicted with a polio-like virus that rendered him partially paralyzed and unable to walk. As he recovered, Preuss undertook vigorous gymnastic exercises and long walks to rebuild his strength. His father, Eduard, an amateur botanist who would die when Preuss was nine years old, took him on rambles in the mountains, which inspired his passion to climb them. As Preuss grew older, he became more interested in climbing. He trained methodically, doing pull-ups from inverted glasses set atop a wardrobe to simulate climbing the steep, loose rock that predominated the region, eventually even doing one-arm pull-ups.

At age twelve, Preuss and a friend snuck away to climb a technical route up—and down—the Gross Bischofsmütze, an 8064-foot-high peak, without a rope. Preuss neglected to tell his mother about his adventure. When she found out, she restricted him to his room in the mornings so he could not sneak off for another daytime climb. It was a futile gesture—he snuck away alone to climb at night instead. While Preuss preferred to climb alone, he also often climbed with friends, including his sister, Mina, and her friend, Anna Freud, daughter of the famous psychoanalyst.

Preuss would go on to complete many important first ascents in the Alps. Just as when he was a child, he usually climbed alone, including, at the age of twenty-five, his first ascent of the *East Face* of the Campanile Basso, a 9459-foot limestone tower in the Brenta Dolomites, an exceptionally risky solo climb due to its exposure, route-finding challenges, and the nature of virgin limestone, which is often dangerously loose. Preuss believed that soloing was safer than roped climbing because, in that era, when a roped climber fell, the rope often failed or yanked everyone tied to it off the mountain. This was not merely a theory; it had happened on the Matterhorn in 1865, and Preuss witnessed it himself in 1912 when Julius Truffer, a guide leading British mountaineer H. O. Jones and his bride up the Aiguille Rouge de Peuterey, fell when a hold broke and pulled his clients off with him.

Pitons and carabiners—metal spikes that could be pounded into the rock and snap links that attached to the rope—came into use around the time Preuss began to achieve notoriety. Although primarily used for safety, climbers began to use them as hand- and footholds. Preuss, however, viewed pitons as unnecessary, even for safety, and as cheating when used as an aid. In his view, climbers should bring themselves up to the level of the climb through physical and mental training. Following Preuss's strict approach meant only ascending routes that one could also climb down, reserving the use of pitons, ropes, and artificial aids for life-and-death situations.

Preuss wrote an essay, "Artificial Aids on Alpine Routes," published in 1911 in the *German Alpine Times*, that argued for pure, unaided climbing and against the increasing use and abuse of pitons. Preuss's position was simple: "With artificial climbing aids you have transformed the mountains into a mechanical plaything. Eventually they will break or wear out, and then nothing else will be left for you to do than to throw them away." In one of his most famous essays, as translated by Randolph Burks a century later, Preuss articulated what became known as his theorems, or rules, of climbing:

1. *You should not be equal to the mountain climbs you undertake, you should be superior.*
2. *The degree of difficulty that a climber is able to overcome with security on the descent and also believes himself capable of with an easy conscience must represent the upper limit of what he climbs on the ascent.*
3. *The justification for the use of artificial aids consequently only arises in the event of an immediately threatening danger.*
4. *The piton is an emergency reserve and not the basis for a method of working.*

5. *The rope is permitted as a relief-bringing means but ought never be the one true means for making the ascent of the mountain possible.*

And what I gladly concede:
6. *The principle of security ranks among the highest principles. But not the frantic correction of one's own insecurity attained by means of artificial aids, rather that primary security which every climber should be based in the correct estimation of his ability in relation to his desire.*

Preuss's critics strongly disagreed with his philosophy. Tita Piaz and Franz Nieberl, two leading alpinists, vigorously contested his theses in a series of essays that became known as the *mauerhakenstreit* or "piton dispute." Among other things, Piaz accused Preuss of "inhumanity" for advocating a dangerous style of climbing that risked lives. Preuss was also charged with inconsistency, as he did not count his rope-soled shoes and ice axe as artificial aids, and was criticized for seducing young climbers into sacrificing themselves to the "terrible Moloch" of his high ideal. The criticism didn't seem to deter Preuss. He even joked about it: "My fingertips were climbed through, adhesive tape had to come to my aid," he wrote in one of his articles, "which even the severe critic probably won't charge as a violation of my theories on artificial aid since I used the adhesive tape with the sticky side facing inward."

Preuss's ideals were not merely words; he regularly dispensed with ropes and safety equipment altogether, establishing first ascents on rocks faces, some thousands of feet high, without artificial aids or even the safety of a rope. In one such attempt, Preuss set out to ascend the south face of the Schüsselkar-spitze in the Wetterstein Alps with a team that included his rival, Tita Piaz. The two climbers disagreed about whether a certain difficult pitch should be climbed with a rope. According to Piaz's account, they both attempted the pitch their way, apparently simultaneously, with Piaz using rope tension and Preuss climbing around him without a rope. Both failed, and Preuss, near his physical limit, seemed close to falling.

"I asked him if he wanted a rope," Piaz wrote of the incident.

"Never!" Preuss responded, and persisted even though his legs were shaking.

"It was like a bad dream," Piaz wrote, describing Preuss as "a genuine madman."

This interaction revealed the fatal egoism and idealism at the heart of Preuss's approach. He steadfastly adhered to his rules, nearly always foregoing pitons, downclimbing instead of rappelling, and eschewing ropes except on rare occasions out of consideration for others.

In 1913, Preuss attempted to make the first ascent—free solo, of course—of the North Ridge of the Mandlkogel and fell nearly one thousand feet to his death, "a victim of his own theories," as Italian climber Ricardo Cassin wrote in *The Alpine Journal.*

When climbers retraced Preuss's route up the Mandlkogel, they discovered his pocketknife on a ledge, the blade open, which led some to speculate that he dropped it while eating lunch on a ledge, reached for it, and lost his balance. A climber of Preuss's skill, his friends insisted, could not have simply exceeded his ability and fallen. Over his short career, Preuss made a remarkable number of climbs, more than 300 of which were solo ascents and 150 of which were first ascents. Some of his routes are rated 5.9 by modern standards, a grade not attained in the US until the 1950s. George Mallory, the famed English mountaineer who died on Mount Everest in 1924, said "no one will ever equal Preuss."

PREUSS'S DEATH AT AGE TWENTY-SEVEN had a chilling effect on free soloing in the Alps, and within a year, two other events would further precipitate a drastic change in the course of mountaineering the world over. The first was the publication of a book titled *Alpinismo Acrobatico* in 1914 by Italian climber Guido Rey that shared the latest climbing techniques employed in the Dolomites—artificial aid methods such as pounding in a piton, clipping in the rope, and being pulled up the wall with rope tension. In the spirit of Preuss's theorems, some climbers dismissed ascents made using Rey's "acrobatique" techniques as aberrations and derisively referred to those who employed them as "ironmongers." Such judgments did not stop the ironmongers, who pioneered many long, challenging routes in the Dolomites and elsewhere in the Alps. They pounded away at their iron pitons and dangled guiltlessly from their ropes and rope ladders.

The second event was the dual impact of a world war and a global flu pandemic. On July 28, 1914, Austria-Hungary declared war on Serbia, which marked the beginning of World War I. Then the Spanish flu hit in 1918 near the end of the war, resulting in an estimated fifty million deaths worldwide—about 1 percent of the global population.

The war gave many people—young men in particular but also young women—a strong sense of nationalist pride, a sense of purpose they had not previously known. They responded with enthusiasm, enlisting in the military or supporting the war effort however they could. However, as the war and then the pandemic raged on and death tolls mounted, their enthusiasm waned. The interminable brutality of it eventually dispossessed them of any romantic notions, particularly for those that were on the losing side.

When the German climbers who survived returned, they felt a need to prove themselves after the shame of having lost the war. They threw themselves at their mountains with unprecedented nationalistic zeal, attempting and often succeeding in climbing one "impossible" face after another. This aggressive spirit of conquest reached its zenith on the north face of the Eiger in the mid-1930s. After several attempts, the *nordwand* began to be referred to as the *mordwand*—the murder wall—as the bodies of so many would-be national heroes piled up. Finally, in 1938, a German-Austrian team succeeded. The four climbers were fêted as national heroes and granted an audience with Adolf Hitler and other high-ranking national party officials, who were happy to exploit the climbers for Nazi propaganda.

But even as the Eiger wall was being conquered, a group of Italian climbers was beginning to surpass the Germans in difficulty, commitment, and boldness—one of whom fellow Italian climbing legend Riccardo Cassin would eventually call "the great master of artificial climbing."

BORN IN TRIESTE, ON THE ADRIATIC COAST of Italy, in 1901, Leonardo Emilio Comici was a tall, athletic, and artistic young man who had studied ballet, worked in shipyards, and engaged in amateur caving. After Comici and his fellow speleologists became the first to reach a depth of 500 meters (1640 feet) in the deep caves near his hometown, some of his friends suggested he try rock climbing. Comici soon abandoned caving entirely.

After developing his technique while climbing the walls of Val Rosandra, a canyon near Trieste, the twenty-six-year-old Comici headed to the Julian

Alps, a small range of limestone peaks along the Italy-Slovenia border. There, in 1927, he climbed one of the peaks of 8747-foot Jôf Fuart from the north side. The next year, he climbed the north face of Cima di Riofreddo, a 2300-foot route up a problematic wall, with Giordano Bruno Fabjan. It was one of four first ascents Comici did that year, only his second year of serious climbing.

Comici's background in caving had helped him advance quickly as a climber, but it was his pure love of the mountains, of being up in the air, that drove him. "On the mountains we feel the joy of life," he wrote, "the emotion of being good and the relief of forgetting earthly things: all this because we are closer to the sky."

In 1929, Comici and Fabjan made the first ascent of the northeast face of Sorella di Mezzo in the Sorapìs group, which took them two days, and involved the most challenging climbing either had ever done. Their route was beyond the perceived limits of climbing difficulty—the first Grade VI climb in Italy—and Comici won recognition as the one who had led the most challenging sections of the route. Two years later, Comici and Giulio Benedetti climbed a new mixed free-and-aid route up the northwest face of Monte Civetta, including a 3200-foot wall, the largest rock face in the Dolomites.

In August 1933, Comici climbed what would become his most iconic and controversial route on the Cima Grande, the highest of the three limestone towers that make up the Tre Cime di Lavaredo. The north face of the Cime Grande forms a pyramid that leans forward oppressively, presenting an overhanging wall that, from a distance, appears nearly blank. Many climbers had tried the face, but none ventured far before retreating. This was partly due to the overhanging nature of the wall; beyond a certain height, rappelling down seemed as unlikely as continuing upward.

Comici studied the Cima Grande and picked a direct line on the right side of the massive wall that he could follow, he believed, more or less directly to the top. He was prepared to make his first ascent quickly, knowing that rival climbers from Germany and Austria had their eyes on the prize, but couldn't find a willing partner. Then a guide named Angelo Dimai invited Comici to join him and his brother, Giuseppe, on their planned attempt. Comici agreed.

The trio attacked the wall, with Comici leading the most difficult pitches, pushing the route up the intimidating lower half of the wall. They'd brought a full arsenal of equipment—dozens of pitons, hooks, slings, and carabiners—and employed them liberally. As a testament to Comici's skill and *fortissimo*, the trio passed most of the difficult climbing on the first day and, after a bivouac, they reached the top late the following morning. The "impossible" wall had been climbed.

Pitons had been in use on the big walls of the Dolomites for some time, but in the race to be the first to climb a route, climbers sometimes used aid to beat out the competition. Comici, who, as David Smart reveals in *Emilio Comici: Angel of the Dolomites*, was trying to fit in and enjoy the role of masculine hero under Benito Mussolini's fascist regime, was not immune. The war may have been over, but nationalistic pride demanded that any unclimbed line in the Italian Dolomites be climbed first by Italians, by whatever means necessary. Comici, who is credited with inventing many of the methods and devices used in big-wall climbing today, including multistep aid ladders, fixed belay anchors, haul lines, and hanging bivouacs, helped open up previously unclimbable walls. Italian climbers who trained using Comici's techniques were soon climbing difficult routes that rivaled and even surpassed the accomplishments of the Germans.

Comici also conceived the *direttissima*—an idealistic notion that the most aesthetic line up a mountain is also the most direct route up its steepest, highest wall, the theoretical line of a falling drop of water from the summit to the ground. Although the *direttissima* was appealing to many climbers, it was also controversial because forcing a line straight up a cliff sometimes meant climbing blank rock using equipment instead of teasing out a route that followed the natural features of the wall. Comici's concept may have been borne out of a pure mind (he himself rarely forced a plumb line up a mountain), but in practice it became a platform for further nationalistic competition as climbers vied to climb the biggest, steepest faces, by the most direct, difficult lines, by any means possible. Eventually bolts were drilled into the rock and all-bolt lines appeared, including Cesare Maestri's 1970 machine-bolted route up the iconic Patagonian spire Cerro Torre.

To Comici's surprise, his route on the Cima Grande drew criticism from some Italian climbers who said he relied too much on pitons and direct aid and wouldn't have been able to climb the route without them. Even his companions on the climb, the Dimai brothers, were critical of Comici's tactics and thought they could have done better but were not given a chance to try it without so many pitons. The criticism bothered Comici, especially the accusation that he could not have climbed the wall by fair means.

IN 1937, COMICI FOUND HIMSELF alone in the Brenta Dolomites of northern Italy. Despite his reputation as an aid climber, he also enjoyed climbing alone unroped. On a whim he decided to climb the *Fehrmann* route on the 1200-foot Campanile Basso. Climbing alone and unroped, he reached the summit of the tower in just over an hour, then downclimbed the regular route and promptly free soloed the *Preuss* route, still regarded as one of the most challenging and dangerous routes on the peak. Then he soloed down, reversing the *Preuss* route.

That same year, Comici hiked alone to the north face of the Cima Grande and did the unthinkable: he soloed the 1800-foot wall, taking the line of his 1933 ascent. He spent three and a half hours on the wall, climbing carefully but confidently upward, using a rudimentary self-belay and pitons on the early pitches. Eventually he discarded his rope and pitons and continued free solo, clinging to thin holds on the overhanging wall as he climbed higher, passing a German party on his way up. The route, currently rated Grade VII (5.10+), is not especially difficult by modern standards and has been free soloed in its entirety, but it was unprecedented and audacious for Comici's time—few would have believed it if there hadn't been witnesses.

While Comici developed and employed many modern aid-climbing techniques, he was said to dance like a ballerina while free climbing, an ideal to which he aspired. "If you are absolute of technique, you can easily express your feelings, just like in music and dance," wrote Comici in *Alpinismo Eroico*. "In difficult passages, I abandon myself completely to the impression of living in the rock, and that the rock lives in me."

He also shared his feelings in a letter to a climbing partner, Severino Casara. "When I climb alone, I always look down to get drunk on emptiness, and I sing with joy," he wrote. "If I don't have breath to sing, because the difficult passage cuts me off, then the song continues quietly in my head."

In October 1940, some friends asked Comici to go climbing with them on the training wall at Selva di Val Gardena in Vallunga. Although he was busy with office work, Comici obliged. He accompanied the group to the wall, climbed up an easy route to a ledge, and turned to assist the others in follow-ing him. To better observe them and show the way, Comici tied a sling with a piece of cord, attached it to a piton, and leaned out, holding himself by the cord, as he pointed out the route.

Unfortunately, the frayed cord broke and Comici fell. Efforts to save him failed. He was dead, a piece of rotten cord still clenched in his hand. Comici was buried at the foot of the cliff where he died at age thirty-nine.

CHAPTER 4

The Katoomba Suicide Club

The aboriginal people of Australia undoubtedly could have climbed the continent's mountains if they had needed or wanted to, and sometimes did for cultural or spiritual reasons. However, like many native cultures, they have consistently discouraged or even forbidden outsiders to climb mountains and rock formations that they consider sacred embodiments of their ancestors or landmarks of their songlines, including Uluru (formerly Ayers Rock). Despite these taboos, the history of climbing in Australia, as in most colonized territories, is Eurocentric.

One such individual in this history was Freda Du Faur, a young woman living with her family near Sydney, who taught herself to climb on the sandstone cliffs of nearby Ku-ring-gai Chase National Park. After developing commendable rock-climbing skills on her own, she traveled to the New Zealand Alps in 1908, where she learned ropework from Peter Graham, a New Zealand guide. It was with Graham and his younger brother that Du Faur would climb 12,218-foot Aoraki (then called Mount Cook) in 1910, marking not only the first female ascent of the mountain but the first by an Australian. Du Faur would make many first ascents of the New Zealand Alps over the following years, including the grand traverse of all of Aoraki's peaks in 1913.

When Freda Du Faur first started planning overnight mountain climbs, the idea of a lone male guide accompanying her created something of a scandal. Out of considerations of propriety, an additional team member was added as a chaperone, and she wore a modest ankle-length skirt on all of her climbs. Such modesty was the norm for women climbers in Australia until the 1930s, when the culture of climbing shifted dramatically.

BY 1910, ALL THE GLASSHOUSE MOUNTAINS, a group of volcanic plugs along the Sunshine Coast of Australia north of Brisbane, had been climbed except one—Coonowrin (known locally as Crookneck), a tall rock that was said to be unclimbable. In March of that year, Henry "Harry" Mikalsen, a twenty-three-year-old who had grown up within view of the Glasshouse Mountains, worked out a route to the summit by himself. As the *Brisbane Courier* reported on June 2, 1910: "The feat was not accomplished without difficulty and danger." The article continued, "He stayed for an hour on the summit, and made the descent without mishap . . . as his home is at the foot of the mountain, he was watched with anxious eyes and could be seen the whole time." On this ascent, considered one of the first important recreational rock climbs in Australia, Mikalsen climbed over loose, blocky rock with several steep and even overhanging moves where an unroped fall could have been fatal.

Two years later, three sisters—Jenny, Sara, and Etty Clark, dressed in voluminous gym attire for the sake of modesty—accompanied by three young men—Willie Fraser, Jack Sairs, and George Rowley—rode their bicycles to the Glasshouse Mountains and climbed Coonowrin, choosing a more direct route up the peak. Although they climbed mostly unroped, scrambling up the grassy cliffs, they tied in and belayed past a steep, exposed wall. It was a wise decision. "The rope was let down through a crack in the rock at the side of which [one of the women] was standing," it was reported in the *Queenslander*'s account of the climb on June 8, 1912. "As she stepped off onto another little corner the rock gave way and left her swinging for a moment in mid-air, some 100 ft above the ground. Fortunately, the rope was good, and in strong hands, and she soon gained a fresh foothold and . . . clambered into safety."

Their use of a rope made the group something of an outlier in Australia at that time. Much of Queensland's early climbing culture was influenced by the ethics of Albert Armitage Salmon, who founded Australia's first climbing club in 1926. That same year, Salmon had made, with Alan Clelland, an unroped ascent of the east face of Tibrogargan, a steep, exposed rock buttress that had not previously been climbed or even seriously considered (today it is considered low Class 5 in difficulty). Although he had taken up rock climbing just three years earlier, and had no formal training on or knowledge of ropes and equipment, Bert Salmon (as he was known) would become known as the spiritual father of Queensland climbing.

Salmon, who followed the "leader must not fall" philosophy, believed roped climbing was more dangerous than unroped. At first, Queensland climbers were simply behind the times, unaware of modern roped-climbing techniques, but even after they were introduced, Salmon and his cohort shunned ropes on many of their climbs—even when others felt it was appropriate to use them.

Eric Payten Dark, a government health officer from New South Wales, came to hold a different view of roped climbing. He had begun climbing while in medical school after seeing a photo of Mount Lindesay, a striking volcanic peak on the Queensland–New South Wales border with a unique tiered summit ringed by cliffs up to 800 feet high. Dark became obsessed with climbing it and, in 1913, he succeeded, venturing alone to the rocky summit. In 1923, he moved to the Blue Mountains and began climbing there, scrambling unroped on the sandstone cliffs. Eventually he met other climbers and, in 1929, they formed the Blue Mountaineers, the first rock-climbing club in New South Wales, which they nicknamed the Katoomba Suicide Club.

Initially, the Blue Mountaineers climbed in relative isolation, unaware of Bert Salmon's growing influence in Queensland. However, Dark was aware of, and began to employ, European roped climbing techniques. The Blue Mountaineers roped up and belayed on difficult rock, experimented with pitons, and used an ice axe that they called their "unethical instrument" as a rudimentary belay anchor. But Dark adhered to the fair-means ideal espoused by English climbers such as Alfred Mummery, insisting that ropes and equipment only be used for protection and never for assistance while climbing.

The Blue Mountaineers allowed women—including Dark's wife, Eleanor, one of the founders of the club—but membership requirements were somewhat exclusive and its rigorous insistence on following safety protocols tended to make women feel unwelcome. This was not the case in Queensland, however, where climbing had evolved into an inclusive and fun activity that attracted as many women as men. In fact, women were equaling men in their ascents of the most difficult routes; as described in a 1934 article published in *The Truth*, "the Queensland girls have left the rest of Australia far behind in this exacting and exciting sport."

A 1931 article titled "Rock-Climbing: A Health-Giving Sport for Women," published in the *Australian Women's Mirror*, detailed the benefits of rock climbing without once suggesting that practicing the sport without a rope or protection was in any way dangerous. In fact, at least among the Queensland contingent, large groups of men and women, and sometimes even women climbing without men, were regularly making mass ascents of steep, exposed rock without a rope or protection. Participants did not think of these climbs as dangerous or life threatening; they were simply fun, even healthful.

LIKE ANY EXCLUSIVE GROUP, the Katoomba Suicide Club had an initiation rite: All new members had to climb the *Fly Wall*, a steep, difficult 30-foot sandstone face noted for its small holds and a difficult dynamic move. In 1934, Queensland climbers, including several women, visited the Blue Mountains for the first time. Dark and the Blue Mountaineers were gracious hosts, showing the Queensland climbers their favorite areas and encouraging them to try difficult climbs. The Queensland climbers, though, had heard about *Fly Wall*, and wanted a crack at it. Dark and the other Blue Mountaineers took them out to the route and told their guests to rope up and belay. The Queensland climbers had other ideas.

"I put the rope on," Salmon recalled of the incident in the *Sunday Mail*, "and then I took it off!" Dark was insistent that Salmon only climb the wall while using a belay.

"You won't!" he called down.

"I'm going to try anyway," Salmon responded, and clambered up the wall. "I tried my level best for Queensland and for my own reputation," Salmon said, "and I succeeded in climbing to the top of the wall without the rope. That was the first time it had ever been done!"

Salmon's climbing partner, George Fraser, went next. He tied into the rope and began to climb, but then he changed his mind. "Blimey," he said, "I'm going to climb it without the rope, too!" He climbed back down and discarded the rope. He repeated Salmon's free solo of *Fly Wall* to the amazement, and consternation, of the Blue Mountaineers.

But it was not only the male contingent of Queensland climbers who upstaged the Blue Mountaineers. One Sunday morning, Salmon and a twenty-one-year-old woman named Muriel Patten climbed the first of the Three Sisters rock formations, notorious for its difficult climbing. It was the first ascent of the First Sister by a woman. Naturally, Patten climbed the route without a rope. As reported in the *Katoomba Daily*:

> *Miss Muriel Patten, a petite and daring Brisbane girl, claims a record: that she is the only woman to scale the first of the Three Sisters. One section of this climb is extremely difficult and hazardous: particularly for a lady. . . . A big crowd was present at Echo Point and watched intently the progress of the daring climbers—Miss Patten in particular.*

Spurred by Patten's successful ascent of the First Sister, Jean Easton made the second female ascent later that year with a party of Blue Mountaineers. Unlike Patten, though, she used a rope.

Although unroped climbing was seen as a fun and healthful activity in Queensland, the dangers it presented were well known. On New Year's Eve 1928, the newspapers had reported that one of Salmon's frequent companions, Lyle Vidler, had been found dead on Mount Lindesay. Ever since he and Salmon had climbed a route up the east face of the mountain the previous Easter, Vidler had been obsessed with a new route up a feature called the Great Chimney, a vertical cleft in the mountain's 400-foot north face. Despite Salmon's suggestion that he give up the notion of trying it alone, Vidler had taken the train south a week earlier, intending to try the climb during the Christmas holiday. Three days later, a group that included Salmon drove to the mountain to search for their young friend. Unable to find the missing climber, Salmon climbed to the summit alone but found no trace of Vidler. He returned to the base of the cliff to search there.

As reported in the *Brisbane Courier*, Salmon climbed 50 feet up the chimney and saw Vidler's body far above him. "When I reached the place, I found that the body had been caught between the base of a large stinging tree and one of the walls of the rock chimney," Salmon told the *Courier*. "It was held from under the armpits by vines and a number of dead branches." He concluded, "From the moment I reached him I was convinced that Mr. Vidler had been killed instantly."

Salmon suspected a hold had broken while he was climbing high in the chimney. Vidler was the first person known to have died while rock climbing in Australia. He was twenty-two years old.

CHAPTER 5

No Compromise

In the late 1960s, Henry Barber's parents sent him to a mountaineering school in Colorado. Climbing was new for the Boston teen, who had only done some introductory climbs with the Appalachian Mountain Club, but he soon aspired to be like the centered, confident Colorado mountain guides he thought were "cool." One day, while aid climbing in Boulder Canyon, Barber watched a climber free solo a nearby route, which blew his mind. Later, a group of climbers invited him to try a thin, overhanging 5.10+ crack on a toprope. To everyone's surprise, he pulled it off. That got him fired up. When he returned home, Barber began climbing anything that could be climbed— buildings, quarries, boulders, crags—sometimes without a rope.

Like many free soloists, Barber's earliest climbs—first at Quincy Quarries near his home in Boston, and later at the Shawangunks in upstate New York—were solo because he lacked a partner. If he couldn't find someone to climb with, he climbed by himself. Even when he did have a climbing partner, Barber climbed with a level of intensity that tended to wear others out, leaving him to climb alone when he wanted to get in a few more routes at the end of a day. But, as his confidence grew, he began to solo because he enjoyed it.

In 1972, Barber visited Yosemite for the first time and immediately made an impression by climbing *New Dimensions*, a 400-foot 5.11a on the Cookie Cliff that was then the hardest free climb in Yosemite. He returned the following year and established the new hardest route in Yosemite, at 5.11c, making the first free ascent of *Butterballs*, a coveted thin finger crack high on the Nabisco Wall, which he climbed on his first try, without falls. He also nabbed the second free ascent of *Foops* in 1973, which gained him the admiration of his idol, John Stannard, who did the first ascent of the 5.11c overhang in 1967 and regarded Barber as a protégé. Stannard, one of the most technically proficient free climbers of the late 1960s and early 1970s, was staunchly opposed to using pitons or bolts as protection, an ethical stance that Barber wholeheartedly adopted. Although Stannard was impressed by Barber's free-climbing ability and enthusiasm, he was concerned about Barber's habit of free soloing hard routes.

One of Barber's most notorious free-solo climbs was his 1973 ascent of *Gorilla's Delight*, a 200-foot 5.9 in Boulder Canyon, Colorado. According to the guidebook, it was 5.7, involving some thin climbing on a slab high up but nothing very difficult. When Barber reached the slab, he thought it looked tenuous and committing, but went for it anyway, relying on the 5.7 rating in the guidebook. It turned out the slab involved slick 5.9 friction that he barely pulled off. "I was absolutely terrified, just barely making it," Barber recalled in the book *On Edge*. "I was way out of control, and once you're scared, the whole game starts to become very dangerous."

Despite his close call on *Gorilla's Delight*, Barber had absolute confidence in his ability to climb down from anywhere on a route. If he encountered a spot that was too difficult or risky, he'd reverse the route even if he was 1000 feet off the ground. Barber put that confidence to the test during his 1973 trip to Yosemite, where he made a free-solo ascent of the *Steck-Salathé* route on Sentinel Rock. He wanted to climb the 1,800-foot 5.10a as a tribute to his friend, Roger Parks, who had fallen and died on it the year before. Barber hadn't done the route previously, which suited him fine; as a general principle, he believed that it was safer to free solo a route without prior knowledge and, in fact, most of his free solo climbs were done on-sight.

"I on-sighted because I didn't want any predetermination that I could make it," he told me in the fall of 2021. "I wanted to be fully engaged, have all my senses firing." This, he believed, made him less likely to make a mistake. He also practiced downclimbing religiously, which made him confident he could backtrack from anywhere on a route if he ran into unexpected difficulties.

Barber had been thinking of free soloing the *Steck-Salathé* before he went to Yosemite in 1973. After looking up at the wall every day from Camp 4 while in the Valley in 1972, he'd decided to try it the next year. He trained by soloing other walls, first at the Gunks, then in Yosemite, doing multipitch routes and linking thousands of feet of rock, climbing up and down, building up his confidence on wide cracks, immersing himself in the mindset of soloing a big wall.

Even so, he had doubts as he climbed *Steck-Salathé*, wondering if he could pass certain sections of the route he'd heard about. At one point, in a deep chimney known as the Narrows, he slipped and got wedged in the crack but was able to wriggle himself out. He finished the climb without further incident, and felt elated, wishing he could have shared the experience with someone. But on the descent, suffering from the effects of heat and dehydration, his thoughts became fuzzy. He puzzled over what the climb had meant to him and wondered why he didn't feel exhilarated or thrilled at having done something so unprecedented.

Barber claimed he didn't solo the route to get attention, but he got it anyway. Word of his climb spread like wildfire and was reported in the next issue of *Summit* magazine. Everyone started calling him "Hot Henry." *Summit* soon published an article lauding Barber's free-solo climb. In the next issue, a letter to the editor complained, "Why was the magazine giving attention to such ill-considered acts as solo climbing?" Royal Robbins, one of the pioneering Yosemite climbers of the 1950s through the early seventies, responded in the next issue, calling Barber's free solo of the *Steck-Salathé* "visionary."

Soon after the *Steck-Salathé*, Barber dropped out of college and started climbing full time, as many as three hundred days per year, roped up when he had a partner, without a rope when he didn't. He traveled around the world— England, Australia, Germany, and across the US—supplementing his income as a gear representative with money from slide shows and media adventures, including TV shows featuring him climbing. In 1976, Barber signed on to free solo several Welsh sea cliff routes for a US television program called *American Sportsman*. As a professional climber, Barber saw films as good for business, something he could use to promote his lecture tour and finance his worldwide climbing trips.

The film included footage of Al Harris and Barber climbing *A Dream of White Horses*, which provided some drama when Harris went off the 5.8 route and nearly took a huge fall. After they finished the climb, the producer asked Barber if he'd repeat the route without a rope. Barber agreed. It was almost a fatal decision. He made it across the traverse easily, but near the end of the route, while stemming up a final steep corner, his balance was thrown off when a cameraman swung over to get into position and hit him with his rope. Barber started to fall—a 200-foot drop to a surf-pounded ledge—but caught himself and finished the climb.

His close call should have been a harbinger, but Barber decided to go ahead with a free-solo climb of a more difficult route called *The Strand*, a steep, sustained sea cliff crack rated E2 on the British scale (5.10a). The 200-foot route was well within Barber's ability and would provide a dramatic conclusion for the film. As a condition, however, Barber insisted that he be left alone. No one was to talk to him or ask him to do anything; he would just climb the route when he was ready, take as long as he needed, and be done with it without any outside distractions. Of course, that's not what happened.

First, there was a long delay while the cameras were being set up. Barber had come mentally prepared to free solo the route, and to retain his focus during the delay, he free soloed a nearby 5.8, which did not go well. High on the route, he was startled by a seagull that dive-bombed him and plucked off his hat, an incident that led him to question why he had agreed to free solo *The Strand* and why he was still going ahead with it. Meanwhile, the sun was now shining directly on the route, which the film crew felt was not optimal; they decided to delay filming for a few more hours until the light was better. Barber killed time by eating lunch and drinking beer.

Finally, after a delay of several hours, they were ready to film, and Barber, still wondering if he should be doing this, started up the climb. Almost immediately, a cameraman asked him to repeat a section of the climb. He thought of climbing back to the ground and walking away, but didn't. He'd agreed to do the climb, and everyone was here—what would people think if he walked away?

He repeated the moves for the camera and continued climbing. It was hot and oppressive on the wall; the rock was loose; the seagulls were annoying; everyone was watching. Things were unraveling, yet Barber remained steadfast, believing he could adjust his mindset and persevere despite the distractions. He tried to regain his composure as he climbed, but never did. He found his mind wavering and was unable to focus.

People on the ground sensed something wasn't right; the route was only 200 feet high, yet it was taking Barber much too long to climb it. He wasn't flowing up the rock—he was struggling. Barber's girlfriend, Kim Blanch, walked away, unable to watch, fearing he was going to fall and die.

Barber regained his composure at the crux, but lost it again after realizing he'd just climbed a section of difficult layback moves that he probably could not downclimb. He considered stopping there and asking someone to drop a rope to him, but his ego wouldn't let him, so he kept climbing, and things kept getting worse. His feet, which were starting to swell in the insufferable heat, hurt badly from being jammed into the crack. This discomfort created mental strain, a sense of urgency—precisely the wrong things a free soloist wants to experience in the middle of a difficult climb. Still, he carried on, even after shaking so badly at one point that he had to back down to a stance and regroup. Then, as he finally pulled over the top, relieved to have pulled it off, the producer asked him to repeat a section at the very top.

"Before the climb, I felt tormented, asking myself, 'Why am I doing this? Why didn't I just say no?'" Barber told me. "I felt incredible pressure. Nobody put that pressure on except for me. I fucked up because I said I would do it and I should have said 'I don't want to do it.'"

Despite successfully getting in his zone and completing the climb, he later came to a definitive conclusion about the whole affair: "This is bullshit."

BARBER CONTINUED TO FREE SOLO, just not for the camera. When he visited the Elbsandstein region of East Germany in 1976, he free soloed the *Perry Crack*, a serious 5.9 that American climber Oliver Perry-Smith had first climbed in 1907. The route, which had only a single protection ring, was considered too dangerous—several climbers attempting it with a rope and belay had fallen and died. Barber's free solo perplexed locals, even though their own style of climbing, with marginal protection on steep sandstone, was often just as risky.

One day during the East Germany trip, Barber free soloed an arête on the Meurerturm that Bernd Arnold, one of the leading climbers of the region, had shown him. It was a "Master" route, Arnold told him, one that only the best climbers were even allowed to attempt. Unaware of the details of the route, Barber climbed up without a rope and found himself gripping tiny edges that seemed poised to break off. The route turned out to be rated a 5.10d, well within his ability but unexpectedly sketchy; though Barber pulled it off, he was badly shaken. He felt lucky to have survived.

No one had seen him do the climb in the mist, but he left chalk marks on the route, and the locals figured it out. "They were stunned. Totally stunned," recalled Barber. The climbers in the region had already thought Barber was unsafe because of his bold leading, taking long runouts between pieces of protection on the friable sandstone. Now this.

Although Arnold's climbs were viewed as "calculated-risk death routes," as Chip Lee wrote in his biography of Barber, he was concerned by Barber's willingness to climb unroped. He felt Barber was "capricious and unsafe," and that he relied on an "inflammable mixture of adrenaline, confidence, and fear to surmount difficult, unprotected leads," according to Lee. Herbert Richter, another of Barber's East German hosts, was also concerned. "Henry is perhaps still too young . . . or he trusts his ability too much," he said of Barber. "In any event, he sacrifices safety by not using the necessary precautions. . . . But one must remember that Death only looks away into the corner once in a while."

ONE DAY IN JOSHUA TREE in the early 1970s, a young Southern California climber named John Long suggested a route to his climbing partner, eighteen-year-old John Bachar. "Let's go do *Double Cross*," said Long. Bachar agreed and started heading to his car to get his rope and gear for the 80-foot high 5.7, but Long walked toward the route with just his rock shoes and chalk bag.

"Oh, no, we're not using ropes," Long said. Sensing Bachar's hesitation, he asked, "If you toproped it one hundred times, how many times would you fall?"

"Uh, none," Bachar replied.

"That one question changed my life," Bachar said later in an interview with *Rock and Ice*. "After I soloed *Double Cross*, there was just this weird twitch inside of me."

Soloing was not new, in Joshua Tree, Yosemite, or elsewhere. Quite a few climbers of the 1960s and early 1970s, including Henry Barber, free soloed regularly, but climbing without a rope was new to Bachar, barely out of high school and already one of the best rock climbers in the US. The urge to free solo—the "twitch"—soon became an obsession.

John Bachar was born in 1957 near Los Angeles. His parents divorced when he was seven years old. Bachar recalled his father, a member of the Sierra Club, taking him and his younger brother on backpacking trips during his childhood. In his early teens, Bachar read *The White Spider* and *Annapurna*, which sparked his interest in climbing. He'd heard about people climbing El Capitan in Yosemite. "It was all mysterious and intriguing because the stone was foreboding and not where humans went," he said. "Who are these weird people?"

Bachar first climbed at Stoney Point, a hill covered with sandstone slabs and boulders 30 miles north of Los Angeles, at age fourteen, and soon became a regular. He visited Joshua Tree for the first time two years later, and led his first route, a 5.6. Within a year, he was practically a J-Tree local, leading 5.11 and climbing with the likes of Mike Graham, Tobin Sorenson, Dean Fidelman, and other members of a tribe that viewed climbing as a way of life. When the spring season in Joshua Tree ended the tribe would move north to spend summers in Yosemite.

Bachar attended UCLA briefly, intending to become a math professor like his father, but despite earning good grades, he dropped out in 1976 to climb full time. "I was throwing away a huge possibility for my life by leaving college," he admitted, "but I realized that I was one of the best." He promised to give all he had for climbing. "That's what I'm going to do for the rest of my life."

When he arrived at Stoney Point, Bachar had been scrawny, barely able to do two pull-ups; two years later, he was cranking out sets of twenty-seven. A year after that, he was establishing new 5.11 routes. His improved ability was no fluke; it was in large part the result of his mathematical approach to training and performance. By his midtwenties, Bachar was devoting several hours each day to working out. He also trained mentally, with relaxation and visualization exercises, learning how to stay focused on the problem at hand—the circle of rock around him, as he put it—to stay in control, to be able to climb down from anywhere. And he was always calculating, breaking down a route, analyzing its features, and rehearsing the moves mentally, if not also physically, before climbing.

Bachar was strongly influenced by John Gill, the so-called Father of American Bouldering. A mathematician and gymnastic training fanatic, Gill saw bouldering, which he defined as "one-pitch climbing of great difficulty, usually done close to the ground and unroped," as an end unto itself. Gill, who introduced the use of gymnastics chalk to rock climbing, had established boulder problems in the 1950s and 1960s that were technically harder than anything that would be done before to the late 1970s—the equivalent of 5.13 when 5.9 was considered the top of the scale—and rope-free ascents of short climbs up to 5.12 in difficulty. He is especially revered for his unroped 1961 ascent of the Thimble—a 30-foot-high pinnacle in The Needles of South Dakota—a 5.12 that he had not rehearsed ahead of time. Gill's ethic was to solo a problem if possible, toprope it if it was too dangerous to solo, and strive for as perfect an ascent as possible. Bachar adopted this approach wholeheartedly while taking soloing to a whole new level.

"It's a sport of self-mastery," Bachar said of free soloing in *Backpacker* magazine in 1986. "Knowing that one wrong move can kill me makes me more aware of what I'm doing. I concentrate on my breathing, try to cut out the internal dialogue, focus only on the rock—and relax."

BACHAR HAD SOME CLOSE CALLS during his climbing career. In 1979, during a trip to Colorado, Bachar made the third ascent of *Clever Lever*, a 5.12a in Eldorado Canyon. It begins with 30 feet of difficult gymnastic climbing across an overhang with a long move to a jug. From there the climber's feet cut loose and they have to hook a heel over a flake and lever up, after which the route becomes relatively easy. Bachar initially led the pitch without falling, but as his feet swung out, the rope came tight for a split second. Unsure as to whether the rope had kept him from falling, Bachar returned later, alone and without a rope, to find out.

This time, Bachar climbed up, reached for the jug, and cut his feet loose, just like before, but this time, the force of his swing ripped his fingers from the jug and he fell 30 feet, out of control, onto the sandstone slab below. He managed to twist in the air and land feetfirst, facing downhill, but his momentum pitched him forward, resulting in a long tumble down the slab. When Bachar finally stopped, a rock he had dislodged during his tumble hit him in the back. He was lucky, suffering only minor injuries, and was able to limp away. Bachar quit soloing after that, at least for a little while, but eventually he felt the twitch again.

A year later, Bachar had another close call. His confidence restored after a spring season of hard climbing and soloing in Joshua Tree, he set out for

Moratorium, a four-pitch 5.11b in Yosemite with hard climbing high off the deck. He'd soloed long 5.11s before but usually after climbing them a few times, wiring the sequences, making sure he had the moves dialed in before committing to them without a rope—not this time.

Things started out well, and Bachar cruised through the first half of the route, including a friction-dependent 5.10d stemming crux at the end of the second pitch. But at the crux of the climb, a thin jam and layback crack in a smooth-sided dihedral several hundred feet off the ground, Bachar hesitated, unable to find a reliable hold, uncertain whether he should commit to the next move. He backed down to a ledge to regroup, then tried again.

Bachar, like most free soloists, was not a "roll-the-dice" type of climber. He did not like to take chances or rely on luck. To avoid feeling out of control, even just a little, Bachar trained assiduously, physically and mentally. But here, with hundreds of feet of open air beneath him, he realized he would have to commit to an insecure move he'd never done before, a roll-the-dice move that would put him at the edge of control. With no other apparent option, he went for it. The pinkie-jam held. He squeaked through the move and finished the climb.

After his close call on *Moratorium*, Bachar quit making on-sight solos of 5.11s. But he definitely didn't quit soloing. If anything, he stepped it up. By the early 1980s, Bachar was soloing even harder routes, including circuits in Joshua Tree and Yosemite that included multiple routes up to 5.12 in difficulty that he climbed nearly every day. Part of his motivation seemed to be to set an example, to prove to other climbers that it was possible to climb hard without resorting to bad style, such as when he free soloed *Baby Apes*, a 5.12b at Joshua Tree to deter another climber from placing a protection bolt on rappel, a new trend that Bachar detested. Placing bolts while leading from the ground up was acceptable, because it preserved the adventure and uncertainty of the climb, and the risk, all things that Bachar believed were important for the integrity of the sport.

Although Bachar fought for years to prevent it, by the late 1980s, the sport climbing craze had infected even the historically traditional Joshua Tree, as typified by a 5.13a called *Father Figure*, established by Scott Cosgrove in 1988. Cosgrove, one of a new generation of young climbers who didn't share Bachar's ethical stance against preplacing protection, put in bolts on rappel to protect the lead. The overhanging 5.11 climbing on small holds capped off by a hard 5.12 crux move 50 feet above the boulders seemed to demand it—it was not the type of route you'd be able to protect on the lead.

Still, Bachar resented how the new generation had abandoned the traditional ground-up approach to climbing. By the mid-nineties, Bachar was pushing forty, and with the exploits of younger climbers gaining most of the attention, he was becoming something of an anachronism. But Bachar was admittedly competitive. Perhaps as a statement, or perhaps merely to prove something to himself, he free soloed *Father Figure*.

IN THE SPRING OF 1982 while climbing with a group of friends on the shady side of the Old Woman rock formation in Joshua Tree, I heard a scuffing sound and turned to see a lone climber standing quietly at the base of *Spider Line*, a thin, overhanging 5.11d crack. He had shaggy, shoulder-length hair and was wearing gray shorts, a blue chalk bag, and gnarled old rock shoes. Oblivious to our presence, he chalked his hands, rubbed them together meditatively, and breathing deeply, looked attentively up at the line. And then he started climbing, slotting his fingertips in the thin crack, toeing in on barely discernible ripples, and pulling himself up, move by move.

We stood mesmerized, watching as he climbed, move after flawless move, quietly, without any apparent effort, as if the force of gravity had been momentarily suspended. In less than a minute, he pulled onto the ledge at the end of the crack and vanished over the top.

Thinking about Bachar's free solo of *Spider Line* kept me up half the night. The next morning, I grabbed my rock shoes and chalk bag and snuck out of camp early, before anybody else was awake. I walked back to the base of the route to try the first moves for myself. I had no illusions about soloing the route; I just wanted to try to understand what I had seen. I pulled myself off the ground and reached rightward for a hold. The difficulty was ridiculous. I struggled to hang onto the greasy, sloping edges and flaring jams. I backed off, looked up dumbly at the line, and walked away.

I worked my way around the Old Woman, bouldering the first few moves of each route, until I reached the base of *Double Cross*. Looking up at the crack, I suffered a nearly debilitating adrenaline rush and had to sit down and breathe deeply for several minutes to fight it off.

After a few deep breaths, I tightened my laces, chalked up, and started climbing. At the top of a flake 20 feet off the ground, I paused. I knew I could climb this route all day and not fall off. But if I made even the slightest mistake, someone might find me dead on the boulders below. I looked up at the crack splitting the pale sunlit wall above me, then down again at the boulders.

"Fuck it," I thought out loud, and continued climbing, reaching the top soon after.

I sat on the ledge for the longest time, watching the silent desert morning unfold, wondering how I was going to get down. Everything was still. I was enveloped by a profound sense of calm. I had done it. Yet it was nothing. I soloed a 5.7. *Big deal.* I wouldn't even bother to tell anybody.

Just then, I caught sight of some movement. A solitary figure appeared on the landscape, walking briefly in the sun and then into the shadow, stopping at the base of *Left Ski Track*, then climbing it quickly, quietly, a study in strength and economy of movement, an embodiment of perfection on rock. His every move was deliberate—a reach, a pull, a step up, as if suspended in space and time. In a moment he was a hundred feet above the ground, stepping from shadow back into sunlight, and then he disappeared.

CHAPTER 6

Survival of the Fittest

In 1986, *Climbing* magazine published "Fool's Goal: Shawangunk Solo Climbs," about the escalation of hard free-solo climbing in the Gunks during the mid-eighties. "A new game had come to town," Russ Clune wrote. "Although nothing was overt, a third-classing competition had started within a small clique of Gunks regulars." By "third-classing," Clune meant unroped climbing. The competition he described didn't involve easy scrambling routes, as the term suggests; the Gunks climbers were soloing hard 5.11s, and in Clune's case, eventually 5.12. It was fascinating to read about, and a bit frightening.

I first met Clune, a lanky, dark-haired, freckle-faced upstate New Yorker with a distinct East Coast accent, at Joshua Tree in the spring of 1985. While climbing a handful of routes with Clune and his friends, I observed that he was a methodical and bold leader who took to thin cracks and faces with marginal protection. Having grown up in the Gunks, Clune was used to that kind of climbing, and zipped right up everything, placing wired nuts in narrow slots and running it out where a fall could have had serious consequences. I didn't see a competitive side to Clune. He wasn't trying to outdo anybody else; necky climbing was his kind of fun.

Of course, like most climbers, Clune *was* competitive, although the competition described in his article was friendly, albeit potentially deadly. As a small group of climbers began to solo harder and harder routes, they became obsessed with free soloing three ultra-classic Gunks routes: *Foops*, the 5.11c roof problem first free climbed by John Stannard in 1967; *Open Cockpit*, a steep, technical 5.11c face and crack pitch climbed by Steve Wunsch in 1973; and *Supercrack*, an overhanging 5.12c crack first free climbed by Wunsch in 1974.

Free soloing was nothing new in the Gunks. Henry Barber had made a habit of it during the early seventies, and a lot of climbers enjoyed running laps on easier routes without a rope. The area lent itself to free soloing, given the abundance of short routes on good rock with easy approaches and descents. Still, for the most part, only a handful of climbers pursued hard free soloing seriously. Clune didn't start soloing until after he'd been climbing for a few years, when he began venturing unroped onto easy routes—5.2 and 5.3 "scrambles," as he called them—to reach the start of more difficult routes, usually not as an end in itself. But eventually, he graduated to more challenging climbs. In the early eighties, he upped the game, going out with Russ Raffa in the afternoon and soloing 5.7s and 5.8s—well within his ability—as a way to help him develop mind control, which was important for climbing routes with long runouts above dubious protection. Free soloing hard stuff came later, in the mid-eighties, Clune told me, when a small group of Gunks climbers started pushing their limits.

Jeff Gruenberg struck first with an unroped ascent of *Foops*, which involved passing an eight-foot horizontal overhang that stuck out 40 feet above a jumble of granite boulders, a short-but-committing crux that required absolute confidence to execute. Gruenberg also soloed *Yellow Wall*, a 200-foot 5.11c, another Gunks classic and a bold free solo that helped to prime the competition. "The one thing that really still sends shivers down my spine is thinking of Jeff soloing *Yellow Wall*," Clune told me. "There's a couple holds on it that were never all that secure and I was like, 'Holy, Jesus!' That one was . . . scary."

Inspired by Gruenberg's solo of *Foops* and *Yellow Wall*, Clune got up the nerve to free solo *Open Cockpit*, a technical, dead-vertical thin crack and face line, just barely beating Barry Rugo, who soloed the route three days later. "The heat was on," Clune wrote, "two down and one to go." Of the holy trinity of free solos in the Gunks, only *Supercrack* remained. Originally referred to as *Wunsch upon a Climb*, the 70-foot route was thought to be the first 5.13 at the Gunks but was later downgraded.

Even so, it was still one of the area's most challenging routes, a technical endurance problem with several difficult, sequential moves. In one sense, free

soloing the route would be slightly easier than leading with a rope and protection, since hanging in place to set gear in the crack consumes energy and
makes failure more likely. However, for most climbers, the consequences of an
unroped fall squelched any thought of free soloing the route. Back then, only
a handful of climbers had free soloed a route of that difficulty, and only a few
locals had seriously considered it. Of them, only Clune tried it.

Clune didn't just go out and solo the 5.12c on a lark. He worked it, relentlessly practicing the moves on a toprope and then leading the route over and
over, to the point that he could consistently downclimb it without falling.
Only then did he gain the confidence to try it without a rope.

Despite people who say you can work the fear out of a route or that it's
not so bad to free solo easier routes well within your limits, Clune doesn't
think you can ever really say free soloing is safe. "It's inherently dangerous,"
he admits. "To ever call it safe is to really shut your brain off to the realities of
it. I mean, is it safe to get up on your roof and fuck around with the chimney,
without a rope? No. The odds are pretty much in your favor nothing will happen, but you know, it's not safe."

Even so, he pulled off *Supercrack*. He described himself as being on
autopilot during the climb, everything going as planned, until an internal
dialogue and jolt of adrenaline interrupted his flow. "*What the hell are you
doing?!*" he remembers wondering, before he quashed the thought, chalked
up, and continued. At the top, he thought, "God, I love this place," followed
by "I'm retired."

MANY CLIMBERS TOOK TO free soloing in the 1970s and 1980s to train
themselves to be able to keep their heads during difficult, runout climbs—to
develop mind control as they called it. Modern sport climbers know the rope
and bolts will catch them if they fall, but before sport climbing, climbers faced
potentially long falls on poor or nonexistent protection. If they couldn't focus
when the going got dicey, they would likely end up hurt or dead. Back then, it
was common to see climbers free soloing at a fairly high level—not so today.

"If you think about the scene in the mid-eighties, it was actually a pretty
good group of folks at the major climbing areas soloing hard by the standards of the day. I think it was just kind of a style of the time," Clune says. "It
happened in Britain, happened in California, happened in Colorado, and it

happened here [in the Gunks]. So, I think it was almost a commonality more than a 'he's-doing-it-therefore-I-must' kind of influence."

He points to Joshua Tree and English gritstone crags, places where there's a community of climbers who hang out and climb together, and where the nature of the rock lends itself to a culture of free soloing. In such a culture, once one climber starts soloing, others tend to follow, then they start upping the game, climbing harder and harder routes, seeing who will follow and who will quit first. Like the day when Clune, visiting Joshua Tree, fell in with the local crowd.

"It was New Year's Day of '84," Clune remembers. "The usual crowd was around, only locals—Largo [John Long], Yabo, Mike Lechlinski, that group— except me because I was with Largo. There was no plan for the day. Next thing you know, we go to some crag and everybody starts soloing." The group started on 5.8s then graduated to 5.9s and eventually 5.10s, continually upping the grade until they were free soloing 5.11s.

When they ended up at *Leave It to Beaver*, a 5.12, Clune decided it was time to stop. To his relief, somebody hung a toprope on it. But Clune remembers the locals' attitude toward soloing: "Everybody did it. The rope was hardly ever busted out."

SCOTT FRANKLIN WASN'T PART OF the free-soloing competition Clune described in his article, but the young East Coast climber was making a name for himself. In 1985, Franklin had established *Survival of the Fittest* as one of the first 5.13s at the Gunks, but after his first ascent, most climbers used a toprope, treating it like a training climb. At that time traditional climbing— leading from the ground up, placing protection on lead—was transitioning over to sport climbing, a more athletic and risk-averse pursuit where climbers used pre-placed protection bolts and worked a route, practicing it obsessively until they had it wired before making the send.

"*Survival* was kind of a pivotal route there because I led it from the ground up, traditional, placing the pins on lead and all that stuff," Franklin told me. "And then as soon as I did it, you know, everyone was done with traditional climbing. They just wanted to toprope it, work it, dog it out, because they couldn't lead it." As a result, the route became a very popular workout. "People were getting really pumped on it and getting stronger, and then we all just started doing it a lot, over and over again because it was a really fun route."

Franklin frequently joined the others in toproping the route as a workout. As a result, he eventually wired it, which got him thinking about trying it without the rope. "I had never done a route more frequently and repeatedly than *Survival*," he says. "And it was such a focal point, too, for all the climbing we were doing around other new routes. . . . I just became more and more focused on my climbing and really trying to push myself, getting stronger, and being a better climber." That's what got him thinking. "Wow. I really should solo that."

"Knowing that I *could* do it physically wasn't the issue," Franklin says. "But that's always the interesting part about climbing—going from the idea of doing something to actually doing it, and executing. "The idea stuck with him." I kind of latched onto it, like, "I'm going to do that. I'm going to solo *Survival*." He didn't share his decision with anybody except his girlfriend, Catherine Beloil.

On one fall morning in 1987, Franklin decided to give *Survival* a try, even though the cold, crisp weather wasn't good for climbing. He hiked up to the wall with Beloil, put on his rock shoes, chalked his hands, and started up. Despite having the route wired, he was still anxious. "I [remember] trying to stay calm, not being too hyped up," he recalls. "I was trying to be really deliberate and careful and climb it the way I climbed it all the time. And it worked. It was surprisingly quick. I remember feeling like, 'Well, that was it! I did it.'"

Like Clune, after he soloed *Survival of the Fittest*, Franklin retired from hard soloing. "I remember being just super-psyched and then feeling a huge sense of relief," he says. It was the only hard route he ever free soloed. Once was enough.

CHAPTER 7

Kid in a Candy Store

It was freezing cold when I pulled into the turnout below Castle Rock near Leavenworth, Washington, one fall morning in the mid-1980s—the sun wouldn't come over the canyon rim for at least another hour. There wasn't another car in sight, which meant I would have the entire wall to myself. Grabbing my gear, I hiked up the short, dusty trail to the base of the 600-foot-high cliff. I changed into rock shoes, tied on my chalk bag, stepped up to the icy cold rock, and began my pre-climb ritual.

First I wiped every trace of dust off the soles of my shoes. The dry dirt and rock dust at the base of Castle Rock is particularly slick. Sticky rubber is useless when coated in dust. I spat on my hands and rubbed my shoe soles until they were clean. I spat on my hands again and wiped them on my pants to get the dirt off and dry them, and then I took my time chalking up, rubbing the white powder meticulously over each finger and the palm and back until each hand was ghostly white. It was obsessive but meditative, a way of preparing my mind.

Then I closed my eyes, took a deep breath, exhaled, dipped my hands once more into my chalk bag, rubbed my fingertips lightly, and started climbing, methodically, savoring each move, until I reached a broad shelf called Logger's Ledge 300 feet up the wall. Before pulling over the edge, I looked down. The parking lot was empty except for my car, which appeared toy-size from this height. From there, 300 feet of easier face climbing led to the top of the cliff.

I sat with my feet dangling over the edge for a few moments, looking six hundred airy feet down to the highway and out over the Wenatchee River, still in deep shade, and up at dark walls of Tumwater Canyon across the roaring river, almost silent from this height. The quiet was momentarily broken by the whoosh of a swift darting past, then another. It was still cold; the sun had only just appeared on the crest of Icicle Ridge, a vertical mile above me. It would be hours before the sun hit the wall. Thinking I would have Castle Rock to myself for a while longer. I hurried down the trail to the base of the rock.

I started climbing again, hoping to get in another two or three laps before the sun hit or other climbers ruined my solitude. Barely 30 feet off the ground, I heard footsteps scuffing up the trail and turned to see who it was.

"How's it going?" Peter Croft said, grinning up at me.

SOON AFTER PETER CROFT WAS born in Ottawa in 1958, his family moved to Departure Bay, a ferry port on the eastern shore of Vancouver Island. The wilderness there was the backdrop of Croft's childhood, including hiking and fishing trips with his father. As a teenager, he and his friends would explore the surrounding woods and swim out to the many small, rocky islands just offshore in the Strait of Georgia. Still, Croft hadn't thought much about climbing until he read Chris Bonington's book, *I Chose to Climb*. After that, he could think of almost nothing else.

Although his dad had taken him climbing a couple of times, it was not until age seventeen that Croft began climbing in earnest on the basalt cliffs and boulders near his home. He soon moved onto Squamish, a "mini-version of Yosemite" as he called it, on the mainland, just north of Vancouver, British Columbia, and established himself as one of Canada's leading rock climbers.

Croft visited Yosemite for the first time in 1979, climbing several classic free routes including *Royal Arches*, an airy 1600-foot route first climbed in 1936 and considered the first "big wall" route in Yosemite. Inspired by the high standards and influenced by the Yosemite climbers' ethical approach to free climbing, Croft returned to Squamish and, over the next couple of years, established several of the hardest free climbs in the area. He returned to Yosemite in 1982, climbing longer, harder free routes including the *North Face* of the Rostrum and *Astroman*, both multipitch 5.11c routes at the cutting edge of long, hard free climbing. Back at Squamish, Croft climbed

University Wall (5.12b) with Hamish Fraser and Greg Foweraker, establishing the hardest long free climb in Canada. He also visited Washington State from time to time, where he had established many of the hard rock routes by the 1980s.

In addition to his reputation for hard free climbing, Croft was also becoming known for free soloing. In Washington, I'd hear about him soloing laps on Castle Rock, romping up route after route in Icicle Creek Canyon, or tagging summits in the Enchantments or Stuart Range. It was hard to believe sometimes that such a person existed.

Like most climbers, Croft had started out with some easy soloing here and there, before eventually pushing into more challenging terrain. He counts his 1982 ascent of *R.O.T.C.*, a 5.11c overhanging finger crack on Midnight Rock near Leavenworth as his first serious solo climb. In the early 1980s, Croft read *Hard Rock*, Ken Wilson's photo-essay compilation of classic British rock climbs. Eager to try them during a trip to England, but lacking a partner, Croft soloed them instead, mostly on-sight. Afterward, while eating fish and chips in a pub in Manchester, he thought about how great it would be to solo some classic routes at home. The end result would become one of the most incredible soloing days yet conceived: on-sight solo climbs of the *Beckey-Chouinard* on South Howser Tower, *Kraus-McCarthy* on Snowpatch Spire, the *Northeast Ridge* of Bugaboo Spire, and *McTech Arête* on Crescent Spire, for a combined 4,800 vertical feet of alpine rock climbing up to 5.10 in difficulty—in addition to descending each peak—in fourteen hours.

Meanwhile, rumors of Croft's trips to Yosemite began to reach us in Seattle. "Peter Croft climbed *Astroman* twice in a day," one had it (incorrectly), followed by "Peter Croft climbed *Astroman* and the Rostrum in a day" (this one was correct). Even though it was unprecedented, we were only mildly impressed. We already knew about how Croft and Fraser had made a record three consecutive ascents of the Grand Wall—3000 feet of vertical climbing up to 5.11 in difficulty—in only nine hours. We also knew that he had soloed the *Steck-Salathé*, then a linkup of *Steck-Salathé* and the *Northeast Buttress* of Middle Cathedral Rock, a combined twenty-six pitches up to 5.10 in difficulty. Croft was roped up for his single-day ascent of *Astroman* and the Rostrum— soloing those long 5.11 routes was unthinkable at the time. But, as his binge soloing of long free routes continued, people who knew Croft suspected he was thinking about it.

I FINALLY MET CROFT IN Yosemite in 1985. The buzz around Camp 4 the night after he arrived was that Croft had driven all night to Yosemite from Squamish and then immediately gone on a rash of free-solo climbs, including the *Northeast Buttress* of Higher Cathedral Rock, a 900-foot 5.9, then *Braille Book*, a 600-foot 5.8, and as a finale, he flew up the first five pitches of *Central Pillar of Frenzy*, adding several hundred feet of 5.9 crack climbing. He did it all during a rainstorm that had driven me and most other climbers off the rock that day. It had even snowed. These weren't the hardest routes in Yosemite, but the idea of driving twenty straight hours and then racing up 2000 vertical feet of 5.8 and 5.9 rock, unroped, in rain and snow, sent a ripple across the Valley.

Then Croft soloed the *North Face* of the Rostrum, an 800-foot 5.11c. Even though we knew it was coming, we were blown away.

"The first time I went up there, there were some guys ahead of me," Croft recalled during an interview with me for *Climbing* magazine. "They asked me what I was going to do, and I lied. I told them I was only going to do the first four pitches. I didn't want to say, 'I'm going to solo the Rostrum.'" He went on to repeat the solo a few days later. The unthinkable had become the routine.

Croft viewed free soloing in Yosemite as a progression. Henry Barber had soloed the *Steck-Salathé* in 1973. John Bachar soloed *New Dimensions*, a 5.11a thin crack, in 1976. After Croft soloed the Rostrum, everybody knew what was next. Still, when I interviewed him in 1985, he denied any such intentions.

"No," he assured me without a hint of hesitation when I asked if he was going to solo *Astroman*. "It's just too thin in some places."

Croft hadn't climbed it for a few years. He thought about doing it roped first, but decided not to, so he could preserve the adventure. To make it even more adventuresome, he planned to start with solos of *New Dimensions*, the Nabisco Wall, and the Rostrum. He did the first two routes easily, but the Rostrum was in full sun already, and the day was hot, so he decided to skip it and focus on *Astroman*. He hung out in the Valley until the route was in the shade and cooled down before he started up.

"As I looked at it from the forest there," Croft told Nick O'Connell in a 1993 interview, "I started psyching myself up, getting it engrained in my head that this wasn't a dangerous thing, that I was totally ready for it, and that it would be a totally successful climb. I saw myself hiking up there and saw myself climbing the whole thing. And then I started getting an overpowering urge to do it. It was hard to stop myself from going up there immediately."

Croft started up around five o'clock in the afternoon. He "dithered around" on the boulder problem pitch, a thin 5.11c layback crack, the technical crux of the climb, but after stalling for a few minutes, climbing up and down, trying to psych himself up, he finally pulled the trigger. After climbing it smoothly, he knew he was on. He topped out as the sun was setting, entirely alone. Sitting down, he took off his rock shoes and soaked it all in.

Croft's ascent of *Astroman* was, up to then, the boldest hard free-solo climb ever done in Yosemite. Combined with his single-day linkup of El Capitan and Half Dome—completed with Bachar in 1986, the first ever—it had become clear that Croft was operating on another level. Yosemite legend Royal Robbins referred to him as "my hero," and called his free-solo ascent of *Astroman* "astonishing." It would be more than a decade before another climber would solo the route, and to date only three climbers—Croft, Dean Potter, and Alex Honnold—have done it. Not that other climbers hadn't thought about it. Some thought Bachar would be the first. He'd been feeling the pressure of the expectation that he would do it, but after Croft pulled it off, Bachar seemed relieved.

"Way to go," Croft recalled Bachar telling him. "I'm glad you did it so that now I don't have to."

ONE DAY IN 1990, CROFT soloed the *Steck-Salathé*, *North Buttress* of Middle Cathedral, *Northeast Buttress* of Higher Cathedral, the *Royal Arches*, the *South Face* of North Dome, and *Arrowhead Arête*, a link-up of seventy-five pitches totaling 7800 feet of climbing up to 5.10 in difficulty, plus approaches, descents, and hikes from cliff to cliff across Yosemite Valley. In typical fashion, he got into Camp 4 after dark, threw down his sleeping bag, and slept; then he was up at first light and got back on the rock, picking up where he had left off.

That same year he joined longtime Yosemite climbing guide Dave Schultz to set a new record on the *Nose*—6 hours and 40 minutes. A year later, Hans Florine and Andy Puhvel climbed it 37 minutes faster. Croft and Schultz responded with a jaw-dropping time of 4 hours and 48 minutes. In 1992, Croft teamed up with Florine to lower the mark by another 26 minutes, leading to speculation about a sub-four-hour time someday. (The current record, set by Alex Honnold and Tommy Caldwell in 2018, is a little less than two hours.)

Also in 1992, Croft and Jonny Woodward made the first free ascent of *Moonlight Buttress*, a 1200-foot sandstone prow in Zion National Park. Originally rated 5.13a, the route was later downgraded to 5.12d (and eventually free soloed by Alex Honnold on April 1, 2008, leading some people initially to believe the story was an April Fool's joke). But Croft has never really cared about ratings—he just wants to climb.

Croft put his ability to log miles of climbing to the test in 1998 with a first ascent of a route up Spansar Brakk, a rock spire in the Charakusa Valley in Pakistan. He and partner Conrad Anker practically sprinted up and down the 8000-foot-long knife-edge ridge traverse that included 5.11 climbing in twenty-three hours round-trip. Two years later, he soloed the two-mile-high *Evolution Traverse* as well as made an enchainment of the four Celestial Arêtes on Temple Crag, linking four 2000-foot routes up to 5.10b in difficulty in a single day.

Croft has remained active, establishing numerous long, hard routes in the High Sierra and working as a rock-climbing guide. (Rumor has it he still solos, too, quietly though, for his own reasons.) Despite his achievements, Croft has remained humble and reclusive, shunning almost all media attention. He makes a cameo in *Free Solo*, assuring Honnold that it was the right decision to bail on his first attempt to solo El Cap.

As guidebook author Bruce Fairley wrote of Croft in a *Canadian Alpine Journal* article, "Even if there were no climbing press, no television cameras, he would still be climbing in the same way that he is climbing today." Fairley also wrote that Croft, "without any conscious attempt to do so, symbolizes a higher ethical position than that prevailing in the community of climbers around him."

Many climbers of that era, including myself, were heavily influenced by Croft's approach: get in as much climbing as possible in a day and on as much terrain as possible, whether 5.2 or 5.10, ideally without a partner to slow you down. During an interview with O'Connell, he explained why soloing appealed to him:

> *There are no interruptions . . . no stopping to place gear. . . . On longer routes, you get a certain rhythm going. You're just reacting to things and*

the decisions you make are almost subconscious. . . . It's all instantaneous. It just flows.

In terms of adventure, the more equipment I can get rid of, the better. . . . For me an adventure is something that I can take an active part in but that I don't have total control over. And the more active a part, and the more intimate the relationship with the surroundings, the better. So it's possible to have an adventure in a car, but it would be better on a bike. And better than a bike would be hiking, and since hiking is generally the same sort of movement over and over, better than that would be roped climbing. And better than roped climbing would be to eliminate all the equipment and climb solo without ropes.

As I sat watching Croft climb the last 30 feet to the top of Castle Rock that morning, it occurred to me that I had never seen him roped up. Every time I had encountered him climbing, he had been soloing.

"Nice day," I offered as Croft topped out on his first lap of the day.

"Sure is," he replied. "Doesn't get better."

"Nope," I said.

That was about all we said to each other the whole day. Croft doesn't talk much anyway. Aside from a hello here or there as he encountered other climbers, Croft climbed quietly, immersed in his own world. He started back down the route he had just climbed; I took the trail.

It went on like that for hours, soloing laps until it got too hot to climb. A few other climbers arrived in the late morning—we sometimes had to climb around them or traverse to another route to avoid them—but they let us alone. They just stopped and watched us silently as we climbed past.

By noon, I had climbed Castle Rock ten times, over a vertical mile of rock, in only a few hours. Croft had probably climbed three times that, counting his ascents and descents. He had already vanished when I decided to call it a day, probably halfway back to Vancouver, although you never knew with him. When it came to climbing, Croft was like a kid in a candy store, wide-eyed, wanting it all.

"It's not as if soloing changes your life every time," Croft told O'Connell, "but it reinforces certain things in your head. It requires that you concentrate pretty hard, and depending on the type of concentration, it can bring different things to you."

One of the things that it brings to Croft is a sense of intense connection with the physical and emotional landscape. "Sometimes when I'm soloing I find the beauty of the climb just staggering. I'm living life intensely and the rewards are intense. If they weren't intense, I wouldn't bother."

PART II

Call of the Void

"Looking into the abyss, we want to live, but at the same time we become aware of our total freedom."
—Jean-Paul Sartre, *Being and Nothingness*

I was born in 1962 in Seattle, Washington. My birth mother, who I did not meet until I was nearly thirty, was eighteen years old. Her strict father, who had sent her to a home for wayward girls, forced her to give me up for adoption. She abused drugs and alcohol, was sexually promiscuous, exhibited acute anxiety and manic behavior, and was diagnosed with ADHD—she was a mess.

As an infant, I was adopted by a middle-class couple in their early twenties. High-school sweethearts, they had married right after graduation, mostly at the insistence of my mother, who was desperate for attention and had a jealous streak a mile wide. Her twin sister was getting married, so my mother got married too—and fast. Her sister soon had two children; my mother tried, but after she had a miscarriage, her doctor told her she probably could not have children of her own. She adopted me to fill the void.

I had many questions and doubts during my childhood. Mostly I wondered why my birth mother would give me up. I saw my adoption as evidence that I must be flawed.

Austin Howell free soloing Built to Tilt *(5.10a/b), Shortoff Mountain, North Carolina* (Photo by Ben Wu)

My adoptive mother had anger issues. She'd been abused as a child, and was in turn vindictive, abusive, and attention seeking, which led to my parents divorcing when I was two. After the divorce, I lived with her, although she would occasionally leave me with my dad for long periods, which made me feel even more unwanted.

One morning in fifth grade, a boy teased me about my lunch box, and I hit him over the head with it. I was suspended from school for several days. When I returned, I responded to a teacher's dismissive comment by calling her a bitch and throwing my books at her—that got me expelled.

My mom, who was going through her second divorce, simply left me home alone every day when she went to work. My only adult supervision was a tutor who taught me math, English, and history a few times a week. I spent the rest of each day roaming around the neighborhood; eventually, a group of high-school delinquents adopted me as their mascot and taught me how to shoot pool, play pinball, and drink beer. When my mom found out, she had a fit.

"What am I going to do with you?" she yelled. "You are ruining my life!"

ONE DAY SHE CAME HOME from work and told me that she was moving to California with a man named Nick and was taking me to live with my dad. I cried quietly in the back seat as my mom drove me to my dad's house. She hugged me and told me that she loved me, that she'd fly me down when she was settled in California. I just stood there crying, thinking it was my fault.

Clearly, I had emotional issues, and so my new school placed me in a special education class. One day during lunch, I stabbed a classmate with a fork because he made fun of my shoes. This time, all of my pent-up rage came pouring out. I shouted obscenities at everyone within range. My teachers took me into an empty classroom and took turns holding me down. After three hours, I was physically exhausted and could barely move.

The next day the school psychologist asked me a lot of questions and had me take several tests. I was allowed to return to school, and for a week I was closely supervised. I ate lunch at a table by myself. A teacher's aide stayed close by the entire day. The psychologist came once a week to see how I was doing.

My stepmother was a lot like my adoptive mother, vindictive and verbally abusive. Worse, she had a biological son she adored and favored. Still, she sensed that something was wrong with my mom and persuaded my dad to fight a vicious custody battle when I was in seventh grade.

I was old enough for my opinion to be considered by the court in awarding custody, so I was called in to testify in private with the judge. The only question I remember was: "If it was your choice, who would you want to stay with, your mom or your dad?" As I left the judge's chambers, I looked down at the floor as I walked past my mom, who was crying at a table with her lawyer. Everyone knew what I'd said to the judge.

My raw emotional state after the custody trial made me an easy target for abuse. One boy named Brad seemed to delight in bullying me—spitting on me, slamming my fingers in my locker door, throwing food at me during lunch, calling me derogatory names. I wasn't his only victim; he and his friends terrorized anyone who didn't fit in with their tribe, especially kids they perceived as weak. They took a special interest in tormenting my friend, Jay, an epileptic who would occasionally have seizures at the bus stop or in the hallway.

One day Brad threw Jay's clothes into the shower after gym class, and something inside me snapped. A surge of energy flowed through me, my heart began pounding, my stomach tightened. I felt dizzy and nauseous, and almost blacked out. In a blind rage, I took a swing at Brad, but missed, and he promptly beat the shit out of me. The best I could do was pull his hair as he punched me repeatedly in the face.

That Christmas, I flew down to California to visit my mom and her new husband. My mom cried the whole time and complained about how it was unfair that she had lost custody, that she only got four days of visitation for Christmas, that the airline tickets were costing her a fortune. On the drive to the airport to send me home, she pulled over on the shoulder of the freeway and broke down.

"How could you do this to me?" she asked angrily, sobbing. She blamed me for the outcome of the custody battle. "Why are you doing this to me?"

Every day that winter on my walk to the bus stop, I crossed an overpass above a freeway. How many times I stopped there, looked down, and thought about jumping, I don't recall. I don't know why I didn't either, but if I had to guess, I would say it was because I had found climbing.

CHAPTER 8

The Imp of the Perverse

When I was fourteen, I asked if I could take a climbing instruction course I had found in the classified ads. My stepmother said no. "Climbing is dangerous," she insisted. I didn't give up. I started climbing onto the roof of the house, and one afternoon, I rappelled out my bedroom window using a rope I found in the basement.

"What are we going to do with him?" I overheard her asking my dad, exasperated.

"Well," he said, "we could let him take that climbing class he wants to take."

She finally gave in. Now fifteen, I was the youngest student in the class. After several weeks of classroom sessions and a day on some practice rocks, they took us on our first real climb, The Tooth, a 5605-foot peak an hour's drive from Seattle. The peak seemed innocuous from far away, a little rock point shaped like a canine tooth, but as we hiked nearer, it reared up menacingly. We were going to climb *that*?! Although I tried not to show it, I was terrified.

The route ascended 400 feet of steep volcanic rock, up corners and short walls interspersed with narrow ledges and gnarled subalpine firs and hemlocks. Our guides climbed ahead and belayed us up one at a time from ledge to ledge. The exposure grew as we climbed higher, and in places we seemed to be perched on the edge of the world, the cliff falling away infinitely far to the boulder field below. We were perfectly safe, the guides said, roped up and belayed from above for most of the way, except for a short stretch about 100 feet below the top, where we had to untie between one belay and the next. It was easy; no need to rope up there, they assured us.

I untied from the rope and followed the guide's vague instructions to "scramble up to where Don is waiting." I climbed more or less directly up to where Don, one of our guides, was perched just below the summit, belaying climbers up. I couldn't see any other climbers, so I just picked out what looked like the easiest line between us and scampered from ledge to ledge.

I arrived at a foot-wide ledge below a short, vertical wall about 10 feet high, capped by a ledge that led 20 feet up and left to where the climber ahead of me was tying into the rope, preparing to climb the final pitch to the summit. I tried to climb the wall directly but backed down. I tried the left side, then the right, but neither option seemed feasible. I rested for a minute then tried again, making a steep move on thin holds, then another, to a point just one move below the ledge. There was a little flake of rock to grip with my fingers. Grabbing it tight, I walked my feet up as high as I could get them, levered up, and reached for the ledge, but found nothing to hold on to, so I reversed the moves back to the narrow ledge.

I looked down at the jumble of boulders lying malignantly in the shadows 300 feet below and thought it would be an awfully long way to fall. Suddenly I felt something, a feeling like the one I got right before I took a swing at Brad in the junior high locker room. My heart began pounding, my stomach tightened. I felt dizzy, nauseous. Afraid I might lose my balance and fall, I gripped the rock tight and held on. I breathed deeply, eyes closed, afraid to look down.

"Is this the route?" I eventually called up to Don when I had recovered.

"Sure," Don called down, more casually than I expected. "Do you want me to toss you a rope?"

"No," I said, not wanting to appear weak. "I think I can do it."

"Right on," he said, turning back to the young, blonde woman tied to the other end of the rope he was holding attentively.

I started up the step again, and this time got my feet onto higher holds that allowed me to reach higher, grab the edge of the flake at the back of the ledge, and flop onto it using my knees and elbows. It was a tenuous, awkward move. I stood up carefully and then inched over to where Don had lowered the rope for me.

"You were supposed to traverse lower down," Don said as I tied in, "but that way was good too. Your technique is horrible, but you'll learn."

I climbed up to Don, who was on a ledge just below the summit, a small slab of rock where a half dozen people could sit comfortably.

"You can untie here and scramble up to the top," he said. "Wait there for the rest of the group."

On the summit, I looked over the east face, down hundreds of feet of jagged rock, and felt a sudden urge to jump off. It felt like a physical hallucination, as if the fabric of space was bending and I was being pulled toward the edge. I took a step back, walked to the other side, and sat down as far away from the edge as I could.

Larry Straker, at fifty-five the oldest student in the class, arrived on the summit shortly after I did and seemed to be enjoying himself. He walked over to the edge as I had and looked down.

"Wow, that's a long way down!" he said, a huge smile on his face.

"Are you okay?" he asked, suddenly looking concerned. "You look a little freaked out."

"I'm okay," I said, smiling weakly.

I DIDN'T SAY MUCH AFTER that. On the ride home, I contemplated the climb. I was aware I could have fallen to my death if I'd made a wrong move while I was climbing unroped, agonizing over thoughts of *what if*, but I'd stayed calm and worked out the difficulties despite the risk. It hadn't seemed that bad. In fact, once I'd overcome my fear, it had seemed fun. I was more concerned by my urge to leap off the summit. *Was I suicidal? No, I'd stepped back from the edge.* So what *was* that?

It turns out that, when standing atop a cliff or high building, a lot of people feel the same inexplicable impulse to jump off. There is even a term for it in French: *l'appel du vide*—"the call of the void." In *Harper's* magazine, novelist Louis de Bernières wrote that each time he approached the edge of a cliff, he felt himself being drawn over. "The vertical became the horizontal, and a terrifying sickness took me at the stomach and throat." American author Tom Hunt experienced it when he visited Beachy Head, a 535-foot seaside cliff on the south coast of England. In *Cliffs of Despair: A Journey to the Edge*, Hunt noted that since 1965, more than five hundred people have ended their lives jumping from Beachy Head. It is believed that some of them didn't actually mean to, but rather they were seized by an unaccountable impulse to jump and gave into the urge before they knew what was happening.

Hunt described how one time while taking his usual Sunday morning stroll along the top of Beachy Head, he felt a sudden urge to run to the edge. "For a moment I actually feel caught in a current that will sweep me over the edge if I keep looking. So I turn away and veer inland, where the feeling disappears as quickly as it came."

Hunt knew he was not the only one who felt it. In the newspaper article that had enticed him to write about Beachy Head in the first place, to explore and resolve the trauma of a suicide in his own family, a police officer taking a reporter for a walk along the edge of the cliff asked, "Can you feel it? There's a funny feeling that the cliff draws you over the edge. I don't know why."

Originally, this phenomenon was thought to be a manifestation of a subconscious suicidal impulse. As de Bernières wrote, "I have never felt this anywhere else, even when mountaineering or when I was a tree surgeon, and I wondered how many people might have been hypnotized into committing suicide unintentionally." In his 1897 book *Suicide*, French sociologist Émile Durkheim referred to such sudden, unpremeditated acts of self-destruction as "automatic suicides" in which "suicidal tendency appears and is effective in truly automatic fashion, not preceded by an intellectual antecedent. The sight of a knife, a walk by the edge of a precipice, engender the suicidal idea instantaneously and its execution follows so swiftly that patients often have no idea of what has taken place."

Today, psychologists reject the idea of "automatic suicide" and refer to these incidents by a less-romantic term: "high place phenomenon" or HPP. In a 2012 study published in the *Journal of Affective Disorders* titled "An Urge to Jump Affirms the Urge to Live," researchers proposed that HPP may be the result of crossed wires, a signal to the brain to engage the survival instinct that momentarily has the opposite effect. The signal warns you of the very real danger right in front of you, and, just to be sure, it gives you a mental push over the edge to drive the message home. Unfortunately, if you're suicidal, you might actually jump. But most people who experience HPP, it turns out, are not suicidal. They step back.

The 2012 study included 431 undergrads who self-assessed their experience of HPP, suicidal ideation, anxiety, depression, and mood episodes. From their responses, the researchers found that HPP was more common than expected, even among subjects who reported no history of suicidal ideation. They also found that people with higher levels of anxiety sensitivity were more likely to experience HPP, and that the likelihood was highest among those who additionally experienced low levels of suicidal ideation. "Individuals who report experiencing the phenomenon are not necessarily suicidal," the study concluded. "Rather, the experience of HPP may reflect their sensitivity to internal cues and actually affirm their will to live."

Not only that, but researchers believe people can overcome HPP by repeated exposure to the void. Their theory is that, by putting themselves in situations where falling is an imminent possibility, and then repeatedly not falling to their death, they come to accept that although the fear is real, they can suppress it, control their mind and actions, and survive. This, it turns out, is the same kind of mental conditioning that allows someone like Alex Honnold to free solo El Capitan.

IN 1845, *GRAHAM'S MAGAZINE* PUBLISHED a short story by Edgar Allan Poe, titled "The Imp of the Perverse," about a man who killed someone to inherit his estate. Although the man has lived for many years in luxury by keeping the murder a secret, he has an inexplicable urge to tell someone and, once that thought has entered his mind, he is compelled by "some invisible fiend"—the Imp—to blurt it out to a passing stranger, thus sealing his fate.

Although Poe's story is not about climbing or HPP, it is easy to draw a comparison, especially in one passage from the story that describes the phenomenon almost exactly as I experienced it on The Tooth.

We stand upon the brink of a precipice. We peer into the abyss — we grow sick and dizzy. Our first impulse is to shrink from the danger. Unaccountably we remain. By slow degrees our sickness and dizziness and horror become merged in a cloud of unnamable feeling . . . a thought, although a fearful one, and one which chills the very marrow of our bones with the fierceness of the delight of its horror. It is merely the idea of what would be our sensations during the sweeping precipitancy of a fall from such a height. . . . There is no passion in nature so demoniacally impatient, as that of him who, shuddering upon the edge of a precipice, thus meditates a

Plunge. . . . If there be no friendly arm to check us, or if we fail in a sudden
effort to prostrate ourselves backward from the abyss, we plunge, and are
destroyed.

Poe's Imp prompts people to act irrationally and do things that are not
only *not* in their best interest but potentially harmful, and some people are
helpless to resist the urge to self-destruction. And as Poe warned, "With certain minds, under certain conditions, it becomes absolutely irresistible. . . .
The impulse increases to a wish, the wish to a desire, the desire to an uncon-
trollable longing, and the longing . . . is indulged." We act knowing not only
that we should not, but *because* we should not.

It's fair to say that impulse control disorder is a factor in both HPP and
the phenomenon described by Poe. In general, people with impulse control
disorder are compelled by anxiety to do risky things—shoplift, rob people,
gamble, free solo hard rock climbs. The impulse can be so strong that they
feel consumed by anxiety, which builds up like a pressure cooker. Stealing the
candy bar, letting it ride, robbing a bank, jumping out of an airplane—whatever they choose to do—brings relief, even elation, despite or perhaps in part
because of the danger involved.

The impulse can take days or even years to build. As Durkheim noted,
"Patients feel the impulse growing and manage to escape the fascination of
the mortal instrument by fleeing from it immediately." But the impulse may
linger, like a rat in your belly, gnawing at your insides until you finally feed it.

ROWENA FLETCHER-WOOD HAS EXPERIENCED HPP recurrently, and
remembers feeling it periodically as a small child while visiting her grandparents. "We would cross a bridge from the multistorey car park to the theatre,
a long, thin snake of a thing with green, wide-set bars that wound over the
motorway," she recalls. "Below, cars streaked past. I felt as a small thing that I
could slip between those bars. I felt terrified, but I also wanted to jump." She's
also felt the impulse while standing on a railway bridge near her home, on
the platform as the trains streaked by, on the Sydney Harbour Bridge looking
down at the water far below, and still feels it sometimes on mountains when
approaching a ridge with the wind behind her or at the top of a climb just
before she leans back on the rope.

Today, Fletcher-Wood is a certified rock-climbing instructor and science communicator with the accolades of an obsessive overachiever, including a master's from Oxford and a PhD from the University of Birmingham. And, as if that's not enough, she's also a new mom. Fletcher-Wood has learned to accept and even embrace her anxiety about experiencing HPP as part of the psychological thrill of climbing. "I enjoy the feeling too much to eliminate it," she admits, although she has learned to control it. "I often play psychological games with myself. For example, every time you remember an event, you relay the memory."

"By subtly changing the memory," she says, "you can change your recollection of an event. That means the next time, you're actually remembering *remembering* it, not the original event."

"Impulsiveness can go hand in hand with anxiety," Fletcher-Wood explains, "and it seems they make each other worse. Impulsive or risky behaviour can lead to decisions that create worry, and anxiety can sometimes lead to irrational and poorly thought-out decisions."

BUT ARE IMPULSIVENESS AND POORLY thought-out decisions always correlated? In 2007, American climber and BASE jumper Steph Davis free soloed the *Casual Route* (5.10a) on the Diamond, a 1000-foot vertical face on the north side of Longs Peak in Colorado, as a way of moving past a difficult point in her life following her divorce from Dean Potter. But, as she described it later in her memoir, *Learning to Fly*, as soon as she had achieved her goal on the *Casual Route*—for which she'd had to overcome both anxiety and fear—the idea of free soloing an even harder route—*Pervertical Sanctuary*—became fixed in her mind.

The route, a steep crack that overhung gently and ranged from finger to offwidth size, was rated 5.11a. It had been free soloed only once before, by English climber Derek Hersey in 1990. Hersey, nicknamed Dr. Death, was known for his bold free-solo climbs; he was considered by many to be reckless and cavalier, pushing too close to the edge too often. Few were surprised when he was killed in a fall while soloing in Yosemite in 1993. Davis was mindful of Hersey's death but did not let that stop her. "My mind locked down obsessively, the way it always did when I got pulled into a climbing project," she wrote. "All of my thoughts and decisions now revolved around *Pervertical*

Sanctuary. I needed to climb it with a deep physical urge that was impossible to ignore. . . . This new, almost presumptuous dream would be the only thing that would matter in life until I did it."

Davis didn't fit the same profile as Hersey; she seemed thoughtful in her approach, mindful of the risks and her reasons for pursuing them, more open and honest about her thoughts, fears, and feelings than men usually are. Curious, I asked Fletcher-Wood whether she felt Davis might have decided to free solo the route impulsively. She said no. In Davis's case, Fletcher-Wood felt it was more of a physiological phenomenon than a psychological one.

"There are two ways to consider the word 'impulsive,' either based on instinctive or innate impulses or drives, or a momentary, emotional decision," she told me. "Mostly when I talk about it, I mean the latter, which of course builds on the former. When researchers study impulsiveness, it's not so much about the quality of the impulses (how good the decisions are), as how much control you have over them."

In her view, Davis wasn't acting on instinctive or innate impulses. She had admitted that her actions were an attempt to control fear and relieve anxiety, and that they were obsessive, of course, in her description of her mind "locking down." But, in Fletcher-Wood's view, there was something more to Davis's impulse to free solo *Pervertical Sanctuary.*

"Like running, there is a serotonin release," she explained. "There's also an adrenalin surge and drop. When we imagine doing something, we engage our cortex, and if you tell yourself the story of doing an action, your motor cortex, if scanned, looks the same as if you're doing it."

Just as remembering a memory can change your recollection of an event, it can also make your mind respond as if you are actually doing it. "So, it seems like even just imagining a climb gives us a massive boost of hormones that are addictive, and Steph was indulging in this, essentially 'increasing the dose' up to actually doing it."

THIS ADRENALINE SURGE AND DROP is part of how Fletcher-Wood has achieved success. "And for the personal note, yes, I tend to create goals [and] targets and obsess about them," she told me. "That's how I achieve things, whether it's getting to Oxford University, finishing a novel, or completing a challenging climb!"

But there can be a darker side to the hormone surge that sometimes accompanies high-risk activities like free soloing. Some people engage in high-risk activities because they help them confront or manage anxiety, depression, and other disorders. Fletcher-Wood admits she fits that description. She has generalized anxiety that she tends to experience physically. "People with anxiety tend to be more sensitive to internal physical signals like stress, stage fright, or fear of heights," she says. "Fear is, after all, a useful survival mechanism—it tells us to get back from that edge."

Fletcher-Wood says she experiences a physical response to fear and anxiety. "Sometimes when I'm afraid I vibrate, but mostly I get tension in my limbs, lower back pain, jaw clenching, that kind of thing. It also includes nausea." But because her response is physical, she can still think straight and work through it.

"Although our instincts primarily tell us to fear and withdraw from danger," she says, "we also have a crucial fascination with dangerous things, which allows us to learn about our enemies and overcome them." She points to a quote from E. O. Wilson, the American naturalist and writer, who said, "We're not just afraid of predators. We're transfixed by them, prone to weave stories and fables and chatter endlessly about them, because fascination creates preparedness, and preparedness, survival."

"So, what does this mean?" Fletcher-Wood asks. "Well, for me it means I have evidence I am afraid of heights. The researchers claim this impulse means you have good survival instincts and, far from feeling suicidal, want to live," she explains. "[Climbing] gives me something to focus physical and mental efforts on, and it feels good to do it and to have done it."

Fletcher-Wood doesn't free solo, but she understands how anxiety and impulsivity can draw someone to it, how the thought "I could solo that" can lead to an obsessive need to carry out the impulse, although she questions whether most free soloists are truly impulsive. "Perhaps the decision is impulsive," she says, but points out that most free soloists carefully prepare before they take action to minimize and partition the fear, and don't act impulsively. "Surely a lot of the thrill comes from the release of anxiety upon success?"

But she acknowledges that rewards and an individual's own loss aversion threshold (the tendency to prioritize avoiding possible losses over acquiring potential gains) can complicate our understanding of how anxiety, impulsivity, and obsession affect a given climber's decision to free solo a difficult route, and cautions that while many people *can* control anxiety this way, and it works for her, it isn't a sure thing.

"I am someone who is very impulsive but have a high loss aversion, so it takes a lot to get me to take a risk, but once I have decided it's worth risking, [I'll] engage a 'fuck it' attitude and take lots of those risks," she says. "This can also be linked to the anxiety of suspension (any result is better than waiting—also see research into boredom, and how people will endure pain rather than be bored!) versus the anxiety of risk."

Would Fletcher-Wood go free soloing deliberately, though? "Maybe," she says. Although she's never intentionally free soloed, Fletcher-Wood has had the fairly common climbing experience of finding herself on easy terrain that she wished she'd roped up for, as well as roped climbing where a ground fall is a real possibility.

"Free climbing is scary, and unless you do something stupidly easy for you, it should be. That's part of the thrill, right? . . . But it's not as dangerous as it's made out to be. Most climbers are pretty good at assessing risk," she insists. "If I think about what could happen, or what is behind me, fear could overcome me. So, I don't."

Instead, she says she thinks "about the feeling at my fingertips, rummaging for and testing that next foothold. If I focus, I will not only be not afraid, I will be better, and afterwards I will be pleased I did it. But that's why I've never gone looking for those situations, [but have] merely taken the opportunity when it's 'happened.'"

Although she doesn't free solo, Fletcher-Wood does engage in other risky activities. For example, on her thirtieth birthday, she swam with sharks. She wasn't afraid of the sharks themselves, she says, just obsessively fascinated with them. What she *was* afraid of was breathing out of an air tank underwater, a fear she had to accept and overcome to be able to fulfill her obsessive goal, which she correlates, in a way, to free soloing. "Although it's not a climb, it's about going out into the world and overcoming your physical impulses to run away and escape in order to enter a space or domain that should naturally be exclusive to you."

As for those who do free solo, Fletcher-Wood isn't judgmental. "Undoubtedly there are the crazies," she says, "the people who don't have a good sense of preservation and get injured and go again, and again. But the numbers show that most climbers, even free soloers, aren't foolish," she adds. "They're very together people who know their sport. The fools, the crazies, and the people who take their lives in their hands, are the townies who decide to walk Mount Snowdon in flipflops."

She has a point. Mount Snowdon, the highest summit in Wales at 3556 feet, is a popular hike with the "townies," city folk who flock to the mountains for recreation. Despite a well-established trail to the summit, the Llanberis Mountain Rescue Team carried out seven rescues on Mount Snowdon in one day in the fall of 2020 and were called to recover the body of a walker who'd fallen to his death from the summit trail—the third fatality on the mountain in as many weeks. In most years, more people die on Mount Snowdon than on Mount Everest. In fact, in most years, more people die hiking Mount Snowdon than free soloing.

CHAPTER 9

Russian Roulette

"I was climbing great, feeling solid," Rick Cashner told Eric Perlman, for an article in *Backpacker* magazine, about the spring morning in 1982 when he was free soloing *Spider Line*. "The next thing I knew, I lay wrecked in the rubble and covered in blood."

Two of Cashner's friends, heading off to do their own morning solo session, had looked back and seen him starting up *Spider Line*, which had become something of a must-do free solo for the Joshua Tree regulars. When they returned a short while later, a tourist told them a climber had fallen. They raced over and found Cashner among the boulders below the route, banged up and bleeding from a gash on his forehead.

A few days later, Cashner was back in Joshua Tree with a cast on his wrist, angry with himself and full of frustration that he couldn't go climbing. But it wasn't long before he was back at it. He had one good arm, after all, and the cast turned out to be not too much of an impediment. He was, if nothing else, persistent.

Cashner was a thin, muscular climber—the kind you'd call wiry—with cable-strong fingers and forearms and a head of thick, scraggly hair that went well past his shoulders. His size, weight, strength, and tenacity made him an expert boulderer and proficient free climber, right up there with the likes of John Bachar, Ron Kauk, and John Long, although he tended to do more outrageous things than everyone except maybe John Yablonsky.

Cashner free soloed often, on all kinds of terrain—face, friction, thin crack, offwidth—frequently in the company of others, usually Bachar. The pair did solo circuits together in Joshua Tree and Yosemite, and speed solos of easier routes, climbing walls hundreds of feet high in just a few minutes— their version of jogging, turning what is usually considered a static, control-oriented discipline into an aerobic workout. And although he took soloing seriously, Cashner approached it with a casual, almost cavalier attitude that resulted in an unprecedented number of unroped falls. He was eventually given the nickname "Crashner"—the guy who kept falling off while free soloing, bashing himself up, then getting back on the rock and doing it again.

As reported in the 1985 edition of *Accidents in North American Mountaineering*, at about noon on August 17, 1984, a climber named Ernie Milan and his partner were preparing to climb *Golfer's Route* on Low Profile Dome in Tuolumne Meadows when they met a lone climber who told them he was going to free solo *Darth Vader's Revenge*, a nearby 5.9 route.

About a half hour after encountering the solo climber, just as Milan had reached the final protection bolt on the first pitch of *Golfer's Route*, he heard a "thumping sound" and looked to see a body tumbling "head over feet" down the steep slab and eventually landing at the base of the wall. Milan yelled for help and another climber, hearing his yells, drove to the Tuolumne Meadows Visitor Center to summon a rescue. A rescue crew soon arrived and evaluated the fallen climber, who had survived but was seriously injured. As reported in *Accidents*, "The victim sustained multiple lacerations, abrasions and contusions, and about six teeth were knocked out." The injured climber was flown by helicopter to the medical clinic in Yosemite Valley, then to Modesto where he was hospitalized.

A few days after Cashner's accident, John Bachar went to check out the scene and look for Cashner's missing teeth. While there, he soloed up to where Cashner had fallen, to see for himself what had happened. Sure enough, a knob had broken. There was a white scar on the rock where it had sheared off.

WHEN THE *WASHINGTON POST* PUBLISHED an online article about Alex Honnold's El Capitan free solo, readers posted comments that questioned his sanity. They wondered who would pay to clean up his body parts when he fell, and expressed the opinion that Honnold and the film would encourage others to try to repeat his suicidal feat. In an article in *Outside* online, Honnold's friend and climbing partner Tommy Caldwell wondered: "Would I be watching my friend perform an act of generation defining mastery or a round of Russian roulette?"

The *Manual of Forensic Emergency Medicine* refers to Russian roulette as "a form of high-risk-taking behavior in which the person shoots himself or herself, making it appear in some ways as a suicide" although "the person participating is not necessarily suicidal." Still, according to a study of Russian roulette conducted by the Office of the Chief Medical Examiner in Louisville, Kentucky, which refers to it as "an act of extreme bravado," although the victim's presumed intent is to survive, it is deemed to be suicide "based on a comprehensive understanding of the inherently deliberate, volitional actions of the decedent." Or as the National Association of Medical Examiners' guideline for determining the manner of death explains, "because the act of putting a loaded gun to one's head and pulling the trigger is inherently dangerous and carries a high risk of death," it's no accident.

In some respects, free soloing may seem like Russian roulette. It's a high-risk activity with an element of chance: nothing bad will happen if things go right, but if things go wrong, you are almost certain to die a swift, violent death. In other respects, free soloing is not at all like Russian roulette. Unlike a game of chance where you put a bullet in a chamber, spin the cylinder, put the barrel to your head, pull the trigger, and hope for a harmless click, free soloing has an element of control; the outcome depends on your physical condition, agility, technical skills, and mental focus. If you happen to kill yourself playing Russian roulette, your death will most likely be called a suicide. But if you fall off while free soloing, it will most likely be called an accident.

MOST FREE SOLOISTS BACK DOWN if they aren't sure whether they can safely navigate a section of rock; sometimes, they don't even leave the ground. When deciding whether to free solo a difficult climb, they often practice the route obsessively until they are confident that their skill is equal to the challenge. As a rule, free soloists, like many other participants in high-risk activities, would not just pick up a gun and pull the trigger. They do not take uncalculated risks.

Neither did the high-wire artist Phillipe Petit. One morning in August 1974, he walked, untethered, along a cable rigged across the 138-foot span between the twin towers of the World Trade Center in New York City. Over forty-five minutes, he made eight passes across the wire stretched 1312 feet above the concrete—an act that was called the "the artistic crime of the century." Despite the clear implications of a fall, Petit believed his high-wire walk was not dangerous, because he had meticulously prepared for more than six years. "I don't take any risk," he said of his performances. "There is no fear because there is no reason to be fearful for me . . . it is a world made for me, full of calm and peace and beauty." The onlookers who watched Petit expectantly from a quarter mile below experienced apprehension and fear, but the artist himself, like most free soloists, felt only a sense of calm, peace, and fulfillment.

If you ask climbers, a lot of them will tell you that the ability to control fear, to control their emotional response to it, to keep their shit together in situations where their lives are on the line, is at the core of why they climb, and why they free solo. "There's an element of feeling we are in control to be able to go out in that environment," Margo Talbot, whose memoir, *All That Glitters*, explores how climbing helped her overcome addiction, said during a panel discussion at the Banff Centre in 2019. "I can't control circumstances, but I can control myself," free soloist Mark Twight said during the same discussion.

In a study about risk-taking and performance in climbing published in *Personality and Individual Differences* in 2008, researchers noted that participants in high-risk sports often mention the need to be in control, and found that mastery and accomplishment are important motivators for rock climbers. Climbers who developed a higher sense of self-efficacy—a belief in their capabilities to prepare for and execute courses of action to achieve goals—were better able to manage their emotional states. This, in turn, meant they were less likely to fear failure and more likely to set difficult goals for themselves and take greater risks—but those risks were more calculated than reckless compared to other extreme-sport participants.

MANY FREE SOLO CLIMBERS WILL tell you that mastering their emotional states—controlling fear—is one of the main reasons they push themselves to extremes. My friend Justin Martin is one of them. When I met Martin, an easygoing twenty-something Canadian, in 2019, he was living out of a van as he made his way back to Canada after a winter in Mexico, hitting all the climbing hot spots along the way. In just his third year of climbing, he'd progressed from a newbie at the gym to a 5.13 sport climber.

Although he denied being a risk addict, he admitted to participating in several high-risk activities that took him as close to the edge as possible. "Every time I walk along a cliff I stand as close to the edge as I can, and I look straight down until I get vertigo," he told me. "I've walked on a high-line, driven 220 kilometers per hour on my motorcycle, I've even climbed into tight caves nearly 100 feet into earth." But he says, "My biggest death-defying aspiration is to squirrel suit. . . . You may think I do this stuff because I have a death wish, but the truth is I do it because I'm scared." Martin believes he is addicted to confronting fear.

By the end of the summer we met, he'd posted a video of himself soloing laps on a 60-foot route in central Washington. When I interviewed him later, he talked about it philosophically, as if he'd been free soloing his whole life. "Once I started to face my fears, I noticed my life became easier, and I was creating memories that are worth remembering," he added. "Soloing is the same way. Before ever touching real rock I never understood the appeal of free soloing, to risk literally everything for a stupid climb, so for me it was a shift in perspective."

I'd seen the shift in perspective happen for Martin. Climbing with him in Wyoming and Oregon, he'd been willing to push his limits on a rope but was cautious even when bouldering 20 feet off the ground. Now he was free soloing and espousing theories about risk and reward. "Because soloing breeds such risk, it has very unique rewards," he told me. "It obviously helps with mental state, facing fears, and keeping calm in stressful situations, but for me I find it's about peace."

Although he's willing to take risks, Martin knows there's a line that he won't cross, but he's not sure where it is.

ACCORDING TO RUSSIAN PSYCHOANALYST and historian Gregory Zilboorg, fear of death is an expression of the instinct of self-preservation, which functions as a constant drive to maintain life by mastering the dangers that threaten it. "If this fear were as constantly conscious, we should be unable to function normally," wrote Zilboorg. "It must be properly repressed to keep us living. . . . We know very well that to repress means more than to put away and to forget. . . ." He explained, "It means also to maintain a constant psychological effort to keep the lid on and inwardly never relax our watchfulness. . . . We are intent on mastering death. . . . The affect of fear is repressed."

Keeping a lid on fear, especially in the face of death, is not easy. In her book, *Learning to Fly*, Steph Davis wrote about her need to control fear and anxiety. She recalls in a striking passage that during her first free solo ascent of the *Casual Route* on the Diamond, despite the mental training she'd done to prepare herself for that moment, she nearly freaked out halfway up the wall. "With no warning, my mind instantly cartwheeled into images of my body falling down the wall," she wrote. "Like an onslaught of invading enemies, tension, paralysis, and weakness rushed into my limbs. I froze in position, like a rabbit in the headlights of a truck."

Fear, Davis knew, was her greatest enemy on a free-solo climb. She had tried so hard to eradicate it from the equation, but fear had found her at the worst possible moment—at the crux of the route. She fought through the panic and completed the climb, but instead of feeling elated, she felt confused. This led to an intense period of self-examination and the realization that recent turmoil—the loss of her marriage and other anchors in her life—had made her numb to fear. She wasn't feeling fear, Davis realized, because she'd already lost everything she had to lose. She'd given up.

Still, Davis knew she hadn't free soloed the route because of a death wish; the fact that she'd responded to the panic attack by hanging on tighter, fighting to say on the rock, convinced her of that. She resolved to work even harder to eliminate fear, to control it, so it would not control her. If she let the fear win, she'd have to give up the things she loved most in life—free soloing and skydiving. She decided to free solo *Casual Route* again, to confront the fear—not of the route, but of fear itself. That second time, the weather was stormy and water was running down cracks in the wall, but she climbed confidently, without any trace of fear.

TETON GRAVITY RESEARCH, AN ACTION sports media company based in Jackson, Wyoming, published an infographic on their website called "Your Chances of Dying Ranked by Sport and Activity," based on research from Best Health Degrees. The study reported that you have a 1-in-560 chance of dying by hang gliding, 1-in-101,083 by skydiving, 1-in-15,700 by hiking in the mountains, and 0.0145-in-100 by "expert climbing." While this chart is interesting, sometimes amusing, and offers some perspective on relative risk, it isn't always statistically meaningful since the data is inconsistent from activity to activity. For example, the reported annual skydiving fatality rate of 1 per 101,083 is based on the number of jumps, while the motorcycle riding fatality rate of 21.45 per 100 million is based on miles ridden, and the airplane fatality rate of 1.27 per 100,000 is based on flight hours. Using the chart, it's impossible to compare the relative risk of, say, driving to the grocery store for a loaf of bread versus walking or riding your bike there, driving to your sister's wedding in Denver versus flying, or climbing a 1000-foot sandstone cliff without a rope versus jumping off it with a wingsuit. To get an apples-to-apples comparison, you have to tease it out.

For example, how dangerous is jumping out of a perfectly good airplane? In 2012, 19 people died in parachuting accidents in the United States, or roughly 1 person per 100,000 jumps. That means, statistically, on average, of the next 100,000 people who jump out of an airplane, 1 of them will probably die. But the risk per participant is a little higher: about 350,000 people completed jumps in 2012, with a fatality rate of 5.42 per 100,000 skydivers.

Compare this to a report published in 2007 that looked at BASE jumping. Out of 20,850 BASE jumps between 1995 and 2005 at the Kjerag massif in Norway, there were 9 deaths, or 1 death per 2317 jumps. If that sounds high to you, consider the annual fatality risk per participant. According to a 2008 study in Sweden, the fatality rate in 2002 was 1 out of every 60 participants, the equivalent of 1667 deaths per 100,000 participants.

We could also look at climbing in the Himalayas. It is estimated that between 4 and 6.5 percent of climbers attempting Mount Everest die during or as a result of the climb. That equates to between 4000 and 6500 deaths per 100,000 climbers. According to NASA's Earth Observatory, climbers attempting K2, the world's second-highest peak, have a fatality rate of 29 percent, but Annapurna I, the world's tenth-highest mountain, is the most dangerous to climb, with a fatality rate of 32 percent. That's 32,000 deaths per 100,000 climbers.

Rock climbing, by comparison, seems quite safe. The 145 fatalities per 1 million rock climbers cited in the Teton Gravity Research infographic equates to 14.5 fatalities per 100,000 climbers. However, since this statistic is based on "expert climbers" without defining the term, it is meaningless. The Outdoor

Industry Association's US-based *2018 Outdoor Participation Report* shows that there were roughly 5 million climbers in the United States of all types (indoor, sport, trad, ice, mountaineering, and, presumably, free soloing). A 2017 report recorded 38 climbing-related deaths in North America in the previous year. On average, around 30 climbing-related deaths are reported each year, though it fluctuates, but if we accept that 38 out of at least 5 million climbers died in 2017, the fatality rate would be 0.8 per 100,000 climbers.

But as Eric Brymer, an Australian researcher who focuses on outdoor and adventure psychology and extreme sports, told me, if people really have a death wish, they should ride motorcycles. He pointed to a study comparing climbers, BASE jumpers, and motorcyclists that found the comparative death rate for motorcyclists (1 in 500) was much higher than that of BASE jumpers (1 in 2317) or climbers (1 in 4000). Free soloists themselves nearly always defend their practice by saying that driving on the freeway is more dangerous than unroped climbing, but that claim is debatable. The motor-vehicle death rate in the United States reached its peak in 1937 with 30.8 deaths per 100,000 residents; in 2017, the rate was 12.4 per 100,000 residents. The pool of residents is much larger than the pool of drivers, so if only driving was factored in, the death per 100,000 rate would be higher—much higher than for rock climbers.

There are no meaningful statistics on the death rate of free-solo climbers. Although it would be fairly easy to determine the number of free-soloing deaths per year, due to limited reporting and the inherent bias in self-reporting (free soloists often don't talk or respond to surveys about their activities), we don't know the number of participants. Nearly all climbers do some unroped climbing—such as not roping up for the easy climbing to get to the base of a wall, unroping for the easy climbing to the top, or scrambling down from the top because it's too easy to bother roping up or rappelling—and most fatal unroped falls happen on easy terrain in exactly those situations.

In 1986, a Colorado climber named Laurel Husted fell to her death while scrambling unroped up Class 3 terrain after completing the first ascent of a new route in the Black Canyon of the Gunnison. A hold broke, and Husted fell 200 feet to the trail below, where she died two hours later in her boyfriend's arms. Was Husted a free soloist, or just a rock climber who was climbing unroped on easy terrain after the difficulties of the real climb had ended, as nearly all climbers do? If unroped scrambling on easy terrain is free soloing, then potentially millions of climbers are free soloists.

John Bachar believed all unroped climbing counted as free soloing. There's an anecdotal story about a climber in the 1980s who, seeing Bachar at the gas station across the street from Camp 4 in Yosemite, confronted him about free soloing.

"Man, how do you do all that crazy solo stuff?" the climber asked him.

Bachar looked him in the eye and said, "You're free soloing right now."

Bachar classified free soloing according to zones of risk. According to Bachar, "Zone 1" was climbing close to the ground, such as bouldering with a good landing, where there was little risk of serious injury or death; "Zone 2" meant climbing high enough that a fall would likely result in a broken something, or even a more serious injury or death in some cases if you landed badly; and "Zone 3" meant climbing unroped high enough off the ground that a fall was likely to be fatal.

Ultimately, though, there's no bright line. You can trip on the sidewalk and hit your head; you can be killed falling from zero feet up. On the other hand, people have fallen from great heights and lived. In 2004, a climber named James Lucas fell 100 feet while soloing *North Overhang* at Joshua Tree and lived. And in 2021, Joshua Ourada survived an estimated 150-foot unroped fall from a route in Yosemite. That's nothing. In 1972, a Serbian flight attendant named Vesna Vulović survived a reported 33,330-foot freefall from a jetliner blown out of the sky by a suitcase bomb.

If free soloing is defined as intentionally climbing a Class 5 rock route unroped, for its own sake, high enough off the ground that a fall would likely be fatal, the number of participants in this activity would be fairly low. If we assume only about 10 percent of rock climbers—that's 100,000 free-solo climbers based on the *Outside* survey—do it, and if an average of three free-solo climbers fall and die in a given year, that would be 3 deaths per 100,000 free-solo climbers per year. But then, free-solo climbers almost never fall.

Using this definition, in some years, there are zero reported deaths from free soloing in *Accidents*. Without reliable data, it's impossible to say what the true number is. And even then, it would be difficult to say just how much free soloing was to blame.

CHAPTER 10

Flirting with Death

In 2004 *Rock and Ice* named John Yablonsky the "king of luck" because "he had more sketchy solos than anybody." Everybody seemed to have a story about "Yabo" to tell around the campfire. For starters, there's the story about him falling off of a route called *Short Circuit*, a 30-foot 5.11c thin crack in Yosemite. As eyewitnesses recalled, his fingers slipped out of the very last moves and he flew backward in the air, seemingly about to smash himself on the rocks at the base of the climb. Instead, he somehow hooked his arm over a branch on a small bay tree, which bent and set him gently on the ground, completely unhurt.

Another time, Yablonsky tried to solo *The Good Book* on the Right Side of the Folly in Yosemite. Although the route ended on a ledge several hundred feet off the ground and normally required rappelling to descend, in typical Yabo style, he'd gone without a rope, intending to downclimb the difficult 5.10 route. But on the second pitch, his foot slipped off a wet hold and he went flying. It seemed certain he would fall to his death, but by some miracle he landed on a flake of rock a few feet below and was able to hold on, barely averting disaster. But the Yablonsky story everyone hears is the one about his consecutive free solo ascents of *Leave It to Beaver*, a 5.12a route in Joshua Tree.

I first heard that tale around a campfire in 1982. By that time, I'd already encountered Yabo a few times. He was one of a group of climbers I saw do a gang solo of *Left Ski Track* the morning I'd arrived in Joshua Tree, and later

I'd see him with a group sitting around a picnic table in Hidden Valley Campground or climbing on the boulders below the Old Woman. Yablonsky didn't seem to stand out too much from the others; they were all wearing beat-up clothes, had messy hair, with scuffs and scrapes all over their suntanned arms, and looked like they could use a shower and a good meal. Then I heard the story:

> *The first time Yabo soloed the* Beav, *he had no problem, but he took the easy way at the top, traversing right instead of finishing straight up. But that didn't satisfy him. He had to do it the hard way. So he gets back on it, and this time he's sketching and shaking the whole way.*
>
> *At the top, he could have traversed off again, no problem, but he hangs there for a minute and then throws this horrendous dyno and misses! Everybody's thinking, 'Fuck, he's toast!' But he somehow catches himself on the jug and hangs on. So now we're thinking, yeah, he'll traverse off. He has to. He's totally pumped and shaking. He has nothing left. But no!*
>
> *He hangs there for a minute, shakes out, and then relaunches the dyno. Just as he throws for the jug, his other hand slips off. But somehow, at that exact moment, his fingers latch onto the upper hold. He's full-on deadpoint, dangling there by the fingers of one hand, legs flailing in the air, and we're sure he's going to deck, but he just looks down and laughs like a lunatic and then pulls over the top. It was crazy. Batshit crazy. But that's Yabo.*

Randy Vogel, a Joshua Tree local, witnessed both solos. He felt comfortable enough to take a photo of Yablonsky making a move high up during his first solo ascent of the 5.12 route, but recalled in the online forum SuperTopo that his second ascent was "out of control" and "had everyone so gripped, no one could shoot a photo, least of all really watch." John Bachar was there, too, and concurred with Vogel's assessment. "First lap looked like he was doing a 5.8," he recalled. "Second lap, he threw a dyno near the top, 'chicken wings' and all. . . . Whew!" Rick Sumner recalled being there that day and ducking behind a rock, "refusing to watch what I thought could well be a suicide in progress."

One person who was not there to watch was Lynn Hill. In her book, *Climbing Free*, Hill told part of the *Beav* story that wasn't shared around the campfire. According to Hill, Yabo had a crush on her that she didn't reciprocate. He'd previously threatened to solo a cliff and jump off if she did not requite his love. She dodged his advances but noticed that Yabo tended to take enormous risks when they climbed together. Concerned by his behavior, she began to dissociate herself from Yabo as much as possible. But the next time she encountered him, he repeated his suicide threat and punched himself in the eye.

A few weeks later, she met Yabo at Joshua Tree, and her presence there seemed to drive him over the edge, culminating in his near-suicidal soloing binge. "The entire spectacle was intended to impress or to horrify me," Hill wrote, "and it did, along with all his other friends, who begged him to stop his soloing frenzy before he smashed himself to pieces on the boulders below."

PERHAPS ONE WAY TO MAKE sense of Yablonsky is to consider the story of his traumatic childhood, when an unstable mother with a suspected substance-abuse problem deserted the family when he was five years old, leaving him with an overbearing father. A hyperactive child prone to temperamental outbursts that continued into his teen years, Yablonsky once punched a hole in the wall of his home in a fit of frustration. He would eventually be diagnosed with bipolar disorder, but, like many others, Yablonsky found an escape from his unhappy childhood in climbing; it gave him a direction to focus his energy. He soon dropped out of high school and ended up in Yosemite.

By 1974, Yablonsky was a full-time Valley resident, although he didn't make many friends, not at first. Everybody thought the shy teenager with long hair that hung over his eyes was strange. It probably didn't help that Yablonsky had a nervous laugh and would sit around banging on a tin can or hitting sticks together doing a bizarre chant. But Yablonsky didn't go away; he was always there, desperate to belong, and was eventually accepted as one of the larger tribe of Southern California climbers.

As people got to know Yablonsky, they discovered he had a visionary aspect that was uncanny, as if he was able to tap into a spiritual connection with the universe. One day, Bachar was sitting with Yablonsky in Hidden Valley Campground in Joshua Tree when Yabo said he'd had a vision the night before while sitting on a rock looking at the start of a route called *Spider Line*. "A spider had lowered out of the crack above and was hovering in front of him," Bachar, in a SuperTopo post, recalled Yablonsky telling him. "He then told me that this meant he could safely solo *Spider Line*! I didn't know what to tell him."

At the time, the route, rated 5.11d, had only been toproped a few times; no one had ever led it free. The crack was shallow and flared, and the rock slippery in places. It was hardly the kind of route someone should be trying to free solo, especially someone who was receiving late-night spiritual advice from a spider, and Bachar told him so.

"I tried to convince him to chill out and get in really good shape," Bachar recalled. "In a couple weeks he'd be ready for it."

Yablonsky couldn't wait that long. A few minutes later, Bachar heard a "weird yelping sound" and looked over to see Yabo halfway up the route, barely hanging on. It was a typical Yabo horror show: full-on desperate, feet slipping out of the crack, legs swinging in the air, with Yabo "shaking like a leaf" as Bachar recalled. Some climbers who saw what was happening walked away, unwilling to watch, sure their friend was about to die, but in typical Yabo style, he hung on and latched onto a flake, eventually taking off his T-shirt while hanging on with one hand before making the final moves.

When he came down, Bachar confronted Yabo. "You could have died!" he admonished him.

"Who are you guys to tell me anything?" Yabo shouted back. "I just soloed *Spider Line*!"

YABO WAS ALSO THE HERO of many campground hijinks, always willing to take a dare or perform some odd service in exchange for money or a meal. Hill recalled a night in Joshua Tree when the group around the campfire dared Yabo—who was broke and needed money—to make a nude moonlight free solo of *North Overhang* for five dollars. "Not having a penny to his name," Hill recalled, "Yabo unhesitatingly took the meager bet, stripped, and set off up the climb clad only in rock shoes, a chalk bag, and a wool cap." He did the climb, much to the amusement of the gathered crowd, who hooted and hollered when Yabo went to find his clothes and discovered they'd been stolen. Unperturbed, he walked over to a boulder and pulled out a set of clothes he'd stashed there. "I might be crazy, but I'm no fool," he told his onlookers.

But there were also stories about Yabo's dark moods and violent behavior, usually sparked by a relationship that was not working out, a girl who did not love him back. "If anything could affect John it was a pretty girl," one friend wrote on SuperTopo. "He would go off and solo routes right at his limit," another recalled, "especially when some girl had broken his heart." On more than one occasion, he became so emotionally worked up that he physical harmed himself. And then on September 4, 1991, he died of a self-inflicted gunshot wound after a violent, emotional breakup with his girlfriend.

THE 2018 STUDY "PSYCHIATRIC ASPECTS of Extreme Sports: Three Case Studies," published in the *Permanente Journal*, looked at people who repeatedly risk their lives for fun. The stated purpose of the article was to aid sports psychiatrists in treating their risk-seeking patients. "Because flirting with death is critical to the extreme sports ethos," the study said, "practitioners must gain further understanding of this field and its at-risk participants."

Although the report acknowledged that many people were attracted to dangerous activities for the experience of "life-affirming transcendence," it focused on the negative psychological motivations of participants who have "a genetic predisposition for risk, risk-seeking personality traits, or underlying psychiatric disorders in which impulsivity and risk taking are integral to the underlying problem." Notably, all three of their case study subjects were deceased.

One of the case studies, a man they called Allan, was presented as a "weekend warrior" type—forty-eight years old, married, three teenage children, successful businessman—who died in a hang-gliding accident. While he appeared "normal" from the outside, Allan had been clinically diagnosed with persistent depression, possibly due to feelings of being shackled to his family and business responsibilities, and sought out hang gliding for the dangerous thrill it provided, a way of escaping the meaningless tedium of his existence.

The other two case studies were not weekend warrior types, and neither was said to be suffering from simple depression brought on by the tedium of the grind. According to the study, rock climber and wingsuit jumper Dean Potter had relatively unstable relationships, a high genetic predisposition for risk-taking, impulse control disorder, ADHD, generalized anxiety disorder, conduct disorder, parent-child problems, and narcissism. Dan Osman, another rock climber, was little different; the study said he had ADHD, severe conduct disorder, and cluster B personality traits. They were both described as either "very" or "extremely cavalier," and as being fatalistic, intimately aware of and embracing closeness to death for the excitement and challenge, and enjoying the ability to "cheat" death or feel "bulletproof."

I WAS SITTING AT MY DESK one afternoon wondering if I could sneak out early and go climbing when one of the partners of the Seattle law firm where I worked called me. "Come into my office," she said. "I need you to look at something." For a moment, I wondered if I was in trouble. Had she read my mind? I hurried to her office to see what she wanted.

"Look at this," she insisted, pointing at her monitor. She played a YouTube video of a rock climber speed-soloing a 400-foot granite wall. The climber almost ran up the wall, leaping through the air at one point to grab a hold, and reached the top in less than four and a half minutes.

"I know you rock climb. Do you do that?" she asked, pointing at the climber on the screen, genuinely concerned.

I assured her I did not, at least not the racing-up-cliffs-like-a-track-athlete-without-a-rope part.

"Do you know him?" she demanded.

"Sure," I said. "That's Dan Osman."

"My gosh," she said, "I can't understand why somebody would do that. Is he still alive?"

"No," I told her.

"Well," she said, "that's not surprising."

DAN OSMAN WAS BORN IN 1963 in Orange County, California. His father, a former SWAT team officer and a descendant of a samurai family, trained him to follow the Bushido code, the moral code of conduct of the samurai that stresses living virtuously with courage, compassion, respect, honor, and self-control. He was a hyperactive but inattentive child; his mother, a world champion barrel racer, gave him the nickname "Danny I Forgot."

Osman, who was already studying martial arts, started rock climbing at age twelve. He progressed slowly, like many climbers did in the mid-seventies, working his way through the grades over the course of years. By the early eighties, though, Osman was leading routes rated 5.12, and began establishing hard new routes in Southern California and Nevada. Then he started free soloing them.

Osman had what Matthew Renda, author of the article "The Wizardry of Dan Osman," published in the *Tahoe Quarterly*, described as flair, athleticism, courage, and a "truculent disregard for danger" combined with talent and determination. Others described him in less complimentary terms: reckless, crazy, cavalier, suicidal, someone who had a death wish. Everyone, though, worried Osman might push his limits too far one day.

As the 1980s progressed into the 1990s, Osman developed a reputation as a brash, hyper-energetic climber who was not only willing but eager to take risks, a reputation largely due to his appearance in the first four *Masters of Stone* films, which featured a compilation of notable climbers—John Bachar, Ron Kauk, Todd Skinner, Rick Cashner, Dean Potter, Steph Davis, Alexander Huber—at work on some of their hardest and most outrageous climbs. The fourth film, released in 1997, featured Osman's speed solo of *Bear's Reach*, a 5.7 route on Lover's Leap, in 4 minutes, 25 seconds. It cemented his reputation as possibly the craziest climber alive.

Although the video is purely a stunt performed for the film, it is hypnotic. Osman stands casually at the base of the 400-foot wall wearing red shorts, a blue shirt, rock shoes, a chalk bag, sunglasses, and a watch. He looks at the watch, pushes a button, and then *bam!* He starts flying up the wall, hands and feet in constant motion like a competitor in a pole-climbing competition at the county fair, a flurry of nonstop motion. Halfway up the wall, he leaps upward, completely out of contact with the rock, and extends his hands to grab a flake of granite. It's an intense moment, replayed in slow motion in the film for dramatic effect. You know if he misses the hold, he will most likely fall to his death. Of course, he catches the flake, clamps down on it with both hands, and rockets upward, sprinting over the final few feet of the wall, springing onto the ledge, and stopping his watch.

If you do the math, you will see that Osman wasn't really climbing all that fast. Climbing 400 feet of rock in 4 minutes, 25 seconds, is a rate of just over 90 feet per minute, or roughly one mile per hour. Most people can crawl across the ground on hands and knees faster than that. But that's fast for free soloing. John Bachar and Rick Cashner used to "jog" up 600-foot 5.8 routes in Yosemite at a rate of roughly 100 feet per minute. The current world record for speed climbing a 15-meter course is 5.208 seconds, which is roughly 500 feet per minute or 10 miles per hour, but that's with a toprope on a fixed course that the climber has practiced countless times. Speed climbers are so fast that it's common for them to miss a hold and fall—something a speed soloist can't afford.

In the *Masters of Stone* films, Osman did several free-solo climbs and performed other outrageous stunts for the camera. For the 1993 installment, he free soloed a 5.11 in The Needles of Southern California. For the 1994 film, he free soloed three hard routes including a 5.12 at Lake Tahoe. Osman was clearly a masterful climber; other than the speed-climbing stunts, he climbed methodically, in control, making difficult moves look easy, sometimes adding dramatic flair such as hanging upside down, his legs wedged into a gap, arms hanging free while resting halfway up. He wore his trademark sunglasses. He flashed his hang-loose sign. He was clearly having fun.

"Soloing is just a game," Osman is reported as saying. "It's a serious one, but it's a game. The price of messing up is your life, so you better know what you're doing."

As if free soloing wasn't enough, Osman started playing other games with his life. In one of the videos, he takes a fall off of Cave Rock, while roped up, theatrically trailing streamers of chalk dust from his hands. In another, he enters a jump riding a skateboard. And in another, he leaps off of Utah's Rainbow Bridge, one of the largest natural bridges in the world.

Osman seemed to enjoy falling as much as he enjoyed climbing. As the saying among climbers goes, "If you're not falling, you're not trying." Most climbers rope up and place protection so that when they inevitably fall, they don't hit the ground. But most climbers are afraid of falling, and they usually stick to routes where the risk of coming off the rock is low. Learning how to fall and how to suppress their fear is a necessary component of the sport for most elite climbers. But Osman took it to a new level.

While working on a new route in 1989, he kept falling off and realized his fear of falling was holding him back. Falling on purpose would allow him to confront and master his fear of it, he decided, and besides, it was fun. He'd have his belayer let out slack and then leap backward from the anchors, falling as far as 50 feet. Then he started tying a rope to the top of the wall, tying in, and leaping off. Each time, he felt fear—anxiety, goose bumps—and each time he embraced the fear and, usually, he jumped.

In the film, you don't see him rigging the rope and anchors, preparing mentally for the jump, visualizing it, looping the rope so it doesn't strangle or decapitate him. You don't see him changing his mind and deciding not to jump. What you see is Dano doing radical aerial stunts—cartwheels and flips—as he leaps from or rides a bike or skateboard off a bridge or cliff like it's no big deal. You see a big smile on his face, the hang-loose sign flashing as he falls into the void, without a trace of fear.

As reported in the study, despite Osman's reputation for careful planning and execution while free soloing and rope jumping, his life was "marked by impulsivity, disorganization, forgetfulness, illegal jumps, brushes with the law, and episodes of brief jail time." He was forgetful; he'd get to talking and end up being late to work or he'd drive too fast and get speeding tickets. He also took risks that some thought were reckless.

Osman eventually started using longer ropes to make bigger jumps, mostly from bridges that spanned deep canyons. In 1996, on his thirty-second birthday, he made a 660-foot jump off a bridge in Northern California, but wanted to go bigger. Bridges were only so high, so he turned his attention to overhanging cliffs with no protruding ledges or buttresses, like Leaning Tower in Yosemite, which rose 1300 feet from the valley floor to its pointed summit and overhung the entire way. Eventually Osman rigged a rope and jumped off Leaning Tower. His rigging was complex and required careful setup so that the extra-long rope did not catch around his neck or body and slice through him. He also needed to be sure it unfurled properly and stretched without break-ing. To mitigate the impact of such a long fall, the rope had to be anchored in a way that allowed Osman to swing out away from the wall at the end of his free fall, dissipating the force generated by a human body falling at terminal velocity. It was not a jump that could be approached impulsively or with a cavalier attitude.

After Osman took several jumps off Leaning Tower, he encouraged oth-ers to try it. Most refused, but some gave it a try, including Dean Potter, who jumped once and decided it wasn't for him. "My climbing has always been about control," Potter said in a 2013 interview, "so throwing myself off the rocks like that—thinking maybe I live, maybe I die—pretty much freaked me out. But Dano was a master at this stuff." Potter explained, "He had these elaborate drawings, and while we were working on Leaning Tower, he'd get up all excited in the morning, saying he hadn't slept all night thinking about the rig."

Although Osman had achieved notoriety for his free-solo climbing, he gained national attention for his rope jumping, especially after he set a world record in the fall of 1998 with a 1000-foot jump from Leaning Tower. His jump was filmed for the upcoming *Masters of Stone* video. "When this is all over, I am really looking forward to spending some time with my daughter and family and basically park it on the couch for a while," he said in an interview after the jump. "I've been going at Mach speed for quite a while now and I think it's a matter of time before things start catching up to you."

After he'd set the world record jumping off Leaning Tower, Osman was pulled over by Yosemite Park police. He was arrested after he was found to have multiple outstanding parking tickets. Unable to bail himself out, he spent two weeks in jail, an eternity for someone like Osman. When he finally got out, he was amped up. He knew he needed to remove his ropes and rigging and promised park officials he would do so.

"I think he went up intending to take it all down," Eric Perlman, producer of the *Masters of Stone* films, told the *Tahoe Quarterly* in 1999, "saw that beautiful, intricate network of ropes manifested directly from his wildest imagination, and figured, 'Why not just jump it a few more times?'" On November 23, 1998, Osman and his friend, Miles Daisher, took a few jumps. Then, as Daisher reported, Osman added some rope to the line, moved his entry point, and went for a new world record.

After the accident, it was determined that Osman had misaligned the ropes; when he jumped, the rope used to retrieve the jump line crossed it instead and cut it 900 feet into the jump. Osman was thirty-five when he died. His daughter, Emma, was just seven years old.

THERE'S A YOUTUBE VIDEO OF Dean Potter making the first free-solo ascent of *Heaven*, an overhanging crack in Yosemite rated 5.12d, in 2006, that gives a glimpse of what he was like: peaceful yet aggressive, calm yet furious, focused yet explosive, and withdrawn yet intense. His emotions would be pent up one moment, erupting the next, his whole inner and outer being compressed into two minutes of climbing near his physical and mental limit.

Potter looks almost scared as he excessively chalks his heavily taped hands and then rubs them on his shorts. He's anxious and focused inward, mentally preparing to do battle, to fight for his life, and it shows. As he begins moving up the overhanging 40-foot crack, he climbs competently but not smoothly, setting and resetting his finger and hand jams obsessively, jerking on them to make sure they're solid before making the next move. There's real tension as he nears the top, and when he pulls over, he lets out a primal scream and pumps his fists while he walks quickly up the steep slab, as if the intensity of the last two minutes has compressed his pent-up emotions to the point that they explode.

Born in 1972 in New Hampshire, Potter had what at first seemed to be a normal childhood. His father was a military man, strict but caring, while his mother, a nurse who also taught yoga, embraced a more alternative lifestyle and was described as flighty. They separated when Potter was seven years old. He had difficulty in school, and although he was not clinically diagnosed, his behavior was consistent with ADHD. He tended to be shy and withdrawn but felt resentment toward his peers because he thought they were excluding him. He eventually made friends with another boy, and they snuck into the air force base where Potter's father was stationed and climbed a 200-foot cliff. Potter grew up to be a big, energetic kid, six foot five, and strong. He attended the University of New Hampshire and made the varsity crew team but soon dropped out to pursue his real passion: climbing.

Potter ended up in Yosemite during the 1990s and was soon making bold ascents, earning a reputation as a risk-taker. Although he was a proficient free climber, Potter didn't try to compete with the best climbers on difficulty alone. Instead, he focused on risk—free soloing, slacklining high off the ground, and wingsuit jumping as a way to earn recognition. *Outside* magazine once called him "the modern master of risk-taking on rock."

It wasn't just the hard free-solo ascents or crazy speed solo ascents that had him climbing 5.11 and even 5.12 rock without a rope, miles off the deck. Potter was intense; he was rebellious. He did everything all out, elevated everything to the extreme. In a 2011 *Outside* magazine article, his partners described him as "on a different level," "a warrior constantly searching for the next peaceful battle."

A master slackliner, Potter would walk across lines suspended thousands of feet above the ground, sometimes without a tether, "some of the scariest stuff I do," he admitted. Potter regularly BASE jumped with a wingsuit, setting a world record in 2009 when he jumped off the Eiger and made an 8900-foot descent that lasted almost three minutes. And Potter invented the sport of "freebasing," combining free soloing with BASE jumping by wearing a small parachute while free soloing big walls including the *Deep Blue Sea* route (5.12+) on the Eiger in 2008 and the *Alien Roof* pitch (5.12b) on the Rostrum in 2010. Although freebase climbing seemed to be a safer way to free solo, like a lot of things Potter did, nobody else seemed to want to try it.

Potter was also vying to become the first person ever to free solo El Capitan, and in 2012 worked out a route he called *Easy Rider* that started at the top of El Cap and descended to a ledge system that led to the upper pitches of *Freerider*, a contrived route that included several pitches of 5.11 climbing more than 2000 feet off the ground. Hearing that Potter was thinking about linking the *West Face* route and *Easy Rider* to claim the first free-solo ascent, Alex Honnold, who had also been thinking about free soloing El Cap, beat him to it. He free soloed the *West Face*, an 1800-foot 5.11c. Although it wasn't considered a major El Cap route for the purposes of claiming the first free solo ascent, Honnold had effectively snuffed out Potter's chances of claiming the prize. It seemed doubtful that Potter was prepared to free solo one of the "real" El Cap routes, but you never knew what he could or couldn't do.

Aside from his competitive streak, Potter had a spiritual side that bordered on the mystical; he claimed to have visions. According to Potter, he fell while climbing his house at age five (when the family was living in Palestine for several years), lacerating his head. A group of Bedouin women soon arrived, chanted mystical songs, and threw salt on the blood to ward off evil spirits. This, Potter claimed, also drove away his fear of heights. He also claimed to have had several visions involving flight and ravens, including of being a shamanistic raven in a sacred area of Hueco Tanks State Park.

After a BASE-jumping accident in 2003, in which Potter was seriously injured, he told people he had taken on the spirit of a swift that was also injured in the accident and died before his eyes. Some people thought his visions were fueled by drugs, but he denied it. On his website, he said he was "fascinated with the lines between life and death, sanity and insanity," and pushed himself right up to those lines so he could learn.

On May 16, 2015, Potter and friend Graham Hunt, wearing wingsuits, flew off Taft Point in Yosemite. He'd done the jump several times before; it required some skill to maneuver through a notch between two granite walls. It wasn't anything he couldn't handle, but the margin for error is razor thin in high-level wingsuit flying, as in free soloing. This time, for reasons no one has definitely ascertained, Potter and Hunt didn't make it. The salt had run out for Potter. The climbing community was shocked by Potter's death but not surprised. He'd been on a collision course with fate for years.

While the authors of the 2018 study concluded that Osman and Potter were "extremely cavalier," even fatalistic, the people who knew the two men would disagree. They knew that despite the risks they were taking, both had safety firmly in mind. They didn't simply rush toward danger but diligently (even obsessively) planned and prepared before taking the plunge. Those who called them friends admired—even loved—the very characteristics the researchers described in negative terms.

CHAPTER 11

Extreme Dudes

Childhood for Michael Reardon Jr. was marked by instability. Born in 1965, his mother abandoned the family when he was four years old. For the next four years, Reardon and his father were often homeless, living out of a car while Michael Sr. searched for work.

In the mid-1980s, Reardon moved to Denver, Colorado, embarking on a career that seemed suited to his temperament and looks: lead singer for a glam-metal band. More importantly, he found the mountains. He'd take his bandmates up into the Rocky Mountains where they'd scramble cluelessly around on rocky ridges and revel in the landscape.

Reardon left the music scene and moved to California in 1988 to get serious about his life. He obtained a BS degree from UCLA and started an internet company, then earned a JD from Pepperdine. California was also where Reardon did his first real climb, a 1000-foot 5.9 route at Tahquitz Rock, California, with a coworker named Steve Werbelow, who Reardon described as a "crusty old climber." Halfway up the route, Werbelow handed Reardon some gear and told him to lead the next pitch. "Put these in when you're scared," he said. Reardon did as he was told and, even though it was his first real climb, he found the experience uplifting. "Instead of being scared, the sharp end woke me up like a religious experience," Reardon wrote on his website. "Adrenaline and excitement combined and without any falls, we dragged our way to the top with enough time to stop by and climb a 500 foot 5.7 afterwards."

Reardon wanted to climb more but didn't have any friends or equipment. That didn't stop him. He bought a pair of used Firé rock shoes, tried them out on the local rocks, and then returned to Tahquitz to climb the 5.7 route again, by himself, completing his first free solo on his second day of real climbing.

Reardon climbed as much as he could with older, traditional climbers, working his way quickly up the rating scale. Soon he was establishing first ascents of routes rated 5.13 and even a 5.14 at Malibu Creek Canyon. There was no doubt Reardon had the skills to do hard roped climbs, but what he really loved was free soloing.

In 1999, while still in law school, Reardon produced the first of his *Climb On!* videos, a series about rock climbing in Joshua Tree. He went on to direct a film about Bachar and soon became a larger-than-life character in the climbing community, one who'd gone from homeless kid living out of a car to glam rocker to self-styled entertainment lawyer and Hollywood producer. Reardon was sometimes theatrical to the point of outlandish, leaving plastic farm animals, Barbie dolls, and oversized panties along routes and in summit registers as proof of ascent, or hanging upside down and mugging for the camera in the middle of free solo climbs. He occasionally climbed naked and encouraged others to do the same. His wife described him as a "big kid" even though he was just five feet, seven inches tall and weighed a slight 150 pounds.

Reardon was known for engaging other climbers in rapid-fire stream-of-consciousness conversation that included a lot of subtle (or not-so-subtle) bragging about the climbs he'd done or was going to do. He also maintained a website, freesoloist.com, where he frequently posted reports and photos of his free-solo climbs as well as his "Stupid Summer Stunts" and "Mojo Club" (climbing naked and posting about it was a requirement, with bonus points for free soloing naked above a "struggling helmet and hexes crew" or women performing stem problems in the nude).

As Reardon soloed more, he began to climb harder and longer routes, eventually climbing dozens and sometimes hundreds of routes in a day (he reported free soloing more than 280 routes at Joshua Tree in one day in 2004) or free soloing as much as three vertical miles on one occasion. In 2005, Reardon claimed to have made an on-sight free-solo ascent of *Romantic Warrior*, a nine-pitch 5.12b route that is considered the classic challenging route in The Needles, a feat recognized as an "Adventure of the Year" by *National Geographic Adventure* magazine. "You get so cluttered up with gear and tools that you lose the purity of the experience," Reardon told the magazine. The next year, he on-sight soloed *Shikata Ga Nai*, an 800-foot 5.12a.

Most climbers took Reardon at face value, citing the long-standing tradition of believing someone's claim that they'd done a climb unless evidence proved otherwise. Others saw Reardon as a show-off, hyping free soloing to boost his reputation and make a buck, and doubted he'd done some of the free solos he claimed. Reardon took the criticism personally. "Everyone likes to play voyeur and critique," he wrote on his website. "If you solo and talk about it, you are doing it for ego. If you never talked about it and are suddenly discovered, you are underqualified. It's a lose-lose proposition for those that are unwilling to stand up to those that scream so loudly." Reardon, who had indisputably soloed some ballsy routes, including *The Vampire*, a four-pitch ultra-thin 5.11a face route at Tahquitz Rock, started posting pictures of himself on the routes other climbers had questioned, including one of him unroped on the crux pitch of *Romantic Warrior*, clinging to a thin flake with one hand, flipping off his detractors with the other.

Reardon posted several times on his blog on the *Climbing* magazine website in the spring of 2007, usually to let people know he'd free soloed something outrageous and was getting media attention for it. On April 5, 2007, he posted: "Yes it's true, I soloed 1000 routes in 30 days at Joshua Tree a couple months back. Brilliant photographer Damon Corso was with me for the experience and made Joshua Tree look absolutely magical—check out the eleven-page adventure in *Urban Climber* Magazine!"

Reardon documented his Ireland trip in a series of blog posts that reveled in the delight he found in visiting and climbing in his ancestral homeland. After Corso joined him, the two went on a tour of some of the most spectacular climbing spots in Ireland. On Friday, July 13, 2007, Reardon was up early, as usual, ready for another day of climbing. He'd wanted to free solo the windswept sea cliffs of Valentia Island off the Kerry coast, for photos. Reardon knew well the force of the swells coming off the Atlantic. In a blog post written that February, after he and his wife Marci had visited Ireland, he'd written, "During the winter months, the Atlantic pounds furiously against the walls and regularly sweeps hundreds of feet up on the land." That was during the winter, though. Although the sea was rough for a summer day, and it took some effort to get to the routes, he was finally able to time his approach to avoid the worst of the waves. He did his climbs, and Corso took his pictures, when a series of big waves rolled in. Reardon was waiting on a ledge in an inlet for the set to pass so he could cross safely when a rogue wave curled in and swept him off. Corso tried to throw him a rope, but he was already too far out to reach it. Corso ran to the coast guard station nearby; they were on the scene within fifteen minutes, but they were unable to find Reardon.

Marci and Reardon's daughter, Nikki, flew to Ireland as soon as they heard about his disappearance and were in attendance at his memorial on top of the cliff where he vanished, attended by 150 people, many of whom had only known Reardon briefly but had been infected by his spirit. "If anything I kind of wish he'd gone while climbing," Marci told the *Irish Examiner*. "I was like, a freak wave? Really, that's how it happens after everything?"

ACCORDING TO ERIC BRYMER, who began studying extreme-sports psychology more than twenty years ago, extreme-sports participants, including free soloists, have usually been explored from a negative perspective—one that is focused on what's "wrong" with them. Participation in this type of activity, Brymer notes, is often treated as "extreme dudes" who take unnecessary risks and have "no fear" in their battle against nature. While studies have shown that everyone engages in a certain level of sensation-seeking, extreme-sport participants are often portrayed as out-of-control individuals understimulated by their normal surroundings seeking a so-called adrenaline rush, or as self-centered teenage boys who take unnecessary, socially unacceptable risks to gain attention, the way Osman and Potter were portrayed in the 2018 study. But as the authors of "Psychiatric Aspects of Extreme Sports" note, "The lay perception that extreme sports participants are primarily thrill-seeking, adrenaline-addicted youths may be oversimplified."

In some ways, we can blame the media and advertisers for this stereotypical portrayal. The image of the thrill-seeking daredevil is portrayed and reinforced in advertisements featuring radical dudes with No Fear® as they Do the DEW® while performing *Jackass*-style stunts—wiping out on skateboards, swimming through alligator-infested waters, and head-butting a bighorn sheep. In her 2005 dissertation "Advertising in the X Games," Brandy D.

Grady noted that "Generation Y members (mostly young males born between 1979 and 1994) seem fascinated with sports that incorporate risk [and] involve adrenaline-inducing action and have a high risk of physical danger or even death." She argued that they were attracted to those sports—or at least the portrayal of those sports—because they looked cool.

According to Grady, the portrayal of extreme sports as cool in marketing led to an increase in interest and participation. These ads targeted the stereotypical thrill-seeking teen male desperate to maintain self-esteem and project a positive self-image—to be "cool"; to not be "The Loser." And it works, so naturally, companies trying to engage that segment of the market are willing, even eager, to perpetuate the extreme-sport-participant-as-thrill-seeker stereotype. But according to Brymer, this stereotype of the "radical dude" adrenaline junkie reinforces the false assumption that the thrill of risking death is what motivates those desperate to connect with the image of glamour and "coolness" associated with high-risk sports.

Of course, the advertisers don't admit this; they want you to believe they're making a deeper, more spiritual connection with their target audience. No Fear, a successful clothing company that sold "attitude wear"—baggy shorts and a line of T-shirts with slogans about pushing the edge—claimed its brand was about state of mind. "We're about the mental process," Jim Hancock, No Fear's advertising manager, told AdAge in 1995. "We're about taking on the challenge and fear that's in every and any kind of task and overcoming." Some of No Fear's ads featured rock climbers, including Dan Osman performing a human flag—holding his body in a horizontal position while gripping the rock only with his hands—while free soloing a 5.11 route in The Needles. PepsiCo, the owner of the Mountain Dew brand, made a similar pronouncement in a 2015 press release: "Do the DEW . . . represents the attitude of a community that really seeks to live life authentically." But to most people, the stereotypes portrayed in advertising media make risk-takers seem like deviant, adrenaline-fueled fanatics intent on killing themselves.

It's little wonder then that when some people see a film like *Free Solo*, they come away with the impression that Alex Honnold is damaged, depressed, mentally ill, even suicidal—all terms reported in online comments of the film. "Just a movie about a psycho that pushes for extreme danger," wrote one commenter on Amazon. "This guy clearly has been born with something wrong with him," wrote another. "We don't understand people who seek these thrills," someone else wrote. They imagine, based on marketing depictions of radical thrill-seeking dudes and years of studies arguing for the negative psychology underlying extreme sports, that Honnold must have some sort of psychological defect that has resulted in a death wish.

THE IDEA THAT EXTREME-SPORT PARTICIPANTS, including free soloists, have a "death wish" is nothing new. In their 2005 essay titled "Risk Taking in Sport," two researchers (both named Matthew Pain, one a lecturer in sports and biomechanics, the other a researcher and applied sports psychologist) considered whether American climber Jim Wickwire had a death wish. "According to the Freudian interpretation, risk-taking individuals like Jim Wickwire have a death fulfilment wish; as such, the repetition of life-threatening behaviors are classified as expressing suicidal tendencies," they wrote. "Wickwire himself is still unsure why he pursues his dangerous hobbies, stating that 'The people who engage in this [sport] are probably driven to it in a psychological fashion that they may not even understand themselves.'"

The American Psychological Association's definition of death wish is "an unconscious desire for one's own death, as manifested in self-destructive or dangerous behaviors," which is usually associated with depression or other mood disorders that lead someone to engage in high-risk activities. This definition of "death wish" is derived from Sigmund Freud's "death drive" theory. Freud (borrowing from Alfred Adler and Wilhelm Stekel) argued that humans have two fundamental instinctive drives: one toward creation and life that he called *eros*, another toward aggression and destruction called *thanatos* (a term coined by Stekel to describe morbid obsessions that include a death wish and destructive impulses). The "death drive" theory proposes that, because life is a struggle and death is inevitable, we sometimes subconsciously give up the struggle. This, Freud argued, could manifest itself as a subconscious desire for self-destruction, leading to depression or even suicide.

People who have a death wish may not actually wish to die. In her documentary, *Voices of Suicide*, Linda Firestone interviewed people who attempted suicide and survived and found that, at the moment they made their actual attempt, they "immediately reconnected with themselves and did not want to die." Some people may willingly put themselves in danger, where self-harm or death is a likely outcome, sometimes as a form of self-challenge for the life-affirming feelings that result from successfully facing life-or-death consequences. At the very least they claim that's why they're doing it and are unwilling to admit or reveal that they are driven there by conscious or subconscious feelings of resignation.

Freud's death-drive theory, like many of his explanations of human psychology, has not withstood the test of time. "It is as if Freud supplied us the sick half of psychology and we must now fill it out with the healthy half," wrote Abraham Maslow, the famed American psychologist in his 1968 book *Toward a Psychology of Being*. Maslow, like many scholars of psychology, made it his life's work to explore, complement, and often criticize Freud's theories. These days, the death drive theory has been largely supplanted by the idea that neurotransmitters in our brains—physiology rather than a psychological drive toward self-destruction—are responsible for our moods and self-destructive behaviors.

Research has shown that low levels of dopamine, serotonin, and norepinephrine result in our being less happy or even depressed, leading to feelings of worthlessness or purposelessness that can snowball into suicidal thoughts or actions. According to Doug Robinson, author of *The Alchemy of Action*, rock climbing and other risky sports can flood the brain with neurotransmitters to create a sort of "high" or at least a more positive view of oneself and one's purpose for living. However, the death drive theory can't be ruled out entirely. During wartime or when homicide rates are high, suicide rates tend to drop; when homicide rates are low, suicide rates rise, suggesting humans—at least some of them—have an innate drive toward death.

"Most seasoned climbers would . . . balk at this Freudian interpretation," Pain noted, "and indeed, results of research studies into the mental health of risk-takers indicate no differences from the general population." Pain concluded that risk-taking in sport leads to increased confidence and self-esteem which can lead to success in other life endeavors. "Risk-taking cannot, therefore, simply be explained away as a self-defeating psychosis," Pain continued. "In fact, strong evidence suggests that the inclination to take risks is hard-wired into the brain and intimately bound to arousal and pleasure mechanisms. Such behavior might even have ensured our survival as a species and underpinned our rapid population of the earth."

"Death wish? That's nonsensical," Geoff Powter said during a panel discussion at the Banff Centre in 2019. "People who solo for the *right* reasons are healthier than a lot of people are by any measure of mental health." Powter, a clinical psychologist and writer living in Canmore, Alberta, started climbing in the 1970s. His early experiences were not trauma-free. He witnessed a climbing fatality during his first month of climbing, and later took a serious fall. Neither incident deterred him. Climbing, he felt, was worth the risk and he didn't shy away from risk. During his career as a climber, now in its fifth decade, Powter's climbed hard rock and ice routes including light-and-fast Himalayan expeditions and high-level free solos, including twice soloing CMC Wall, a 5.11 route on the 1000-foot limestone wall of Yamnuska, near Canmore.

"Evolutionary psychologists and biologists argue that risk-taking is something that we have a natural inclination and attraction towards," Powter says. "If we're not getting it through wars, or not getting it through high levels of mortality, like in a pandemic, then we turn to other things that give us the same experience like free soloing. And it's a natural kind of state." But he doesn't think it's only the death wish driving this need to take risks. "As wrongheaded as this is going to sound, when we're in times of war, we have a clear sense of purpose."

"In extreme sports that offer excitement, adventure, exploration, heroism, and self-knowledge," Pain wrote, "we might just have found the substitute [for war]." The idea that extreme sports provide a substitute for war is not new. A lot of extreme-sport participants cite this as a rationalization for their participation. "Peace leaves certain men unfulfilled," Mark Twight, one of the most extreme of extreme-sport participants, wrote. "If this weren't so, they would not challenge themselves with life-threatening activities to help determine their identity during peacetime—and for some, climbing takes the place of battle." While no one can credibly say that extreme sports offer a moral equivalent of war, it is clear they offer a strong sense of purpose to the individual participant, a sense of purpose that often overrides all else in their lives.

WHILE HIGH-RISK SPORTS PARTICIPANTS MAY be purposefully putting themselves into dangerous situations, they are for the most part mindful of the risks and take extreme steps to mitigate them. "The construct known as 'risk' has always been a part of life," Brymer says. "It is only relatively recently that the lack of certainty and the need to control our surroundings has been boxed as a construct and labeled, let alone labeled as something deviant."

It was when Brymer was teaching adventure sports while working on his masters in sports psychology that he started to notice a disconnect. "I read all the literature about people engaging in extreme sports because they were desperate for risk, but I was working with people who were very different from what the literature was saying. They were very, very careful."

He decided to take a phenomenological approach to find out why these risk-takers didn't fit the mold, to find out if instead of there being something wrong with them, there might be something right. "There's an assumption some people have that, if you're not like me, there must be something wrong with you." Brymer told me. "The important thing to realize is that there are many characteristics of people who get involved in extreme sports. There isn't a particular type of person. It's a reflection of everyday life."

The fact that rock climbers tend to take carefully calculated risks only when they feel confident in their ability to manage those risks means, in Brymer's view, that they aren't deviant at all—not even free soloists. Brymer defines an extreme sport as one "where the most likely outcome of a mismanaged mistake or accident is death. If something does go wrong, it is most likely terminal." This quality makes free soloing a good vehicle for discussing socially acceptable risk. According to Brymer, "Risk is a culturally constructed phenomenon stemming from modern society's deep-seated aversion for, and obsessive desire to be 'liberated' from, uncertainty." Risk-taking entails any activity that creates fear or anxiety in most people, such as public speaking, which some surveys claim people fear more acutely than death.

"People would look at tigers pacing in a cage and wonder what was wrong with them," he told me. "Then they let them out into a more tiger-like environment and they started behaving like tigers." It's the same with people, he says; society has put us in cages that we're afraid to venture out of. "We've put ourselves in a cage and wonder why we have psychological problems," he says. He thinks we should open the cage and start doing things that involve risk, which has been a part of human existence since the beginning. "Risk-takers are the normal ones," he told me. "I'm more concerned about the safety-seekers. Those are the ones we should be concerned about."

The safety-seekers have incorrect assumptions about free soloists, Brymer says. They don't understand that free soloists plan, train, prepare mentally to avoid mistakes, and eliminate risk before their climbs. But mostly, they incorrectly believe that free soloists have somehow controlled or eliminated fear. "They don't really eliminate fear," Brymer says. "They learn to use it, to have a more positive relationship with fear that allows them to do something that other people are afraid to do."

"Fear is information," he continues. "It tells you, 'Take this seriously.'" For some people, fear tells them what they're doing is dangerous and they walk away; others approach more cautiously and let the fear teach them."

Brymer thinks our relationship with fear has left us lacking something that shaped us as a species. "Fear was a part of everyday life for humans for thousands of years," he says. "Now we've caged ourselves. Existentialists have been telling us this for years. Having a positive relationship with fear opens up purpose in life. All of the doors of the cage suddenly open."

But risk-taking in extreme sports is viewed differently than in other pursuits. Fundamentally, this is because most people don't understand risk and don't see that risk-taking has any positive value to the individual or society. But our ability to manage and confront risk has been one of our most important strategies for survival—perhaps not on the individual level, but as a species. In our modern world, though, the need to take risks in order to survive has been all but eliminated. Still, some of us still have the "twitch," as John Bachar called it, a compelling sense of curiosity about how far we can push ourselves, an irrepressible urge to find the edge and take a step beyond it, to override our fears of the unknown and feel that we have a chance to overcome our fate.

"Participants know that the slightest mistake could mean death," Brymer says. "Free soloing is not a sport where you can succeed 90 percent of the time; you have to do it right 100 percent of the time, because even 99.5 percent of the time still gets you hurt or dead."

The ability to maintain control, Brymer asserts, is fundamental to the experience of free soloing because it leads to a feeling of empowerment, which is sought by many extreme-sport participants, including Steph Davis. She is literally holding her life in the balance; if she is able to maintain control, stay focused, keep fear at bay, and if she has prepared adequately to meet the physical and mental challenge of holding on and executing the moves, she can successfully complete the climb as she has done many times, which can create powerful emotions.

"That certainly doesn't mean that everyone who free solos does it for the right reasons, but I absolutely don't believe that mental illness is the driving force for the vast majority of people who solo, or, for that matter, paddle dangerous rivers, ski difficult lines, or take a big financial risk," Powter explains. "In very, very few of those cases do those people intend to lose everything they're betting. The high consequences of the game sorts out the unhealthy pretty quickly."

And even when people have decided to climb something alone for slightly less than ideal reasons—hoping to sort out a problem in their lives, struggling with their ego or identity—Powter doesn't think it is necessarily a bad thing. "There's a healing power in taking chances," he says. "It can clarify things, it can oblige you to look for a larger purpose, it can force you to develop some skills and become more proficient."

Those goals—finding a larger purpose, taking active steps, not letting fear control you, and connecting with your sense of capacity—are the things Powter points out a therapist would recommend as clinical targets for a person who is depressed.

"The technical term is developing greater self-efficacy—learning that you have control, and that what you do actually matters," he says. "I can't think of too many situations in which what you do matters more than when you're free soloing. Every foot placement, every flex of a hundred muscles matters more than anything else ever has, and that's an incredibly liberating power.

"Depressed people have often lost faith in the power of their agency," he adds, "They start to believe that the things that they do don't matter, and that's contagious, because they start acting in very self-limiting ways."

Still, Powter isn't suggesting that someone suffering from depression or any other mental struggles take up free soloing as a cure. "It's critical to understand just how acutely aware the soloists are of the risks they're undertaking, and how tuned in they are to their own mental state as they manage those risks," he says. "They worked through the puzzles of risk and fear and uncertainty before they start up a climb, and they understand the meaning of the experience and the role of their ego in managing that meaning."

"If you don't have that meaning sorted out," he says, "you probably shouldn't be up there in the first place and you're probably going to run into some troubles when you are."

CHAPTER 12

What If I Let Go?

After judo practice one day in 1968, Leeds University student John Syrett was accosted by Don Robinson, who insisted that he try climbing on the artificial climbing wall he had constructed in a narrow corridor of the gymnasium. Consisting of pieces of stone cemented into brickwork, it was primitive by modern standards but effective. Syrett, who had never climbed before, was soon a fixture on the wall and began to excel in making difficult moves.

"It's probably safe to suggest than no one (not even himself) realized that John Syrett was creating a new paradigm for climbing in Britain," Irish climber Mick Ward wrote for *UK Climbing*. While nearly all rock climbers of the day trained on real rock when it wasn't raining, Syrett was able to train hard every day for two years on the indoor wall. As Ward noted, this "probably put him massively ahead of almost any other climber in the world apart from John Gill. . . . When John Syrett ventured outside, he transitioned in the most spectacular manner imaginable."

One November day in 1970, Syrett casually made the third ascent of *Wall of Horrors*, an E3 6b (5.11+) on Almscliffe Crag, a gritstone route legendary for its difficulty and level of risk. The route had no protection for the first 30 feet, making it effectively a free-solo climb. The next year, he made the first ascent of *Joker's Wall*, an E4 6a (5.11+) route at Brimham. According to a climber who was there, Syrett first tried leading the route, but took a ground fall when his only piece of protection pulled out, so he climbed it on a toprope to test the moves then free soloed it.

Gordon Stainforth recalled an epic climb on the Aiguille du Peigne he made with Syrett in 1972. They'd made a long rappelling retreat and had one more rappel to go before reaching the snow slopes below, but they couldn't find an anchor, which meant, unless they could find a way down, they'd be stuck there. Their headlamps were turned off, and they couldn't see more than a faint sign of snow below; how far, they couldn't tell. Syrett decided they'd have to leap off or else likely die of exposure and did it. "It worked, and I had no choice but to follow," Stainforth recalled on a UK Hillwalking message board. Although it was only about 30 feet, "It still felt like a long, long way. . . . I mean it actually seemed like quite a while I was falling, but the snow was incredibly soft: I went into it up to about my chest. Most brilliant exit I've ever made from a mountain."

Henry Barber climbed with Syrett during his visits to England and described him as "a great climber." "He was elegant, very cautious, centered, methodical, but free," Barber told me. "He had the spirit of free moving, of flow, on gritstone. He was very confident and smooth, pretty to watch."

Though Syrett partied hard, he also had a quiet side and bouts of melancholy. Once while partying with friends, Syrett cut the tendons in one hand on a broken beer glass, which affected his climbing ability. He still climbed at a high level, and did some noteworthy free solos, but became depressed. Some thought it was because of his diminished climbing ability. Others say that's a myth. "He was depressed about a colleague who was killed alongside while he was working on the oil rigs," Steve Webster wrote on a UK Hillwalking message board. "He was also drinking heavily."

Late one night, Syrett ended up at the home of climber Pete Livesey. "The story we all heard about John's last night with Livesey was that they were talking most of the night, with Livesey not having the slightest clue that John was intending to end it all," John Stainforth recalled. "The story was that he had a rucksack with him with nothing in it except whiskey." Syrett jumped at dawn from the lip of Malham Cove, a 280-foot limestone cliff in north York-shire popular with rock climbers. "From the lip of the Cove, he took the long, savage plunge through empty space, cold air," Ward wrote. "We've all secretly thought of it. He did it. In the twinkling of early morning light, through the eye of a bolt head, he was gone forever."

AS A CHILD, AUSTIN HOWELL showed an affinity for heights, as well as a lack of fear of them; during games of hide-and-seek, he would climb trees around his Texas home. It wasn't until he started college in 2006 that he learned about rock climbing at the University of Houston's indoor gym. Like many college students who discover climbing, Howell's studies suffered. He was at the climbing wall whenever he got the chance, working out the moves of progressively harder problems. Instead of studying, he watched videos of other climbers, including Dan Osman and Michael Reardon. Before long, Howell had dropped out of school and gone on the road, living out of the back of his truck while traveling around the US to every major climbing destination he could. For work, he climbed cell towers, which eventually landed him a job in the Southeast, where he found plenty of rock to feed his obsession.

On his website, Howell was candid about his mental struggles and suicidal impulses. Among other incidents he wrote about, he'd once gone to a rooftop intending to jump to his death but walked away. When he mentioned his rooftop encounter at a counseling session, his counselor asked why he felt so strongly that he wanted to die. "I'd thought about it a great deal," he wrote. "I didn't think I had any good reason whatsoever. I didn't even have a bad reason." He eventually realized he was suffering from depression and anxiety. After seeing counselor after counselor, one gave him an epiphany— his depression was a disease, like cancer, that he could overcome. "Fuck you, depression," he eventually decided. "I'm going climbing."

Howell threw himself into climbing with vigor. He'd always had a penchant for taking risks, for running it out and climbing unroped, but he upped the ante, soloing more often, on more challenging terrain. It made him feel alive, he said, made him want to live. The experience of climbing, especially free soloing, seemed transcendental for Howell. As he wrote in his many blog posts on the subject, he recognized it as a form of meditation, where his mind could shut down as he focused all of his attention on the movement, looking inward, observing his thoughts without distraction.

In 2008, Howell took a nasty fall in a climbing gym, hitting the floor after his belayer failed to hold him, breaking his back. After that fall, while he was in a back brace for four months and unable to climb, his mother gave him an ultimatum. "Basically, she told me I could keep climbing or keep having family support for college," Howell recalled in an interview with *Blue Ridge Outdoors*. He kept climbing—and kept getting hurt. A few years later, he broke both ankles. And in 2015, Howell took a 20-foot fall on the first pitch of the *Nose* route on El Capitan in Yosemite. He'd been roped up, but it hadn't helped. He landed on his head and suffered multiple fractures to his skull, wrist, and five vertebrae. His doctors told him he wouldn't realistically be able to climb again.

Despite his injuries, Howell was soon back to climbing and soloing at an increasingly high level. For him, it had become a matter of necessity; it was what grounded him in life, gave him a sense of peace and purpose and he refused to let it go despite the undeniable risk and his mother's reprobation. "For most people," he wrote, "if they've really found something that's meaningful in their lives, the choice . . . is going to be really obvious. The trick is admitting it."

Howell would eventually boast that he had climbed more pitches without a rope than with one. Eventually, his ropeless climbing garnered attention, which he didn't shy away from. In 2015, he was filmed free soloing a 5.9 route in Linville Gorge called *Dopey Duck* wearing nothing but his trademark hat. Jeff Jackson, then editor of *Rock and Ice* magazine, saw the video and wrote a column about Howell titled "Naked Soloist Is Saner Than I Am," in which Jackson expressed admiration for and even envy of Howell as he contrasted his own long, tiring days of developing and projecting routes with Howell's simple, joyful approach.

To say that Howell was obsessed with free soloing would be an understatement. It was, in some respects, his entire purpose in life. On his website, he posted blog after blog about his free soloing experiences. He made videos of himself free soloing hard routes for YouTube and was working on a film.

The morning of June 30, 2019, was pleasant and sunny, a "splitter day" as Howell described it on social media. He started it off by doing what he loved, free soloing routes on the shady side of Shortoff Mountain in North Carolina's Linville Gorge. As usual, he had on his "Keep Austin Weird" T-shirt and trademark hat, shorts, rock shoes, and chalk bag. His friend, Ben Wu, had hiked up to the cliff with him to take photos as Howell climbed some of his favorite routes, including laps on *Dopey Duck* (5.9) and *Golden Rule* (5.11a/b). Around one o'clock in the afternoon, Wu headed down the trail while Howell continued soloing.

Two climbers on *Dopey Duck* recalled seeing Howell free soloing a 5.11 route next to them, possibly taking another lap on *Golden Rule*. A few minutes later, they heard Howell yell, "No!" They looked up and saw Howell falling over 80 feet and hitting the ground.

A hold had broken, according to witnesses, just 20 feet from the top of the route. According to a press release from the Burke County Office of Emergency Services, rescue crews reached Howell at approximately 1:18 p.m., rappelling in while other climbers performed CPR. It did not take the rescuers long to realize he would not survive; they pronounced him dead just twelve minutes after they arrived. Howell was thirty-one years old.

IN 1978, A STUDY TITLED "Suicide Attempts by Rock-Climbing Falls" suggested that many people try to mask their suicidal act as an accident, such as in two cases where twenty-seven-year-old males died as the result of rock-climbing falls. "These falls, occasionally speculated about as possible suicidal equivalents yet having no recognition as such in the literature, are illustrated as methods used by these impulsive, action-oriented and risk-taking people," according to the study. Basically, the researchers concluded that these were suicidal young men who subconsciously faked their falls to make their deaths look like accidents.

Geoff Powter accepts that while suicidal ideation may have been at the heart of the two specific instances mentioned in the study, that's absolutely not the case with most people who solo. "Psychologists had a hard time figuring out risk-taking," he said, "and thankfully we've evolved far past the point of the title of that article, which both intuitively and academically strikes as nonsense. We understand better now how risk-taking is a life force that leads people to betterment and fulfillment, and I think it's really important to understand that distinction."

Of course, there are free soloists who admit they have suicidal tendencies or at least think about it. As Henry Barber told his biographer:

I suppose I have suicidal tendencies, but everyone does. How many times have you been driving along the road and said to yourself, "What would it be like if I steered into the tree over there?" You're wondering about dying, what it would be like to be somewhere else. I've thought about taking my life thousands of times. . . . In climbing, it's so easy because you're in such a vulnerable position. It isn't to say, though, that I've put the mental processes of taking my life into motion. It's just an interest, and I think that everyone has these thoughts, whether they realize it or not.

Barber admits he has thought about what it would be like to let go, usually when he was gripped, looking for options, looking down at the ground and calculating his chances of surviving a fall. Like on *Gorilla's Delight*, where he was facing a fall onto boulders from more than 100 feet up. He looked down and thought, "What if I let go?" And then he'd responded: "'No, don't even think about that, that's the most absurd thought possible. Ain't gonna happen.' I assessed that [if I fell] I wasn't going to survive. It was very calming."

Though Barber says he's never had any truly suicidal thoughts, he admits that he's talked to therapists who have been worried about him. "I've gone through very difficult times," he told me. "My marriage broke up. I used to go to the top of the cliff, and my therapist said to me, 'Should you be doing that?' And I said, 'Yeah, it's the only place that feels like home.'"

According to Barber, he's thought a lot about the fine line between life and death and the fact that he had the ability to end his life just by letting go. "That struggle is there every time I solo something," Barber said. "The thought of 'What would happen if I let go here?' is only an academic question," he added, "because my body is already into the next move, along with the momentum that's in my mind. Letting go is not even a possibility if I've made the decision to be up there in the first place."

"HAVING SUICIDAL THOUGHTS AND ATTEMPTS, and other mental health issues doesn't mean we can't free solo," says Arno Ilgner, author of *The Rock Warrior's Way*.

"It just means we might be putting ourselves into situations where we could choose to die. The choice to die might manifest itself during the activity." He points to veteran suicide prevention, where they emphasize making guns inaccessible during the period of crisis. "In other words, if veterans have suicidal thoughts and begin acting them out, then it'll take fifteen minutes to get their gun, load it, and shoot themselves," Ilgner says. "That fifteen minutes is important because the suicidal thoughts tend to dissipate in a few minutes. Free soloing wouldn't allow that."

But that's not what Ilgner thinks happened with Austin Howell. "Reports about what happened in the moment he fell point to a hold breaking or a foot slipping or something like that. In other words, it was a mistake, not a choice to die due to suicidal thoughts."

For climbers like me, who found climbing as a way to overcome depression and suicidal thoughts, this rings true. It also resonated with Sonya Pevzner. "Climbing scared the shit out of me, which was good," Pevzner wrote in the *Climbing Zine*. "Scared was alive. Scared meant I didn't want to die." In her article, she describes a life wracked by anxiety and depression rooted in her father's death in a violent car crash when she was an infant, which led her to ambivalence about life, often imagining herself driving into a tree at high speed. Her father had been a climber, and one day Pevzner decided she needed to go climbing to gain a deeper connection with him and deal with her overwhelming sense of loss. Her first attempts at climbing in a Boulder climbing gym scared her, in a good way.

"It's like there was a magic line across the wall, the height after which I perceived a fall to be fatal—that had a paralyzing effect on my climbing," Pevzner wrote. "I dreaded the moment when I would cross that line, when I realized that falling from this height without a rope would mean death. I dreaded it because it made me want, in a desperate and visceral way, to not die. And not wanting to die forced me to choose wanting to live."

Pevzner also wrote about how a rappel off of 9131-foot Mount Shuksan in Washington's North Cascades became another opportunity to confront her fear of falling. Preparing to rappel forced her to confront the reality of what would happen if she fell. "Falling would mean death, real, horrific death—the kind where your body goes splat on the rock and your blood pools and reflects the mountain that just killed you," she wrote. "The first moment of each rappel gave me a jolt of adrenaline. My life was literally on the line. I really, really didn't want to fall."

The fear of death by falling, she realized, was personal in a way her suicidal ideation had not been. She could safely imagine killing herself by driving her car into a tree as a way to deal with her grief, but it was just a gruesome fantasy. But hanging from a rope hundreds of feet up a rock face, relying on knots she had tied, her grip on the rope, feeling the weight of her body above the gravity of the void, knowing that if any part of the system failed, or if she let go, she would fall to her death—that was real, immediate, and personal.

She knew in that moment that she didn't want to die, especially on a mountain, but she would keep climbing if only to feel the fear and remind herself how much she wanted to live.

PART III

Over the Dreamjunk Wasteland

Does my calm repel? Defy? I outgame God and Gravity,
those old hags knitting galaxies. I sit in their spacious laps,
a nonesuch, my moxie a law to myself one hundred feet
    above
contradiction, that dumb mud that undoes me.
It's neck or nothing, yeah.

> —Pamela White Hadas,
> "Ringling Bros. Present: The Lucky Lucie Lamort"

In "The Only Blasphemy," John Long recounts his experience of free soloing *Left Ski Track* at the end of a day of soloing with John Bachar. According to Long, he botched the crucial sequence, barely pulled through the 5.11 crux, escaped falling to his death on the boulders 50 feet below through sheer luck, and had an epiphany about the folly of free soloing for the wrong reasons. It is one of the most influential articles about free soloing ever written.

If Long intended the article as a cautionary tale about the dangers of free soloing, it failed. Instead, it inspired a lot of climbers to solo the route. It became almost a rite of passage for any would-be hard man

Todd Skinner free soloing Left Ski Track *(5.11a), Joshua Tree* (Photo by Jeff Smoot)

visiting Joshua Tree. By writing about his day of free soloing with Bachar—including the story of Bachar's first free-solo climb, which became, in effect, Bachar's creation myth—Long had unintentionally roused the passion of countless others to follow the path of the master, to the point that every aspiring climber thought about soloing *Left Ski Track*, including Russ Clune, a visiting East Coast climber, and me.

I was traveling with Todd Skinner in the spring of 1985, and we'd stopped at Joshua Tree for a month before heading to our next destination. Of course, in Joshua Tree, free soloing was part of the itinerary. Skinner had his own circuit of routes he would free solo regularly, which included *Left Ski Track*. One morning, Clune and I followed Skinner on his circuit, starting with easier routes, working up to progressively harder routes, eventually arriving at the base of Intersection Rock. It was nearly exactly the way Long described his day of soloing with Bachar. Before I knew it, we were standing below *Left Ski Track*, watching Skinner float up it. I wondered if I might be getting in over my head.

"I've never soloed a 5.11 on-sight," Clune said as he tightened the laces of his Firé rock shoes and tied on his chalk bag. Russ had also joined Todd on his circuit and was feeling good—good enough to solo a 5.11 he'd never climbed before.

"Me either," I admitted, looking up at the crack hesitantly. I'd never climbed it before either, and although I wanted to, I was having doubts.

"This route's very solo-able," Clune said. "Just the one hard move at the bottom and you're up."

"Unless you fall," I said.

"No way," he said, smiling broadly. "It's gravy."

Clune started up the angling crack and was soon at the crux, 30 feet off the ground. With his long arms and strong hands, he reached up and latched onto a thin edge and pulled through the hardest moves with little more than a grunt. He continued along the crack easily, following Skinner up the vertical wall.

I stood looking at the route for the longest time, visualizing myself doing the moves, but I couldn't bring myself to do it. Soloing a 5.11, even an "easy" 5.11, even when you've done the moves before, is not something you approach casually. It would be foolish to risk my life because of peer pressure, to avoid appearing weak or indecisive. That was the moral of Long's story, wasn't it?

I wandered among the rocks beyond the campground, alone, for the rest of the afternoon, trying to reinflate my ego. I free soloed easy routes to assuage my angst, to prove to myself that, despite balking at joining the gang solo of *Left Ski Track*, I was only being prudent. And so I wandered, seemingly randomly, across the jumbled landscape, but I knew exactly where I was going.

Nearly every day of our visit to Joshua Tree that spring, Skinner and his group would set up a toprope on an overhanging 5.11 and climb laps. It was a great workout, climbing up and down the 70-foot wall repeatedly. We all had it totally wired. We could climb that route all day and never fall off. Still, none of us had worked up the nerve to free solo it. We'd heard rumors that occasionally one of the local rock stars—John Bachar, John Yablonsky, Mike Lechlinski—would materialize and climb it unroped, but although we saw Bachar and others soloing on a daily basis, so far nobody had come along and soloed this route. We knew why. It was sequential, and committing, with difficult climbing up an overhanging face high off the ground on thin holds that weren't entirely positive. No matter how wired we thought we had the route, it would be too easy to slip off at just the wrong spot.

As I walked into the canyon in the early evening, I felt as if I had stepped inside a cathedral. It was eerily vacant. I walked over to the base of the route and looked up at the wall. *I could solo this*, I thought. *Why shouldn't I?* I had climbed the route dozens of times before, up and down, relentlessly, without falling, without even coming close to falling. *So what if it was the domain of hard-core elite climbers? Why couldn't I?* The thought suddenly scared me, because I was thinking I might actually do it, right now, while no one was watching.

Why not? I could climb it with a toprope a hundred times, a thousand times, and never fall off. Hadn't I already done so? The next step was obvious. It could be my redemption.

I wasn't quite sure I would, though. I agonized over it quietly and decided no. Still, I didn't walk away. I stood there, staring at the wall, and started rationalizing. *Maybe I could just solo through the crux, to the big patina edge above the thin moves, not far off the deck, and see how it went.*

I could easily climb down from there. I could do that much, couldn't I? Then maybe some other day, if all went well, I might go a bit higher, up to the break at the base of the overhang and see how that went. Sure, I thought. *I could do that.* I sat down and changed into my rock shoes, lacing them snug; my footwork would need to be immaculate. As I walked the coarse sand to the base of the wall, a familiar wave of adrenaline nearly knocked me down.

I put a hand against the wall to steady myself, took several deep breaths, and tried to stay calm or at least look calm, even if no one was there to see me. I looked up the wall and at the sky above it. It seemed so enormous, so infinite. *Was the amphitheater really this big? This vacant?* I had never felt so alone here before.

I chalked up, meditatively rubbing the chalk on each finger, between my fingers, on my palms and thumbs, and the back of my hands, massaging it into my skin, focusing on covering every inch of skin from my fingertips to my wrists like a white glove, unnecessary for a face climb but part of my exacting ritual. Looking up once more, I thought *yes*, inhaled deeply, exhaled, shook my arms, and started to climb, pulling onto the ramp and walking up to the ledge and chalking up once again to dissipate my nervousness before moving rightward, pulling sideways into a little dish between the patina edges, pulling up on two thin, sloping edges, using the counterforce of an opposed foot and knee, and reaching up to grasp the big edge that marked the end of the hardest moves.

I put my other hand on the same hold and chalked up again, hesitating there momentarily, looking down 30 feet to the ground, remembering my promise to climb only this high and then climb down. Then I looked up. *Maybe a little higher?* I thought, negotiating with myself. *Maybe just to the roof, then down? Yes. I can do that.* I shuffled my hands rightward on the patina edge, hooked my left heel on the other end, and rocked up to reach a higher hold before locking off and standing up on the edge where I could now let go with one hand, then the other, to shake out and chalk up once again.

I could easily have climbed down from here, but I was possessed. Climbing perfunctorily up the perfectly spaced edges, I was soon halfway up the wall where a horizontal crack divided the vertical climbing from the overhanging, with no thought of stopping. *This is it*, I thought. *This is for real.* I traversed left several moves and contemplated the bulging rock above, the flakes that I would have to climb out onto and pull up on, the rounded knobs I would have to pinch and lever on, the empty space between me and the desert floor that seemed so far below. I could not climb on autopilot any longer; I would have to focus.

From here on, the consequences were undeniable. One false move and I would end up in a wheelchair or dead. *Do I have the route too wired?* I wondered. *Will I mess up the sequence?* It could end so beautifully—or disastrously.

At that moment, I heard voices and looked down to see two young women dropping their packs, pulling out their ropes and gear, and preparing to climb a route across the cove. I recognized them; they were the German girls from the next campsite. *Why were they here? Had they seen me? Did I want them to see me? No. Absolutely not.*

The spell was broken. A new wave of adrenaline washed over me and I knew I was done. I was now quietly freaking out. *Climb down quickly!* my mind screamed at me. *Hurry!*

I traversed back to the right, my arms shaking, heart pounding. I took a last, lingering look back at the overhang. *Yes*, I convinced myself, *going down is the right thing to do.* I started quietly down the vertical wall back to the ground, one move and then the next, keeping my shit together despite the feeling that everything was wrong.

Halfway down the wall, my feet secure on the big patina edge, with only the crux sequence left to reverse, I froze as the voice returned. *You are here*, it told me. *You will never be here again. This is your moment. It's now or never.* I had dreamed of soloing this route since the first time I had climbed it and here I was, adrenaline surging, fighting the urge to flee.

Despite my resolve to climb down, conscious that I was in no state to be soloing, I started back up, one move and then the next, unwilling to stop myself. I climbed back up to the break and traversed to the overhang and chalked up. I breathed to calm myself knowing the whole time that I should not be here, should not do this. But still, I reached up and grasped a flake and pulled up and let go of the safety of the wall below.

Even though I knew I could climb down from any point on the wall, it seemed irrevocable now. I had crossed the threshold. Even if it was physically possible, there would be no turning back.

At that moment I heard a gasp. The girls had seen me, were watching me, and I did not care. Even if I fell, there would be no witnesses to my death because I was no longer there, it was no longer me climbing but some insane fool whose eyes I could see through, whose fingers I could feel through. I no longer existed outside of holding on and letting go, pushing, pulling, reaching, swinging, higher and higher up the wall.

And then there were no more holds to grasp, no longer any air beneath my feet, only solid, weathered monzonite, horizontal now, glowing pink in the low evening sun, a light breeze flitting across the desert, a lizard scampering into a deep fissure, a swift darting by. I scrambled to the highest point of the rock and sat there for a long time, gazing into the sun. I felt blank, like all and nothing, like light and heat and gently moving air, vibrant and in tune with everything around me, more alive, more unreal, than I had ever felt before. I wondered if Russ and Todd had felt like this when they reached the top of *Left Ski Track*. I doubted it. I smiled at the thought of it. I smiled at everything.

After the sun set, I scrambled down and wandered the desert floor in the afterglow until it got too dark to see. I returned to camp to find there had been mild concern since I'd gone missing at the base of Intersection Rock. Skinner had come back to find me and I was gone. The German girls had returned to camp just after sunset; they'd reported seeing somebody soloing who had disappeared. Was it me, Skinner had wondered. It had been dark for more than an hour, and I had not returned.

"Glad to see you're alive," Skinner said as I walked into camp and sat down on a boulder in front of the campfire. "What have you been up to?"

"Nothing," I said. "Just wandering around."

Skinner wasn't buying it. He knew I'd done something. Eventually I confided in him.

"That's awesome!" he gushed. "What was it like?"

I could not answer except to say, "It was good."

CHAPTER 13

Riding the Edge

One of the main sociological theories of participation in high-risk activities is "edgework," a term coined by American sociologist Stephen Lyng to describe voluntary risk-taking activities that explore the edges, or cultural boundaries, between sanity and insanity, consciousness and unconsciousness, and life and death. Lyng sees edgework as a way to escape the feeling of alienation brought about by dull working conditions stemming from class immobility; he likens participation in edgework to individualism and anti-institutionalism. Participants seek to escape the disenchanting living conditions of their class but enact the characteristics of this self-same class—persistence and goal-orientation—to successfully transcend those living conditions.

The term "edgework" comes from a passage at the end of Hunter S. Thompson's 1967 book *Hell's Angels*:

With the throttle screwed on there is only the barest margin, and no room at all for mistakes. It has to be done right . . . and that's when the strange music starts, when you stretch your luck so far that fear becomes exhilaration and vibrates along your arms . . . until the next dark stretch and another few seconds on the edge. . . . The Edge . . . the edge is still Out There. Or maybe it's In.

In *Deep Survival: Who Lives, Who Dies, and Why*, Laurence Gonzales describes his own journey to the edge while speeding dangerously across a flat, dry lakebed in the desert on a motorcycle. "I was going about as fast as I dared . . . when the landscape, the jagged rocks and the alkali lake in the windstorm, and the high blue of the sky overhead all at once came together into a coherent picture," Gonzales wrote. "I became one with the terrain and the motion." It was a transcendental moment, a ride on the shimmering edge of the fabric of perception and reality, an ascent, he called it, "with angels out of the temporal hell of the flesh." But he realized that if anything went wrong, the illusion would shatter.

Edgework theory posits that, in any extreme sport, participants willingly engage in risky actions beyond the edge of control to escape feelings of alienation and alleviate the sense that they are stuck to the grindstone without any chance of escaping it—so that they might figuratively ascend with angels and rise above the temporal hell of a mundane existence. Like "Allan," the forty-eight-year-old businessman who sought out the life-risking thrill of hang gliding in order to escape the perceived meaningless tedium and burden of his existence. Like Mark Twight, who wrote about being disturbed by the lack of authentic values in the modern world, who used climbing "to fight the monotony and alienation of industrialized life, and to validate myself." Extreme climbing, Twight said, gives people "a way to imagine something, a way out of what they are seeking to escape."

There are three theories of edgework: psychoanalytic theory, Type T theory, and sensation-seeking theory. The psychoanalytic theory views extreme sport participation as a pathological and unhealthy narcissistic tendency where participants are victims of unhealthy psychological developments. Type T (the "T" stands for thrill-seeking) theory suggests extreme sports are a positive outlet for a participant's deviant personality trait, allowing them to fulfill their need for uncertainty, novelty, ambiguity, variety, and unpredictability. Type T participants "prefer high levels of stimulation, complexity, and are distinguished by flexibility in thinking styles," according to Kari Knutson and Frank Farley, authors of a 1995 study titled "Type T Personality and Learning Strategies." The sensation-seeking theory views extreme-sport participation as the result of an inherent need for novel experiences and intense sensations, where individuals seek new thrills and excitement in an attempt to alleviate boredom, what Michael Bane refers to as "riding the edge jaggies for all they're worth."

"I came to risk sports looking for Indiana Jones," Bane wrote in *Over the Edge: A Regular Guy's Odyssey in Extreme Sports*. "Instead I found a group of puzzled people with a tiger by the tail, interested not so much in mythology as in touching and holding an experience as ephemeral as spider silk, ghostly as morning mist over a Montana river." Bane, an admitted couch potato who undertook adventures that pushed him to his limit—including kayaking a waterfall, swimming in shark-infested waters, and climbing Denali—wrote about the lure and transformative experience of approaching the edge.

The edge has its own gravity, like a great dark star on the edge of the known universe. We approach the star only with the greatest of caution, because its gravity has the power to rip away our preconceptions, our sure knowledge of the way things are, to let us see the way things might be. The dark star has the power to give us back our feelings, sometimes in exchange for our lives.

This is the theme of *Lines of Flight*, a 2009 film that explores the relationship between the existential drudgery of industrialized labor—mixed with a sense of disenfranchisement with mass production and consumption—and the escape offered by free soloing on gritstone outcrops in northwest England. The film, produced by Martin Wood, a professor at Melbourne Institute of Technology and an accomplished free-solo climber, contrasts archival footage of the region's industrial past—steelworks, garment factories, assembly lines—and commuters mindlessly shopping or scurrying to work with the quiet internal sanctuary of the solitary climber engaged with the difficulties of a steep crack or arête, risking his life for no reason other than to escape and transcend his fate.

Several climbers are featured in the film, working their mundane jobs and then working off their disenchantment by free soloing various extreme routes. Andy Cave typifies them: he went straight from school to work in the coal mines. After discovering the gritstone outcrops near his home, he started climbing, which usually meant free soloing, and eventually became a certified guide. Following his line of flight, he was able to escape the drudgery of work in the mines and find his true path.

Some researchers theorize that while edgework participants think they are transcending their class situation, they are really expressing morbid psychology traits and exhibiting sensation-seeking behavior, seeking thrills through risk. Doug Robinson, author of *The Alchemy of Action*, argues that climbers experience a "high" resulting from the body's natural chemical response to fear and action. As the Pain study "Risk Taking in Sport" explained, "Dopamine is a neurotransmitter commonly associated with the pleasure system of the brain, providing feelings of enjoyment and reinforcement to motivate us to do, or continue doing, certain activities. It is released by naturally rewarding experiences . . . and also survival behaviors like fighting and scavenging." Pain and Robinson confirm that activities, like rock climbing, that are "extremely engaging, intense, and novel" can trigger the release of dopamine. "Thus," the Pain study suggested, "the same mechanism that rewarded our ancestors for acting to stay alive may also underpin the highs afforded by extreme sports." Based on this, one could argue that free soloing to experience flow or a high is not edgework but simply classic sensation-seeking.

BANE SAYS THAT ONE OF HIS MOTIVES for seeking out risk was to find "some part and parcel of our mythology, cowboy or samurai." The mythological cowboy and samurai warrior evoke self-reliance and action in the face of death. Both lived in hostile environments where death was an ever-present risk. Both had to be skilled, watchful, aware of their surroundings, and quick on the draw—six-shooter or sword—or be dead. Free soloists often compare themselves to samurai warriors who lived and died by the sword and had to have complete control of their minds and actions in order to survive. It's a fanciful comparison, given that most rock climbers have about as much in common with samurai swordsmen as they do with professional tennis players—except perhaps when it comes to the concept of flow.

According to Mihaly Csikszentmihalyi, author of *Flow*, enjoyment of high-risk activities for their own sake derives not from the risk itself, but the ability to minimize risk through skill and attention and the ability to control potentially (or actually) dangerous forces or outcomes by rigorous discipline and sound preparation, and that, by doing so, participants can enter an altered state of consciousness called flow. Csikszentmihalyi defines flow as "a state in which people are so involved in an activity that nothing else seems to matter;

the experience is so enjoyable that people will continue to do it even at great cost, for the sheer sake of doing it." He describes it as an optimal experience that evokes "a sense of mastery—or perhaps a sense of participation in determining the content of life—that comes as close to what is usually meant by happiness as anything else we can conceivably imagine." Csikszentmihalyi studied various types of people, including rock climbers, who were not seeking danger and risk per se, he wrote, but climbed for the experience of flow.

In his book, Csikszentmihalyi introduces a hypothetical character named "Alex" to illustrate why the complexity of consciousness increases as a result of flow experiences. Alex (in this case a fictional tennis player, not the rock climber) attempts to navigate the landscape between anxiety and boredom to achieve flow. At first, because his skills are poor, Alex can achieve a sort of flow experience simply by meeting low-level challenges such as hitting the ball over the net or returning a volley. But as his skills improve, Alex gets bored just hitting the ball over the net, and as he begins to play against better opponents, he discovers his skills are lacking, which increases his anxiety, both of which prevent Alex from achieving flow. To return to flow, Alex must set higher goals to increase the challenges he is facing and also improve his skills to successfully meet those challenges. He could theoretically reduce the level of challenge, but according to Csikszentmihalyi it is difficult to ignore challenges once you are aware they exist.

Attaining flow requires that we control our consciousness, focus our attention on the activity, and shut out all irrelevant and extraneous thoughts so that we can become completely present in the moment, the here and now, in a space where we do not worry about life's problems, where what we are doing right now is our entire world. It requires a meaningful goal, action toward that goal, and complete engagement in the action. The goal must be meaningful and engaging—it must present a challenge to be overcome through application of focus and skill and provide clear and immediate feedback.

Climbing, it turns out, is a nearly perfect vehicle for flow, which may be one of the reasons it has become so popular. For the climber, the goal may be to successfully climb a difficult rock pitch without falling. It is a meaningful, challenging goal that requires skill and focused attention because you will fall off if you fail to hang on. It provides immediate feedback. For the free-solo climber, who chooses to climb the pitch without a rope or protection, the goal is even more meaningful and challenging and requires even more intense focus. The feedback is also starkly clear and immediate—you don't just fall if you fail to hang on; you probably die.

There's more to flow than being completely engaged in an enjoyable activity, though. According to Csikszentmihalyi, flow is a response to ontological anxiety (existential dread), "a fear of being, a feeling that there is no meaning to life and that existence is not worth going on with." In that sense, then, those who seek flow through risky activities such as free soloing are, in fact, engaging in edgework. The payoff of the flow activity is transcendence of anxiety and dread through an exalted state of consciousness and a feeling of complete control. "Those who attain (flow) develop a stronger, more confident self," Csikszentmihalyi wrote, "because more of their psychic energy has been invested successfully in goals that they themselves had chosen to pursue."

Geoff Powter agrees that free soloing can be one of the most powerful paths to flow because of the immediacy and consequences of the risk. "The state of flow is the psychological state in which you are much more directly connected to your body, much more directly connected to the environment around you," Powter says. "It includes a heightened sense of place and a heightened sense of purpose that allows you to go on autopilot and deeply feel a transcendental sense that you are doing what you're *meant* to be doing in that moment."

While accepting that this isn't true for everyone, Powter has seen that risk is a crucial ingredient in his own search for flow, and he knows that there's some evolutionary basis for that notion.

"Risk of physical harm transports us to a place that we're evolutionarily designed to be in," he says. "For almost all of our history we have very much had to deal directly with risk and fear and death. It's only been in the last few hundred years that we've been exposed to far less risk, and our mental and physical selves really haven't caught up."

A lot of us are puzzled, he says, when we experience risk. "We run from it rather than understanding it. We judge the presence of it in our lives, thinking that it's wrong to have it in our world, and we act as though we should be able to completely eliminate it, and even feel that we have failed when there's risk around us."

He's quick to point out, though, that facing and understanding fear and risk does not eliminate the fear, but just moderates the extent to which the fear stops someone from thinking or acting. "It's an incredible feeling," he explains, "to experience fear and work through just how real that fear is." Fear and consequence, he points out, are *not* the same thing. "You can be afraid of falling, but that doesn't mean that you will fall, and really learning that distinction is very liberating."

"There are very few things that have clarified that equation as vividly as soloing," he adds. "It offers one of the very few times where what I do right now in this very instant determines whether I live or die, and I think that there's something deeply, deeply intrinsically human about that awareness, and having that kind of control."

Eric Brymer also understands the appeal of using free soloing to achieve flow—the slowing down of time, the mind calm, the floaty feeling—the "ineffable elements" that climbers experience and seek again and again. But despite Csikszentmihalyi's claim that flow requires increasing the challenge to maintain the required level of engagement, Brymer says that "you can get the ineffable elements when you're free soloing, or not . . . but you don't need to push limits to get them."

But when it comes to free soloing, he thinks it's dangerous to up the game to continue to experience flow. "You can't keep doing that," he says flatly.

CSIKSZENTMIHALYI DOESN'T TAKE FULL CREDIT for the theory of flow. He notes that the concept of flow was described in the East long ago. It comes, in part, from samurai warrior culture. Takuan Sōhō, a seventeenth-century Japanese Rinzai Zen Buddhist priest who authored *The Unfettered Mind* (*Fudōchi shimmyō roku*), wrote about flow: "The mind must always be in the state of flow . . . for when it stops anywhere that means the flow is interrupted and it is this interruption that is injurious to the well-being of the mind. In the case of the swordsman, it could mean death."

Flow as described by Sōhō means to clear the mind of all distractions and dualistic thoughts, bringing it into a heightened state of alertness, readiness, and openness to experiencing things as they are in the present moment. This is essential for a swordsman engaging an opponent, when allowing the mind to be distracted by thoughts of anger, fear, or self could result in death. It is difficult for Western minds to achieve this state; we are used to multitasking, parallel tasking, projecting, forward thinking. But the Japanese martial arts and Zen practice are intimately connected and have long sought to cultivate a state of mind engaged in the immediacy of the moment that is analogous to flow.

Bruce Lee, the legendary Hong Kong American martial artist, actor, and one of John Bachar's idols, explained, "I'm moving and not moving at all. . . . It is not, 'I am doing this,' but rather an inner realization that 'this is happening through me,' or 'it is doing this for me.'"

"The mind must be wide open to function freely in thought," Lee wrote. "A limited mind cannot think freely. . . . Awareness is never exclusive; it includes everything."

By saying "go with the flow" we mean diving into and becoming part of the river, which requires discipline, self-knowledge, and a high level of skill developed through mindful practice that, once achieved, leads to feelings of competence and self-efficacy, as well as a state of reduced anxiety and conflict. In the context of sword fighting and free soloing, this state requires the elimination of fear of failure and even death. Thus, according to Pain, "in direct contrast to the Freudian position, we put ourselves at risk not because we have a death wish, but because we wish to confront and overcome our deepest fears."

CHAPTER 14

Total Control

Hazel Findlay, a British climber in her early thirties, has free climbed El Capitan by four different routes including *Freerider* and the original *Salathé Wall*. She also repeated Ron Kauk's route *Magic Line* (5.14b) in Yosemite in 2019. A graduate of the University of Bristol, where she studied philosophy, Findlay now lectures and writes about mindset and mental-management, and coaches climbers to help them overcome fears and limitations. Although she's not a prolific free soloist, she starred in a short film called *Free Flow*, released in 2018 (the same year as *Free Solo*), in which she free soloed several routes in the Llanberis Pass region of north Wales, a glaciated valley lined with steep, fortress-like cliffs composed of rough volcanic breccia and the site of many fabled rock climbs in English climbing history.

In *Free Flow*, Findlay runs up the path, scrambles up to the base of Dinas Cromlech, and starts climbing *Cemetery Gates*, a 200-foot arête on the right wall of the crag, rated E1 5b (5.10a). She narrates as she climbs meditatively, searching out ripples and undulations in the rock. "I use my body to turn the volume down," she says. "I let my fingers and toes find the right places and that is all I need. The emptiness is what I'm here for."

I asked her if she was describing flow in the film. Her answer mirrored what Csikszentmihalyi described in his example of the tennis player Alex. "I've experienced a sort of flow soloing, but I have more often when climbing at my limit on lead," she answered. To access flow, she added, the challenge level needs to be high enough to bring her into a kind of hyper-focused state. "Often when I'm soloing, the climbing is so easy my mind can wander, and if your mind wanders, then you are not in flow, whereas when I'm climbing at my limit, I have to be more focused. . . . However, I have experienced a sort of low-level flow when soloing that is closer to being present than being in flow. It just feels like I am really "here," nowhere else, and very connected to what I'm doing in a relaxed way despite having it all feel very wild as well."

Although she is clearly in control during the climb and never in danger of falling, Findlay moves purposefully in places, making a move then trying one hold after another before committing. She wasn't having any trouble; she was just being very careful. "I led it the year before, and I knew it would be okay to solo," she says. "They let me pick the routes, and I climbed them on lead first to make sure they were easy enough. I didn't feel anxious before. I felt happy to climb a cool route." But, as she admits, she wasn't in flow because the climb, for her, did not present enough of a challenge to lock her mind in to the exclusion of all else. She was merely present, which was enough for her.

"Before I started climbing I focused my visual attention on small bits of rock to become present," she says. "I also connected to my body by listening to my breath. And I tried to feel the rock under my skin." While climbing, she allowed distracting thoughts to come and go without distracting her. "I reminded myself that I am not my thoughts and shifted my attention back to something that is happening in the present moment."

"I try to stay present and let my body do what it already knows how to do," Findlay added, describing her mindset while soloing. "Just as you can let your body walk down a sidewalk you can let your body climb. It's only when the mind interjects [that] you lose focus," she continued. "You want to be calm but attentive. Relaxed but not absent-minded. Really you just want to be present with the feedback you're getting from your senses."

To achieve flow, Findlay says she has to climb more challenging routes, and she prefers pushing the limits of difficulty with a margin of safety. That's why she hasn't made free soloing a habit; the kinds of climbs where she achieves flow are also those that she's not willing to do without a rope.

"I'll say that those people that died free soloing made soloing a habit and they probably went into autopilot and became complacent," she says. "I don't solo that much."

In Findlay's view, "presence" as a concept doesn't rise to the same level as flow; you don't get locked into being so focused on an activity that you lose yourself in it, you are just in the here and now. It's a lower level of flow that others, including Henry Barber, talk about. As they see it, if you're upping the game to get to flow you're going to end up dead.

This idea of presence is different from the usual theory of "presence"—that media are designed to provide users with an illusion that a mediated experience is real. It is more a concept of "being present"—mindful, focused, attentive to what you are doing. It may be a better explanation for what many people find appealing about free soloing; it doesn't check all the boxes for a flow experience, but it doesn't have to. When you're present, it's *you* doing the moves, and you're fully aware, without having that floaty feeling that comes with flow, whereas a flow experience can take you into an alternate reality; you climb but are detached, and more likely to make a mistake.

ENGLISH CLIMBER JIMMY JEWELL HAD a nice, flowy style. Born in 1953 in south Wales, Jewell started climbing after joining the Birmingham Cave & Crag Club in 1972. His first club trip was to Llanberis Pass, where Jewell was led up a four-pitch route called *Direct* on Dinas Mot. He managed the first three pitches of moderate climbing well enough but couldn't manage the difficult crux section on the final pitch—he had to pull himself up the rope, hand over hand, to complete the climb. After his first real climbing experience, Jewell progressed rapidly. Just eighteen months later, he led *Cenotaph Corner* on Dinas Cromlech, *the* classic route at Llanberis Pass, first led by Joe Brown in 1952 and rated E1 5c (5.10b).

As Al Churcher wrote in his 1991 article about English free soloing titled "Two Is One Too Many," Jewell was taken away from hard climbing in the late seventies but returned in the early eighties with a renewed zeal. His "secret training regime" and a fruitarian diet, Churcher wrote, had produced a "powerful climbing machine." Stronger and lighter than he'd been previously, Jewell dedicated himself to free-solo climbing, which made him stand out, especially when he soloed routes close to his limit.

Jewell felt fitness—which made him feel in control and gave him the confidence to free solo—was a crucial component of his craft. He spent a lot of time training. Jewell's friends recall him soloing laps on difficult routes wearing a weighted belt, literally running from route to route to get in as many as possible in a day, and doing massive amounts of pull-ups in the gym. One friend recalled that after hearing that Ron Fawcett, one of the best English rock climbers at the time, was trying to do one thousand pull-ups in a day for training, Jewell immediately started working toward the same goal.

By 1986, Jewell had a well-earned reputation as one of the leading free-solo climbers in the UK. He had climbed several routes for the film *Total Control*, where he was portrayed by director Jim Perrin, as "the main exponent of that deadly game. It was just fun," Perrin intoned, "[and] about having the balls to live out your self-belief . . . that mad streak that's in some people . . . the sheer joy of risking your life."

Despite being thought of as modest and good-humored, Jewell was as competitive and obsessive as anybody. Perhaps more than anybody, as he developed his ability to control his mind and suppress his fear to the extent that he could make even the most fearsome route seem routine. His free solos seemed reckless to some, as if he chose the most sustained and strenuous routes with the loosest rock and highest level of exposure simply to demonstrate that he could go them alone.

In *Total Control*, Jewell free solos several classic routes in north Wales, including *Vector* (E2 5c, 5.10c) at Tremadog, once the hardest free climb in the UK; the *Left Wall* of Cenotaph Corner (E2 5c, 5.10d), a crack splitting a dead-vertical 120-foot wall on Dinas Cromlech; and the first free-solo ascent of *Tyrannosaurus Rex* (E3, 5.11a), a wandering route up the friable 200-foot sea cliffs of Gogarth. In the opening scene, he scrambles up to the base of *Left Wall* in his trainers, changes into his rock shoes, removes his shirt, chalks up, and starts climbing. He's strong but moves fluidly, precisely, not overpowering the rock but floating upward, his lithe arms outstretched, hands jammed in the crack, fingers gripping flakes and edges. (For the film, Jewell climbed *Left Wall* six times in a row, repeating the exact moves even to the point of chalking up from the same holds so he could be filmed from different angles.) On *Vector*, he moved quickly, never hesitating, climbing up the steep wall as casually as if he was taking a stroll in the park. On *Tyrannosaurus Rex*, he practically sprinted up the wall, climbing in just a few minutes what would take hours for a roped team to ascend.

In April 1987, Jewell spent an afternoon climbing a series of long routes at Clogwyn Du'r Arddu—better known as "Cloggy"—a steep rhyolite cliff band located on the upper flanks of Snowdon, considered by locals to be the best crag in the world. After scrambling to the base of Cloggy, Jewell started climbing at 12:30 p.m. He tackled five routes totaling more than 3000 feet of 5.10 to 5.11 (in addition to descending back to the base of the wall after each route), and then he hiked the tourist trail three miles back to the car park. He was sitting at Pete's Eats having a late brew by 4:30 p.m.

A few weeks later Jewell returned to Cloggy and upped the ante. He started with an on-sight solo of an E3 (5.11a) called *The Boldest Direct*, then climbed the *Great Wall*, an E4 6b (5.11c), ticking that route's second free-solo ascent. Those, it turned out, were just warm-ups. To everyone's astonishment, he proceeded to free solo *The Axe*, a loose, overhanging arête described at the time by the *Climbing Club Journal* as "one of the most exposed and 'out there' routes that can be imagined."

Paul Williams, the Cloggy guidebook author, photographed Jewell soloing the route that day. One of those photos became an iconic image of the era, showing Jewell climbing the most overhung section of the route front-lit by the morning sun, his bare torso and arms, yellow pants, and pink-and-blue chalk bag luminous against the darkness of the boulder-strewn cwm a thousand feet below. The photo appeared on the cover of the next edition of the Cloggy guide, and Jewell's sponsors, DMM and La Sportiva, turned the image into a full-size poster. The image was at the same time inspirational and horrifying; it drew you in, made you want to be so bold, so daring, so in control, yet at the same time firmly cautioned against it.

"All you need is chalk and balls man," a grinning Jewell famously said after his free solo of *The Axe*. "It's the purest way to cruise." Whether it was chalk and balls or something else, that ascent helped cement Jewell as someone who was operating on another level. Stevie Haston, a friend of Jewell's and a bold free soloist in his own right, understood its implications, remarking, "*Axe* one week, chop the next."

On October 31, 1987, Jewell and a friend took a shortcut from a pub to the climbing hut at the top of Crag Pant Ifan at Tremadog—up the cliff. The usual way would have been to scramble up a gully, and that's the way his friend went, but Jewell decided to finish the day with a run up a route called

Poor Man's Peuterey instead. Rated only Severe (5.6), the 200-foot "beginner's route" would have been an easy solo by Jewell's standards, even in his trainers carrying a backpack.

No one saw what happened. A friend, Dave Cuthbertson, climbing nearby, heard a voice gasp, "Oh, shit!" And that was it.

THE IRONY OF JEWELL'S DEATH, as so many of his friends and fellow climbers noted, was that he died on a route he could have practically walked up. In fact, he was taking it so lightly that he hadn't even bothered to wear rock shoes. One of Jewell's friends recalled that he had been featured in an advertisement for La Sportiva's Mega, a cutting-edge rock shoe designed to provide high friction and crisp edging. Jewell was pictured in the ad standing next to a pile of skulls in a slate quarry (part of a movie set) wearing a pair of Mega shoes. "Some people don't climb with Megas," the ad said, suggesting those people ended up dead at the base of cliffs. Noting the irony, one of Jewell's friends remarked on a UK Climbing forum, "Jim died not wearing Megas."

Another factor that may have contributed to Jewell's death was the weather. October 1987 was one of the wettest on record in the UK. The Great Storm, an extratropical cyclone of fierce intensity, had blown up the east coast into the North Sea and wreaked havoc over the entire UK, causing extensive flooding, knocking down trees, and killing eighteen people. In addition to being wet, it was also cold that October, even for north Wales. Wet, cold conditions are generally not conducive to rock climbing, as they make it easier for a climber to slip.

"Never become overconfident, even on the last easy stages of the climb," Jewell said in the film *Total Control*. "It's all too easy to pull a loose hold or loose block or become out of balance." He was talking about not letting your guard down just because the hardest climbing is behind you. "The route still commands respect, the rock still demands judgment," he cautioned.

There's a tendency for people to blame route conditions—water, ice, a broken hold, a hornet attack, or something else—for a soloist's demise. When Derek Hersey fell and died from the *Steck-Salathé* route in Yosemite in 1993, many surmised that he had slipped on wet rock after a sudden rainstorm. When John Bachar fell and died while soloing on Dike Wall at Mammoth

Lake, people said a hold must have broken. Rarely is a soloist's death ascribed to poor judgment, haste, lack of focus, or subjective error.

No one knows what happened to these climbers, because no one saw their falls. We create these explanations in part because we can't allow our heroes to die stupid, meaningless deaths. But in Jimmy Jewell's case, his friends and those who wrote about his death didn't shy away from the fact that he had made a careless mistake.

"Clearly Jim paid the ultimate price for his misjudgment," one commented on a UK Climbing forum. "For just a brief moment he lost respect for the rock and he paid for it with his life."

CHAPTER 15

This Is Your Path

Many consider Alex Honnold's ropeless ascent of *Freerider* on El Capitan the most significant achievement in Yosemite climbing, but Honnold plays it down, a response that has earned him the nickname No Big Deal. He describes his simple philosophy about free soloing:

Soloing stems in some part from wanting to engage with a beautiful place in a challenging way. Nothing inspires me more than big sheets of blank rock. Perfection. But the desire to solo a route has to be weighed against the possibilities. Can I physically do it? Am I prepared? Am I absolutely sure of myself? Finally I commit, and once I start there's only complete focus. The only thing that exists is the rock around me and the next few moves of climbing. Yet there's still the joy of movement, the pleasure in moving my body over rock and swinging around freely. And ultimately there's the summit, which feels a lot like the base. I'm still immersed in a beautiful place but somehow it feels even richer.

"He was a horrible kid to raise," Honnold's mother, Dierdre Wolown-ick, recalled in a profile of her son in *Alpinist*. "Always climbing on stuff"—monkey bars, trees, wanting to go up on the roof. The first time she took him to a climbing gym, the five-year-old promptly scampered up a wall when she wasn't looking. "I was scared he'd kill himself," she recalled later. When he was ten, Honnold's father, Charles, started taking him to a climbing gym near their home in Sacramento, California. His son was into climbing, and it seemed like a good way for him to burn off some nervous energy. And he was an excellent gym climber, earning a spot on the US Youth National Team by age 18. Honnold was smart, too, "a huge dork" as he put it, who got straight As in high school and attended UC Berkeley to pursue an engineering degree. But he felt isolated in college, and instead of going to class, he often went to Indian Rock to climb laps.

His father died of a heart attack when Honnold was nineteen, shortly after his parents' divorce, which sent him into what he describes in *Free Solo* as a "bottomless pit of self-loathing." He took a year off to find himself, and one day in late December 2004 ended up alone and bloody after taking a fall on a mountain above Lake Tahoe. If he hadn't had a cell phone to call for a rescue, he may have died there. That spring, after he recovered from his accident, he "borrowed" his mother's Chevy minivan and drove to Joshua Tree, where he started free soloing intensively, a way of turning off and tuning out his angst and grief. He never looked back.

Like many other solo climbers, Honnold started free soloing, he says, because he didn't have any partners. His first free-solo climb was a 5.3 at Lover's Leap in South Lake Tahoe. That climb went well, so he did another, and another. Two years later, Honnold arrived in Yosemite Valley, still a relative unknown in the climbing world, a status that would soon change. First, he soloed *Astroman* and the *North Face* of the Rostrum, both multipitch 5.11s, in one day. Peter Croft had shocked the climbing world with his same-day solo ascents of both routes twenty years earlier, and they were still among the hardest big-wall free solos yet done. To Honnold, it was no big deal. A year later, he free soloed Half Dome, which, despite what Honnold might say about it, was a big deal.

At five feet, eleven inches and 160 pounds, Honnold is lanky. His arm span is longer than his height (a ratio climbers refer to as a positive ape index) and his own mother has called his hands "monstrously huge"; his fingers have been favorably compared to ballpark franks "swollen on a hot grill." But what makes Honnold stand out from other climbers is how he's wired. Scientists put Honnold in an MRI scanner to study his amygdala—the part of the brain that controls emotions—and flashed images at him, gnarly stuff that evokes a strong emotional response in many human beings. But for Honnold, when he feels fear, he's able to lock it away.

In September 2008, Honnold began the biggest free-solo climb of his life—at least up until then—the *Regular Northwest Face* route up Half Dome, alone, without a rope. While the route is not very technically difficult by modern standards, the wall itself is 2000 feet high and nearly dead vertical. An unroped fall from anywhere on it would be fatal. Everything went fine until the last 100 feet. After cruising through the Zig-Zags, a series of steep, thin 5.12 corner cracks, and traversing the immensely exposed Thank God Ledge, all Honnold had left was a 5.12a slab with one hard move, and then an easy pitch to the summit. That's when his fear came unlocked. "It was like I woke up," he said of the incident. He was horrified. As Honnold later wrote in *Alone on the Wall*, "The minute you freak out, you're screwed." He was alone, almost 2000 feet above the ground, clinging to tiny ripples on a polished granite slab, quietly freaking out.

Honnold could have grabbed a bolt and pulled past the hardest move, or yelled up to the hikers on the summit to call for a rescue. But instead he clung there, chalking up for five minutes and psyching himself up to do the move. He needed to smear his foot on a slick slab and trust it to stick long enough to reach up to a positive hold—just one move, that he'd done twice before. He knew he could do it. But he was thinking too much. And then he had one of those pivotal moments solo climbers sometimes have, when they abandon logic and just go for it.

He later admitted that, at the crucial move, he put his fingers through a carabiner clipped to a bolt. He didn't use the bolt to pull past the hard move. That would have been cheating. But if his foot slipped, he could grab the carabiner and avoid falling—at least in theory. A few minutes later he was standing on top of Half Dome with a bunch of tourists who assumed he was just another hiker who'd come up the cable route.

DURING THE FILM FREE SOLO, Alex Honnold likens the free soloist's mentality to that of a warrior.

I think that the free soloing mentality is pretty close to warrior culture, where you give something 100 percent focus because your life depends on it. It's about being a warrior. It doesn't matter about the cause necessarily. This is your path, and you will pursue it with excellence. You face your fear because your goal demands it. That is the goddamn warrior spirit.

Arno Ilgner may be partly responsible for the warrior attitude espoused by many climbers including Honnold. Ilgner is the author of *The Rock Warrior's Way*, a best-selling book on the mental aspect of climbing first published in 2003, and has been training climbers on how to think and live like warriors for almost two decades. He's spent much of his life thinking about mental approaches like Honnold's, and cautions against using them lightly. "I think there are too many people and groups throwing around the 'warrior' word to heighten interest in what they're doing or selling," Ilgner told me. He points to obstacle course races as examples: "Run a little, crawl through a little mud, get a T-shirt, and you're a warrior. This disrespects our first responders who are trained to serve us by laying down their lives," he says. "It also cheapens what it means to be warriors, their role, and their responsibilities."

During our conversation, Ilgner laid out what he believes it means to be a warrior, as a climber but also in everyday life. He considers first responders, like soldiers, police officers, and firefighters, who selflessly move toward threats while others flee, to be warriors. He also outlined the approach he uses in teaching The Warrior's Way—the physical, mental, and spiritual aspects of preparing for battle and for neutralizing threats encountered on the rocks and in everyday life, and how those skills translate to free soloing.

"Death is a central issue," he says. "It can teach us to live our lives in meaningful ways. Free soloing is the realm that can reveal who we are at our core, and quickly. It reveals how we make choices about risks and consequences, and how those risks and consequences impact our ability to focus our attention."

"As I said, free soloing heightens the possibility of death, which reveals how we all understand and deal with our mortality," he told me. "Many people think free soloing is crazy because they don't understand it. They're looking at it from the outside, with no experience with it, and judge it as crazy, simply out of ignorance." Ilgner acknowledges that some people who do know something about free soloing, like climbers, also think it's crazy. "Their basis for making that value judgment is not grounded in ignorance," he says, "but rather in how they relate to their own death. Then they project their value judgment onto those who do it."

"Death is a part of life," Ilgner continued. "But it's difficult for most of us to really understand that fact and to live our lives accordingly." He calls death "the great equalizer."

"It doesn't care if you are rich or poor, prepared for a risk or not, a nice person or an asshole," he told me. "Death will kill you if it's your time. You might die free soloing, in a car crash, from a sudden illness. . . . The list is as long as one's life."

Death can advise and teach people to live their lives in more meaningful ways, Ilgner believes. "It makes us dig deep into ourselves and do some soul searching about why we're here," he says. "It prompts us to ask the difficult questions about why we're in certain relationships, why we're staying in certain jobs, why we're sitting in front of the TV watching endless dramas about others risking their lives."

"Death lays our lives raw before us and free soloing is an activity that does that better than most others," he adds. "Free soloing cuts away the crap."

ILGNER DOESN'T THINK HONNOLD IS throwing the word "warrior" around lightly, though. He interviewed Honnold after the El Cap solo and found Honnold's comments about being a warrior pretty close to the mark.

"We can look at the actual act of free soloing and how it relates to the warrior mentality, as Alex outlined," Ilgner told me. He used the analogy of two samurai in a deadly duel to explain. "The goal is clear: survive by killing the opponent. The consequence is also clear: you die if you lose."

"How should they be motivated?" he wondered rhetorically. "By the goal, the consequence, and motivation," he answered.

"If the samurai are motivated by achieving the goal, then their attention will dwell in the future, because when you're in the midst of fighting, achievement of goals is always in the future," he says. "That distracts their attention from what they need to do in the moment: fighting well."

This reveals the paradox of life, he explains. "We want to achieve goals, but we achieve them not by focusing on them, but indirectly, by focusing on what we're doing in the present."

"Free soloing clarifies the goal," he continued. "Without a rope, one has to climb and not fall to arrive at the top. It also clarifies the consequence: you die if you fall." It also clarifies the importance of doing the necessary preparation work to heighten success and diminish failure, he believes.

"Motivation needs to be driving one squarely toward what's necessary for fighting well," he says. "From my understanding, this is what Alex did."

In Ilgner's view, a free soloist's efforts need to be focused 100 percent in the direction of climbing, without hesitating. This is how Honnold succeeded in free soloing El Capitan. In an interview Ilgner conducted with Honnold after that climb, Honnold said, "Doubt is the enemy, because it distracts attention. One can diminish doubt if one prepares well." Honnold told Ilgner that he "used to think one needed 'mental armor' to keep fear at bay." Ilgner explains, "He applied this technique on his free solo of Half Dome, and it failed him." Honnold "doesn't believe that's the best strategy anymore." He told Ilgner, "Preparing well to expand your comfort zone, so much so, that it now includes the risk you're considering."

To Ilgner, when Honnold said, "This is your path and you will pursue it with excellence," it meant Honnold had made a personal choice based on his love of free soloing. "Free soloing resonates with him, just as big-wall free climbing resonates with Tommy Caldwell," he told me. "Free soloing is in Alex's DNA, and he sees it as his path. That kind of motivation allows him to pursue excellence because it's driven by a love for the activity itself." In a blog he posted shortly after our conversation, Ilgner added: "Free soloists need to love free soloing. That love allows them to express themselves in their own authentic way as they connect to and make sense of their place in the world."

When Honnold said, "You face your fear because your goal demands it," Ilgner agreed. "Yes, the goal *does* demand it. And you face your fear of death by doing the necessary preparation." However, he sees a potential downside to this: that a climber might purposefully put themselves into a dangerous free-soloing situation, using the severity of the consequences as a way to *force* their attention to focus.

"I think a lot of climbers who climb roped up, where the consequence is not death, fall victim to this," he says. "They fear falling, even on safe falls, and use the fear of falling to force them up the rock." That's a poor strategy in his view. "Using the seriousness of the situation to force your attention into the moment leads to climbing to get it over with. That's not a recipe for success."

"Fear prompts the fight or flight response," Ilgner continued. "Fear of falling causes us to 'fight' through to climb or 'flee' to safety. If we haven't addressed our fear of falling, then it'll manifest itself when we get pumped and the likelihood of a fall becomes real. Then the fight-or-flight response kicks in. Yes, if we fight, we'll be motivated to climb through, but we're reacting to the external situation as victims." This, he says, is not The Warrior's Way.

"Warriors are deliberate in how they approach risk," he says. "They learn about the consequence, so they're prepared for it. They decide exactly how they'll focus their attention," Ilgner says, "on processes they control, like breathing, relaxing, continuous movement, and eye focus." One main difference between warriors and what Ilgner calls victims is that warriors live their lives to be present, not to get it over with. "Warriors 'muster' their motivation from within," he believes, "victims do this from without."

What Ilgner was saying reminded me of Dan Osman, who was descended from samurai and was taught the Bushido code of conduct as a young man. He was often deliberate in how he approached risk, such as practicing falling to learn how to control and overcome his fear, which allowed him to free solo at a high level. "Like the kendo practitioner who lays aside his wooden sword to duel in earnest with live blades," Andrew Todhunter wrote in his 1996 *Atlantic* article about Dan Osman, "the free-soloist—in freeing himself or herself from the rope on routes where falling is tantamount to death—becomes a kind of mystic."

Ilgner didn't know Osman but had some thoughts about how he may have approached risk. "Maybe what Dano did is aligned with how samurai are taught and the Bushido code," he told me, explaining that the seventeenth-century samurai Yaygū Munenori of the Life-Giving Sword school heightened samurai training because of the influence of his Zen master Takuan Sōhō.

"Munenori and Takuan were the first, to my knowledge, who used the term 'free mind.' A free mind allows attention to flow freely in the moment to the task that needs it," he says. "At the same time, we don't let attention flow indiscriminately. That could cause us to die." A clear understanding of the task is necessary, Ilgner believes, accompanied by a focusing of attention in the mind to think about the risk and make decisions, then shifting attention to the body, focusing on breathing, relaxing, body movement, eye focus.

"Note that the thinking we do is collecting information about the risk and then making a risk decision," he says. "The climbing we do is acting out the risk based on that information. Attention flows freely and completely to each of these tasks to make sure we're taking appropriate risks."

Osman exemplified certain of these qualities, but not others, Ilgner believes. "A possible explanation could be how we each tend toward either analytical or intuitive tendencies. Analytical people tend to overthink and take action tentatively; intuitive people tend to underthink and just engage. I tend toward intuitive. Maybe Dano had the same tendency. Perhaps he could have benefited from more attention to the preparation part of risk-taking."

Austin Howell is another climber who wrote about the warrior spirit in his blogs about free soloing. His idols were John Bachar, Dan Osman, and Michael Reardon, all of whom adopted the warrior mentality as part of their personae. I asked Ilgner if certain types of people, particularly climbers with emotional or mental challenges, might latch on to the warrior concept and free soloing as a way of coping or transcending their situation.

"Dealing with trauma and these mental health issues makes life harder," he answered. Ilgner free soloed because Bachar did, and due to peer pressure, because his climbing partner wanted to. "We're impressionable, want to be part of group, want to be accepted, feel worthwhile, and so on. So, we're influenced in this way," he acknowledges.

"A part of the training we do is to bring awareness to this need for belonging and find different ways to satisfy it," he explains. "We focus on separating our identity from outcomes so we can shift our locus of control internally where we'll be less influenced by behaviors of others."

Does this work? Ilgner believes so. "Paradoxically, others will respect us more for our independent thinking and actually want us to be part of their groups," he says. "They see a power in our being due to how we're oriented internally, and they're drawn to that sense of power."

CHAPTER 16

The Heroic Quest

On a trip to Yosemite, a graduate student named Jacob Ray Sparks took some friends up the back side of Fairview Dome, a 900-foot granite dome in Tuolumne Meadows. Some in his group were uncomfortable with the increasing steepness near the end, where they had to use their hands in places to navigate the rocky terrain, but they made it to the top. That's where they encountered a free-solo climber.

"As we rounded up to the plateaued peak, we saw a climber come up the opposite, sheer side of the rock, with no ropes and no safety gear," Sparks later wrote of the encounter.

> *His hair was wild and wind-blown; his eyes seemed to stare right through me. Clearly a master of his chosen extreme sport, he transitioned seamlessly from the difficult vertical challenges of the rock face to taking some calm and conscious breaths at the top. . . . He stood strong and tall as if he had encountered menacing monsters and had found some invisible treasure in their bellies. . . . "How was it?" I asked. "Good, good," he said dismissively.*

A few years later, Sparks, who had gotten to know many Yosemite climbers during a stint as a seasonal ranger, decided to write about free soloists for his master's in recreation management at Brigham Young University. The professors tried to talk him out of it, but he insisted. His 2016 thesis, titled "Extreme Sports: A Study of Free-Solo Rock Climbers," provides a glimpse into what those climbers were experiencing.

Sparks was aware that most studies of extreme sports, which had been conducted by individuals who never engaged in the activities they studied, regarded participation as pathologic or otherwise emotionally unhealthy, or the practice of out-of-control sensation-seekers with narcissistic tendencies. But Sparks's encounters with other free soloists and his own experiences made him think something else was going on.

When he tried to talk to the free-solo climber, he'd "seemed disinterested in conversation and consumed by the experience he was having." Sparks tried to infiltrate the tribe by hanging out at Camp 4, the usual hangout for Yosemite climbers, and asking questions, but he found the climbers there reluctant to talk with someone they perceived as an outsider. "Maybe they [were] not eager to be criticized for these actions so often regarded as selfish, suicidal, or reckless," Sparks conjectured. They tested him, asking if he free soloed himself, or at least had climbed the routes they had free soloed. Only after Sparks told them about his own experiences climbing during his time as a park ranger did the free soloists begin to open up.

Sparks's study suggested that while sensation-seeking may be an initial impetus for engaging in extreme sports, it's not what drives more experienced participants. They exhibit greater emotional control and lower anxiety than less experienced participants, and they possess a stronger sense of reality and personal responsibility. This matches the findings of other researchers: such as Eric Brymer, who described more experienced participants as being resourceful, intelligent, independent, and forthright, as well as experiencing an above-average desire for success and recognition. "Extreme sports demand perpetual care, high degrees of training and preparation, and, above all, discipline and control," noted Pain. "Most of those involved are well aware of their strengths and limitations in the face of clear dangers. . . . Individuals do not want to put their lives in danger by going beyond personal capabilities."

Sparks similarly found that most free-solo climbers didn't have a need to seek out risky situations or be out of control. While a couple of the free soloists he interviewed had a "very dark something," a "dark energy," as he described it to me, that trended toward the self-destructive in their psyche, the majority were on a positive path. "They were searching for peak experience, seeking for that pure form of movement and connection, finding challenge at their level of competency, and having an epic experience," he told me. "They didn't want to work at a desk for the rest of their lives. They wanted to experience the fullness of life."

In his thesis, Sparks described his free-soloist subjects as extremely aware of their strengths and limitations, highly trained to meet the challenge and danger they faced, and favoring discipline and control that did not exceed their abilities. "The participants described their motivations in terms of overwhelming enjoyment, heightened focus, and personal progress," Sparks wrote. Free-solo climbing gave them "opportunities for positive transformation with outcomes including gains in courage, humility, egocentrism, and emotional engagement." Brymer went further, arguing that participants in extreme sports are less governed by the superego than the average population, and that the life purpose and opportunity for personal transformation provided by extreme sports literally changed their lives.

"At the end of the day I had an epiphany because I did not die but I really enjoyed it, a whole environment that I never imagined existed was opened to me," one of Brymer's subjects reported. "My life has been radically altered by that choice, by that day. I can trace my change of path to that day." Author Michael Bane wrote in *Over the Edge* that his first extreme experience left him feeling better than he had ever felt, triggering a total life transformation and a quest to go "to places I've only imagined. It will allow me to reach out and touch . . . something. Something desirable, something mythical."

Brymer and other researchers have found that extreme sports can change the "battle against nature" into an understanding of nature as central and meaningful. Similarly, by confronting their fears and taking risks, participants develop a sense of mastery that is more about courage than fearlessness. "We thrive when appropriately challenged," Sparks wrote. "We enjoy sharing an epic tale where we can choose to persevere, focus our skills, and find a stronger self at the end." According to Sparks, when free soloists reach "states of focus and concentrated energy rare in the world today" they are able to fulfill their self-narrative, their heroic quest.

This was true for me. Before I started climbing, I was shy and withdrawn and struggled with feelings of insecurity and inferiority. An average student in high school, I got straight As in college, became a lawyer without going to law school, and passed the bar exam on my first try. But I'm still risk-averse—I prepare obsessively before speaking in public or arguing in court, just as I did while writing this book. Part of me still believes I need to work twice as hard as everyone else to succeed, but I've learned how to focus and do the work, which I attribute largely to my experiences while free soloing. Without the confidence and mental control I gained by confronting my fear and anxiety, I would probably be a mess.

YOU'D THINK MICHAEL LAYTON, A former climbing guide who has had his share of accidents over the years, would have given up solo climbing, but he hasn't. "I've had broken legs and been impaled, and I've had some ground falls," he says. Layton ended up in a wheelchair after breaking both legs while free soloing at Red Rocks. The then twenty-two-year-old couldn't find a partner that day, so he hiked in and soloed a 5.10, carrying a rope. He succeeded in climbing the route, but his rope wasn't long enough to rappel. He started downclimbing instead—when a hold broke he fell an estimated 50 feet. "It should have killed me," he acknowledges. Luckily, he bounced off a ledge and fell down another cliff. He broke all the metatarsals in both feet and, unable to walk, had to crawl out.

"I recovered from that but it kind of scared me off of hard Honnold-type free soloing," Layton says. "Every once in a while, I'll hop on a multipitch 5.8 that I've done before and know that I'm not going to fall [off of], but I've had enough accidents that in the back of my head, I'm like, 'well, what if a bunch of bees come out of the crack, or a bat flies my face, or a hold breaks or someone drops something on me,' you know?"

Unlike many free soloists, Layton agrees he's crazy for free soloing. "Absolutely," he says, "and completely irresponsible and self-centered and selfish." But it isn't suicidal, he insists. "I'd say just the opposite. That the whole point is to come back alive, and if you wanted to kill yourself, there's a much easier way to do it." He balks at the idea that free soloists have a death wish. "We're just testing the machine we were put in, trying to see how far we can push it."

"Here's the thing: My generation never went to war," he explains. "We never had really hard times. Everything's kind of given to us." He feels like his risk-taking is a kind of substitute for having gone to war or having gone through a major disaster. "Nothing like that ever happened," he says. "This is just a way for me to say, this is the genetic potential that I was given; let's see what I can do with it."

In Layton's view, there's an innate need in some humans to have that sort of experience and if we don't get it from war or a survival situation that is imposed on us, some of us go out and find a way to meet that need. "And not everyone has that," he says. "Plenty of people are completely content, which I don't judge at all. All my coworkers, they all barbecue with their families on the weekends and that's enough for them. But for me, I need to see what I'm made of."

Layton is painfully aware that this search to find out what he's made of has a dark side. On May 30, 2021, while traversing a ridge of Temple Crag in the High Sierra—unroped on a ledge system that Layton thinks was probably 5.4—his friend Vik Waghray fell 2000 feet to his death. "He must have grabbed a loose block right behind me," Layton reported. "I made eye contact as he fell, and it will haunt my soul forever."

Layton was stunned. "I lost my voice screaming for him over and over with no response and knowing there was no way I could do anything, going down would have been my death too." He didn't move for a long time. When the shock finally wore off, he soloed carefully back across the ridge where his friend had fallen.

"The reward was not worth the risk," Layton says of that day and the route they were on. "I'd much rather [have] gone to a picnic that day." He says if he could find something less dangerous that he enjoyed, he'd probably do that instead. But he can't. He's still climbing, still soloing, although he admits he finds it hard to go some days. "The night before or morning of [a climb], my stoke can be pretty damn low," he admits. "This isn't new; I've always had a lot of anxiety climbing and sometimes it gets the better of me. But since Vik's death, I've actually found doing big days in the mountains very therapeutic." He continues, "It breaks my heart he won't be able to share in any future experiences with me in the places he loved, so I have to get after it and do them for him." In a sense, honoring his friend has become Layton's heroic quest.

If you ask some free soloists if they have a death wish, they'll tell you they have a life wish. By having the courage to go on the heroic quest, to directly experience everything life has to offer—immersing oneself in experience free from the paralyzing fear of death—the quest becomes essential to one's well-being. Of all the climbers I talked with, Layton had the best explanation of what it meant to free solo because you have a life wish. "You're given this life and this body and you're given free will and so to go into the mountains and solo something is to experience life in a way that not many other people are able to experience," he told me. "I feel like it's living my life to its fullest potential when I'm doing something like that."

Brymer describes this as the "capacity to understand what it means to be human." But instead of "life wish," he describes the concept as an exploration of our form of life. "We're looking at what the potentialities are for different forms of life," he says. "Instead of going out and testing our potential, we've caged ourselves. We're sitting on the couch eating crisps and watching TV instead of experiencing life more holistically. . . . We have the capacity to realize—to see, feel, experience—all of the potential of human life."

LAYTON'S UNDERSTANDING OF HIS LIFE WISH and Brymer's concept of the form of life are rooted in what Abraham Maslow defined as "peak experience." In a 1943 paper titled "A Theory of Human Motivation," he introduced his famous hierarchy of needs, a theory of psychological actualization that was later presented as a pyramid-shaped scale. At the bottom are basic human needs (food, water, security, safety), then belongingness and esteem closer to the top, and eventually narrowing to a peak of self-actualization reached by achieving one's full human potential.

"It is quite true that man lives by bread alone—where there is no bread," Maslow wrote. "But what happens to [our] desires when there [is] plenty of bread and when [our] belly is filled? At once, other and 'higher' needs emerge and these, rather than physiological hungers, dominate [us]. And when these in turn are satisfied, again new and still 'higher' needs emerge, and so on."

Though Maslow's hierarchy has been criticized as lacking scientific rigor, it is still a useful framework for sociological and psychological research; it can also help us understand why some people take up free soloing as a serious pursuit. "People with a stable sense of self-esteem feel a stable sense of self-worth, and they feel a sense of competency or mastery," psychologist Scott Barry Kaufman, who's written extensively about Maslow's theories, said in an American Psychological Association seminar in 2020. "They feel like they're owners—they can control their future. They're the . . . authors of their lives."

Unlike most of his predecessors, such as Freud, Maslow studied mentally healthy subjects instead of people with severe psychological disorders. He focused on what was right with people to try to determine what made them able to self-actualize. In his 1964 book, *Religions, Values, and Peak Experiences*, Maslow explored those extraordinary moments when a person's self-view and physical reality are in harmony, an altered state of consciousness characterized by euphoria often achieved by self-actualizing individuals—he called these moments "peak experiences." They happen when a person feels a sense of "wonder, awe, reverence, humility, surrender, and even worship before the greatness of the experience," when reality is perceived as "truth, goodness, beauty, wholeness, aliveness, uniqueness, perfection, completion, justice, simplicity, richness, effortlessness, playfulness, self-sufficiency," and we feel connected to all of humanity.

In some ways, the peak experience defined by Maslow resembles a religious experience similar to the moment of enlightenment or a spiritual ecstasy—such as the way John Muir described standing on the summit of Cathedral Peak in 1865—both defined as altered mental states characterized by heightened mental and spiritual consciousness accompanied by emotional and sometimes physical euphoria. "Such episodes . . . were not necessarily religious at all," according to Edward Hoffman, an adjunct associate professor of psychology at Yeshiva University who wrote a biography of Maslow. "Yet self-actualizing persons gave descriptions about these experiences that were amazingly similar to the verbiage of the world's great sages and mystics."

Although Maslow's theory of peak experience is commonly associated with the concept of flow, it isn't the same thing. Flow and peak experience often go together, especially in the realm of extreme sports like free soloing, but you can experience flow—the internal mental process of being so immersed in an activity that one loses sense of time, space, or self—without experiencing the ecstasy that defines a peak experience.

Maslow, whose health had never been exemplary, had a severe heart attack in 1967. This transformative experience shifted his view. As he wrote in his journal:

The only trouble [with peak experiences] is that your goddam body can't keep up with you. . . . The acute and climactic peak experiences seem to lessen in number while the "awakened" cognition or unitive perceiving

*seems to increase and even come under voluntary control. The happiness
then tends to be mild and constant rather than poignant and acute. . . .
This type of consciousness has certain elements in common with peak
experiences—awe, mystery, surprise, and esthetic shock . . . but are constant rather than climactic. . . . The words I would use to describe this kind
of experience would be a "high plateau."*

*. . . Transcendence can mean to live in the realm of . . . plateau living.
After the insight or the great conversion, or the great mystic experience, or
the great illumination, or the great full awakening, one can calm down as
the novelty disappears, and as one gets used to good things or even great
things, live casually in heaven and be on easy terms with the eternal and
infinite.*

Some psychologists say that free soloists are overcoming the ontological anxiety that humans have to deal with to be able to live. More simply,
they are denying death by facing it bravely and, in doing so, attempting to
become heroic. According to Ernest Becker, author of *The Denial of Death*,
"human beings are naturally anxious because we are ultimately helpless and
abandoned in a world where we are fated to die." We have "an excruciating
inner yearning for life and self-expression—and with all this yet to die." This
yearning for life and self-expression drives us, but our knowledge that we are
going to die creates fear and anxiety about our purpose in life. What are we
here for? *Nothing?*

As Freud and other psychologists tell us, humans are narcissistic; we care
mostly about ourselves and are often quite self-absorbed. Our primary drive
in life is to transcend the mundane, to become heroic—at least in our own
esteem. If we can achieve an appropriate level of self-esteem, our subconscious
can ignore the reality of death, and we can believe ourselves immortal. This
combination can allow us to do risky things. We know people can die doing
them, but don't believe *we* will die.

"When you combine natural narcissism with the basic need for self-
esteem, you create a creature who has to feel himself an object of primary
value: first in the universe, representing in himself all of life," according to
Becker. This need to stand out, to be a hero at least in our own minds, creates
what Becker calls "the ache of cosmic specialness." Modern society no longer
provides us—especially young people—with a path of meaningful action that

allows us to feel heroic. Some people seem satisfied with what our culture provides and can feel heroic by mastering a video game, making the varsity team, starting a business, or getting married and raising a family. Some have to look elsewhere, outside of mainstream culture, to find it. This desire may explain the boom in popularity in rock climbing over the past several decades.

Climbing culture creates different "domains of symbols" (Becker's term) for many different types of heroism, ways for individuals to fulfill their need to stand out and feel significant. For some people, the mere act of overcoming fear and completing a difficult or scary climb can fulfill those needs. One climber might feel heroic completing their first 5.10 lead in the gym or doing their first V4 boulder problem. For another, it might be on-sighting a 5.12 sport climb or ascending Half Dome or El Capitan. From humble beginnings, climbers graduate to highball bouldering, difficult trad routes, one-day free climbs of El Capitan, light-and-fast alpine ascents, speed climbing the *Nose* or the Eiger, and so on. These cultural roles allow for the creation of mythical heroes in climbing, such as Alex Honnold, who has said that free soloing El Capitan made him feel like a superhero. But we don't have to free solo a big route in Yosemite ourselves to gain a sense of cosmic specialness; we choose our own challenges—whatever it is that gives us that sense of supreme meaning in our lives, of being "a small god in nature" as Becker put it.

Heroism, according to Becker, is a primary response to our fear of death. As such, for an action to be truly heroic, it has to involve a journey to the edge of the void. "We admire the courage to face death," he wrote. "When we see a man bravely facing his own extinction we rehearse the greatest victory we can imagine." Roped climbing brings us to the edge of the void—when we're leading out above protection on difficult climbing or working our way up a huge wall thousands of feet off the ground, the pull of the void is palpable—but roped climbing is so safe statistically, there's only a very slight chance that we won't return alive. Free soloing, on the other hand, takes us directly to the edge of the void and sometimes even a step beyond, when we continue upward knowing we cannot climb down, where our safe return is not at all assured.

Free soloing, then, can be described as a symbolic system within the culture of climbing that meets a need for feeling cosmic specialness. It is a hero system that allows someone to believe they transcend death by relying only on their hands and feet and skill and mental focus alone to climb the rock—refusing to be intimidated by fear, resisting the urge to let go—exemplifying their courage in the face of death. They face fear of death head on, walk the meteoric line along the edge of the void, and nearly always return alive.

Ernest Becker would probably have thought free-solo climbers were crazy; he thought everyone was crazy. "Men are so necessarily mad that not to be mad would amount to another form of madness," he wrote, quoting Blaise Pascal. We are mad, he observed, because of our futile attempts to fool ourselves into believing we can overcome death. Becker wrote:

> Everything man does in his symbolic world is an attempt to deny and overcome his grotesque fate. He literally drives himself into a blind obliviousness with social games, psychological tricks, personal preoccupations so far removed from the reality of his situation that they are forms of madness—agreed madness, shared madness, disguised and dignified madness, but madness all the same.

As Layton noted, not everyone is driven to fulfill a heroic quest. Some are content to barbecue. Becker thought that whether or not someone had that drive depended on their mothers. Children have a natural fear of death once they become aware of their own mortality, he wrote, and realize that, if they were abandoned, their "world would drop away. . . . The child who has good maternal experiences will develop a sense of basic security and will not be subject to morbid fears of losing support, of being annihilated."

The anxiety that leads to activities such as free soloing, Becker might have argued, is produced by "bad experiences with a depriving mother." A child who is well cared for and loved develops "a sense of magical omnipotence, a sense of his own indestructibility." Conversely, a child who is not well cared for, who is abandoned, feels impotent, insecure, and dreadful. Such a child may not only have a heightened dread of death but act out to get attention.

When I think of my childhood insecurities and self-doubts, which first drove me to think about suicide and eventually led to climbing, I think they were caused by feelings of abandonment. Being given up for adoption by my birth mother and then being abandoned by my adoptive mother made me feel impotent, insecure, and worthless. Eventually I overcame these feelings by taking control of myself and my life, at least in my own mind. For me, part of that was free soloing. I had, as Becker called it, embarked on my Oedipal Project, a call to power, a heroic quest to control my own destiny and conquer my fears with my own powers, through self-control, to figuratively "become my own father" and thereby become omnipotent and godlike, at least in my mind. Such a child is not raised, Becker wrote, but brings himself up to have absolute control over his own destiny.

Of course, absolute control is an illusion; no child brings themselves up. But I used to tell people that I raised myself. My parents fed and clothed me and gave me a place to live, but according to my personal narrative, I created myself—a myth of myself as a heroic being—by taking control away from others and vesting it entirely in me. This may have been an attempt to build defenses that could allow me to feel meaningful, powerful, worthy—to feel like somebody. Or it could have been a cry for attention. Whatever it was, it worked.

Nobody could make me do anything if I did not allow it, which led to that nightmarish scene where I had to be held down for three hours after having a mental breakdown in fifth grade, an episode that Becker might have described as "a very serious attempt to transcend determinism" by using my "body and its appendages as a fortress or a machine to magically coerce the world," as "clay to assert [my] symbolic mastery." He might have said the same thing about free soloing.

"IF I REALLY WANT TO take a psychological perspective of my reasons for taking up climbing and free soloing, I think I had a terrible, fucked-up childhood," Ed Mosshart, a Seattle psychotherapist who specializes in addictive behaviors, says. "My father was a violent alcoholic and a mean guy. He used to beat me, and he would even wake me up in the middle of the night in a drunken rage just to knock my head into the wall." Ed's mother committed suicide, and he and his father became homeless for a time. "I know for sure that when I found climbing, I didn't understand what it meant at the time, but it's what saved me."

In the early 1980s, Mosshart and his friends got jobs working as wilderness surveyors, climbing mountains along the border between Idaho and Montana and installing brass caps on their summits. "I got paid to climb mountains," he says, putting a positive spin on what was in actuality a grueling job. "We were in really good shape and were comfortable in the mountains and wild environments, and so free soloing was a natural extension of that. . . . I think that for me, it is about mastering power, in some ways."

"My mind, my personality, my psyche was undeveloped," Mosshart says. He describes himself as an introject based on his experience of always being under the criticism and harsh treatment of his father figure, internalizing his abuse. "He's not around anymore, but I still have that same tentative hyper-vigilance, internally, and personally, and even socially I felt really outcast," he says. "It wasn't just that I just felt that way—I *was*."

"For a period, it was about finding strength," says Mosshart, "but what I found was that through the vehicle of climbing, I was able to access archetypal features of consciousness. I relate less to Freudian or psychoanalytic perspective and more to deity practice. It became about love."

Mosshart's revelation that climbing transformed itself from mastery of power to love certainly has something to do with the fact that he has practiced Tibetan Buddhism for thirty years. His work with deity practice, meditation on a deity or Buddha you visualize sitting in front of you, is a ritual method of achieving a sense of calm or stillness. "It's not what people imagine it to be," he says, anticipating my question.

"You don't literally have a god or Buddha that shows up; it's like you're generating qualities of consciousness that have a tangible feel and energy to them." This is why climbing appealed to Mosshart. "For me, climbing created a constellation of features that activated that warrior-like archetype, and I became strong. It wasn't about my conscious effort where I would finally feel worthwhile or something like that," he explains. He describes it as putting him "on a direct road to power and mastery. . . . I found a strength inside myself I didn't know I had."

The concept of deity practice came up while Mosshart and I were discussing John Bachar and his pre-solo ritual, his meditative chalking up, focusing inward, and breathing—a method of centering that brings you to a mental state where you can start climbing without a rope. "It is something like consciously visualizing, and consciously activating that archetype or that quality of consciousness that is about power, control, strength, and focus and being the one to take control," he told me.

"In deity practice when you do the meditation, you prepare, sort of ritualize, get quiet, get centered with your breaths, and then you start building that visualization and it's progressive," Mosshart explains. "I think that in some ways climbing, especially when we first started, was like that: ritualistic, meditative, about getting centered and prepared. I think soloing is the ultimate expression of that, having that mastery and being able to channel it and focus it."

In the Tibetan pantheon, there are different deities—a deity of wisdom, a deity of healing—and all these different qualities, which are all qualities of consciousness, that Mosshart believes allow us to recognize that the ego is not king. "The ego," he says, "is only the thing that mediates these unconscious or energetic ways of being that Jung called the 'archetypes'—typical ways of being in the world."

With practice, we can, as Mosshart explains, "start to generate the qualities of consciousness of that deity. That deity may have a certain fierceness, so the idea of the meditation—the ritual—is to access that fierceness, because you've got some very dark stuff you're facing in life, or in the world, and you need that fierceness." Mosshart believes that, in climbing as in meditation, repetition and concentration create neural pathways to generate that experience. "After you've done this enough, you can sit in meditation and very quickly . . . get to a still point, and I think that's what we hope to do when we prepare to free solo . . . to be really quiet and very concentrated and then execute."

He sums up his experience, "When I was soloing, there were no external thoughts or distractions. I was like, 'This is it, I'm *only* right here.'"

CHAPTER 17

The Shimmering Edge

Sitting around the campfire at Joshua Tree in the early 1980s usually involved recounting the day's adventures with your friends and whichever rock rats you'd latched onto during the trip, telling stories, drinking beer, and invariably smoking pot. You'd usually run out of beer after a few days, but somebody always had a joint they'd light up and pass around until everybody was pleasantly buzzed. Sufficiently inspired, somebody would say, "Let's go solo something."

We'd grab our rock shoes and chalk bags and wander out to the Peyote Cracks or Echo Canyon or just around to the back side of the Blob, free solo an easy route, and then sit on top and space out watching the moon rise. Sometimes somebody would start howling if they were sufficiently inspired. Then we'd climb down the easy way, feeling our way along the exposed slabs and ledges by moonlight.

In his memoir, *American Climber*, Luke Mehall describes the same scene two decades later. On his first visit to Joshua Tree in the mid-2000s, he was drawn to the many easy routes close to camp that climbers would often free solo at the end of the day. "It became a ritual of sorts," he wrote. "Climb on ropes all day, then finish up with a solo to the top of some dome, watch the sunset, drink a beer, take a puff, and then scurry back down."

Mehall is open about his psychological challenges and drug use. Severely afflicted with ADHD as a child, he became an "angsty spirit who got into trouble and fights" and tried to deal with serious mental illness by taking risks— drinking, driving, taking drugs, rebelling. "I don't think I was born to be out there," he wrote. "But I guess a lot of life is wasting time and figuring out who you are." He found out who he was when he was introduced to climbing, the simplicity of which—the life-and-death-at-your-fingertips nature of it—could bring his mind into sharp focus and keep it there. It appealed to him almost instantly. "Climbing was the only source of light in those dark days," he wrote.

Like many climbers, Mehall initially started free soloing because he didn't have a partner. He didn't fully understand the appeal but found that climbing easy routes helped to clear his mind. Then one day he got scared while soloing 100 feet off the ground and had to downclimb to safety. "My ADD mind could create a hyper focus in most dangerous climbing situations," he wrote. "Free solo climbing was not one of them." It was stupid, his inner voice told him, and he quit doing it.

Then he went to Joshua Tree. Everybody solos in Joshua Tree. You can't help it. There are so many easy and moderate routes on the hundreds of granite domes, slabs, and towers, many of them not very high off the ground, that, as Mehall wrote, "practically beg you to climb them." He started free soloing again, and even got comfortable with soloing routes up to 5.9 in difficulty, including a crack near the campground that gave him an insight into why people do it, writing:

I felt calm and in the moment . . . and thought about soloing it. . . . I started up with feelings of nervousness and freedom intertwined. Once I started climbing, the jams seemed to swallow my hands. . . . Forty feet up, when you're entering a zone where life as you know it would be over if you fell, was the best moment; endorphins and adrenaline released, a feeling of strength and peace overcame me. I could see how that would be addicting.

Still, he couldn't quite grasp how it might feel to be 80 feet up hanging on by your fingertips and toes on a hard route where falling off seemed likely and the penalty was death. "Goddamn, that's gotta be like the first high from a serious drug," he wrote, "or like a bird flying—how could we mere mortals understand the joys that climbing gods experience?"

Doug Robinson thinks he knows the answer. Robinson, who has been described as a modern John Muir, was strongly influenced by Royal Robbins, the Yosemite big-wall pioneer of the fifties and sixties whose adventurous style of climbing relied more on skill and daring than equipment. "I was still a teenager, quivering on modest leads and overdriving pitons to protect myself," Robinson wrote. "It was through [his] writing that he began, indirectly, to mentor me." Robbins introduced the idea of climbing with chocks instead of pitons to preserve the rock, which appealed to Robinson, who had embraced the lifestyle of the 1960s Yosemite climber: a sort of super-hippie challenging himself physically and spiritually against the wilderness. He grew his hair long, indulged in mind-altering drugs, got naked, climbed rocks, and, in doing so, became a student of the relationships between climbing, drugs, and transcendental experience.

It's no wonder Robinson was portrayed in Galen Rowell's 1974 *National Geographic* article, "Climbing Half Dome the Hard Way," as a sort of mountain guru who embraced oneness with the rock as a vital part of his climbing experience. He certainly embodied a more spiritual approach to climbing than many of his contemporaries during the 1960s; he was less interested in climbing difficulty or achieving first ascents than the direct experience of climbing for its own sake to achieve heightened states of presence, mindfulness, and spiritual growth, which he wrote about in several influential articles.

As a teen, Robinson had been a distance runner, and had noticed what he described as a "floaty feeling"—a noticeable change in his perception, thought, and awareness, what we call the "runner's high"—during his runs and after. In his essay, "Running Talus," Robinson suggested that climbers could improve their skills and mental awareness not by climbing, but by running quickly and fluidly across boulder fields. Called *lung-gom* by Tibetan Buddhists, this sort of running meditation allows one to nearly float through mountainous terrain in an altered state of consciousness.

Robinson became aware of a similar altered state of consciousness and presence when he started climbing, which he wrote about in his 1969 essay, "The Climber as Visionary." Robinson believed there was a correlation between the intensity of the high he experienced from taking psychotropic drugs and the state of heightened consciousness and hyper-attentiveness he experienced while running and climbing. He wondered if climbing produced a chemical response in the brain that mimicked or even corresponded to the high experienced by smoking pot or dropping acid. Robinson explored this concept further in his 2014 book, *The Alchemy of Action*, delving deeply into the science of that floaty feeling climbers get on an engaging pitch of rock, which, he claimed, is just like the high you get using psychotropic drugs—only better.

IT'S NO SECRET THAT SOME climbers get high—a lot of climbers, actually. Back in the seventies and eighties, climbers often smoked pot before they went climbing, sometimes even while they were climbing. "The drug of choice was just cheap low-grade weed," John Long told *GQ* in 2013. "Bongs were the ritual. We were just smoking reefers all the time." But that was kid's stuff compared to other things they were doing. A small group of climbers in Joshua Tree and Yosemite made a regular practice of dropping acid and going free soloing.

One of those climbers, Dean Fidelman, is the subject of a short documentary film about it called *The Rapture of Free Soloing on Acid*. Although he was a fixture of the Southern California climbing scene in the seventies and eighties, Fidelman isn't as well known as some of his contemporaries, like Bachar and Long. He was more low-key, climbing as hard as anybody but content to document the scene from behind the lens of a camera. (He's best known these days as an outdoor photographer and publisher of the *Stone Nudes* calendar.) In the film, Fidelman recalls the freewheeling days of climbing with the Stonemasters: "It would be not uncommon for a group of five or six of us to drop acid and then go soloing. . . . Soloing hard shit on acid is amazing."

As crazy as it might sound to take drugs and free solo, those who do it say it calms your nerves and focuses the mind. Robinson, speaking from experience, says psychedelics such as acid and mushrooms improve physical abilities such as balance, coordination, finesse, awareness, and energy. But as Jim Bridwell—the godfather of Yosemite climbing in the 1970s was known to do big-wall routes on El Capitan while on acid—told *GQ* in 2013, "You don't want to be climbing anything serious on acid—when you take LSD, you're taken to a place that you really haven't earned the right to be yet."

Even so, many climbers seem to have been doing it, and none of them fell off and died while soloing, at least not that anyone knows. Not that they didn't come close. John Yablonsky had some spectacularly close calls. His free-solo ascent of *Spider Line* in Joshua Tree is widely believed to have been inspired by an LSD-fueled vision, and he was known to go free soloing on acid at night in Yosemite. He was not the only one. Drug use was prevalent in Yosemite in those days, but Doug Robinson didn't think climbers needed to get stoned. Climbing gets you high, he says.

ANYONE WHO HAS LED UP into the unknown on a rock wall knows that climbing can cause a fear response, what is usually called an adrenaline rush. What you're about to do—enter a situation where your life is at risk—sets off alarm centers in the brain that trigger the classic fight-or-flight response to danger, real or imagined. The adrenal glands release adrenaline into the bloodstream, which causes your heart to pump blood faster, your lungs to expand to oxygenate the blood more rapidly, your digestion to be cut off to make more blood available, your spleen to contract to add even more blood to the system, and your liver to kick in a shot of glucose. This can make you feel sick to your stomach, but your system is actually being hit with a surge of glucose-rich blood that enables your body to run fast or fight hard.

As Robinson explains in *The Alchemy of Action*, the principal chemical actors in this response are adrenaline (epinephrine), which gives you the jolt of fear, and noradrenaline (norepinephrine), a transmitter molecule that raises your blood pressure. According to Robinson, the combination of fear and action climbers often experience at the end of a difficult or scary lead is what produces the chemical reaction that leads to euphoria, or what he calls the "visionary experience." This mix of intense calm, focus, and elation can be exciting, rewarding, and addicting, leading many to call those who are drawn to high-risk sports, like rock climbing, "adrenaline junkies." But while this cliché sounds right, it is biologically wrong. "Adrenaline isn't fun," Robinson says. He prefers the term "stimulus addict."

Dick Duckworth describes this phenomenon in the foreword to Robinson's book as "a metabolic state of being . . . described as 'flow,' 'in the zone,' 'peak performance,' 'self-awareness,' and the like." It's *like* getting high. Without fear, you don't get the euphoric feeling that comes as you climb higher, Robinson says. "Effort plus a degree of fear shifts your brain into seeing more sharply, more clearly—and feeling more deeply," he wrote. "It does that by shifting the dynamic balance of hormones in your head. And then, transforming some of them. The upshot is a change in metabolism that becomes literally psychedelic."

Many climbers describe the feeling they experience while free soloing as "becoming one with the rock," a way of transcending the physical act of climbing to subconsciously merge with the rock in an almost dreamlike way. It's a drug-free hallucination, a "state of merging into infinity" as Reinhold Messner described it. John Gill wrote that by repeating a favorite route, he could achieve "a sort of transcendental kinesthetic awareness . . . an almost mystical experience." "Climbing forces you to focus, which in itself is the essence of meditation," Robinson wrote. "Put yourself into a position where a lapse of attention means pitching from your holds to plummet down the cliff face, and the peripheral tends to fall away."

It's no secret that extreme-sports participants, such as climbers, engage in a focused, controlled effort to overcome a self-imposed challenge that invokes a fear response. Robinson seems to argue that these people are using adventure sports to unleash the flow of natural drugs in the brain, creating a profound, almost mystical experience. In his view, like proverbial rats in a cage, we do it to get that high and then keep coming back for more.

We can see this cycle in studies of addiction and pleasure-seeking behavior in laboratory animals. In early experiments, researchers found that rats placed in a cage alone and given the choice of two water bottles—one with just water, the other with heroin or cocaine—would drink from the drug-laced bottle until they overdosed and died. In the 1970s, Bruce Alexander, a Canadian psychologist, put the rats in "rat parks"—large living areas where twenty resident rats could socialize, play, exercise, have sex, and so on. In that setting, the rats tended to prefer just plain water; or, if they did drink from the morphine-laced water bottle, they did so only occasionally, apparently just for kicks, not incessantly until they overdosed.

The rat park experiment suggested that addiction was fueled by isolation, and that the rats whose environments were enriched by the company of other rats and opportunities for other types of brain stimulation didn't need drugs; some still took a hit of morphine from time to time, seemingly to enhance but not interfere with their social behavior. They were, it seems, already getting high with a little help from their friends.

In the 1950s, psychologists James Olds and Peter Milner implanted electrodes in the pleasure regions of the brains of lab rats. They then put their subjects in cages, where the rats could press a lever to deliver direct stimulation to their brains. These experiments, as Morten L. Kringelbach and Kent C. Berridge described them in their 2010 study, "The Neuroscience of Happiness and Pleasure," raised "the intriguing possibility that bliss could be achieved through the use of 'pleasure electrodes' implanted deep within the brain." When the electrodes were implanted in septum and nucleus accumbens areas of their brains, the rats would repeatedly press the lever, sometimes up to two thousand times per hour, so frequently that they neglected or completely abandoned other activities such as eating or caring for their young. If you could wire rats' brains to deliver a pleasure response, researchers wondered, what would happen if you wired a human's brain?

Robert Heath, a controversial American psychiatrist, sought to answer that question. In the 1950s and 1960s, he conducted similar experiments on humans, including mentally ill patients. According to his paper published in 1972, Heath conducted an ethically deplorable experiment on a twenty-four-year-old man to see if the combination of brain stimulation and heterosexual imagery would cure him of homosexuality. The subject, who suffered from depression and obsessive-compulsive tendencies, had electrodes implanted in nine areas of his brain. When tested, only the septum produced the anticipated result. As David J. Linden wrote in a 2011 HuffPost blog titled "The Neuroscience of Pleasure," when the subject of the experiment was given free access to the stimulator, "he quickly began mashing the button like an 8-year-old playing Donkey Kong." According to Linden's paper, the subject was self-administering an almost constant stream of "overwhelming euphoria and elation and had to be disconnected despite his vigorous protests."

Linden, chief editor of the *Journal of Neurophysiology* and author of *The Compass of Pleasure*, noted that more recent (and morally defensible) experiments on animals and humans have revealed that many of the experiences we think of as being transcendent—the pleasurable feelings we get from things like gambling, religious rituals, running, and climbing—are the result of the same sensations that caused the rats and humans to obsessively self-stimulate. Drinking alcohol, taking drugs, binge shopping, internet gambling, and jumping out of a perfectly good airplane all activate what Linden describes as our dopamine-using pleasure circuitry. "Evolution has, in effect, hardwired us to catch a pleasure buzz from a wide variety of substances and experiences," he wrote, "from crack to cannabis, from meditation to masturbation, from Bordeaux to beef." And, of course, as Doug Robinson tells us, rock climbing.

Robinson doesn't believe most climbers really want to live right "on the edge"; they just want to be close to it so they can feel the fear needed to trigger the biological reaction that gives them that high. He suggests the danger of climbing is overrated, that when we're on the rocks, roped up, belayed, and placing protection, we *seem* to be on the edge—encountering what the brain perceives as danger and thus triggering the high we're after—but in reality, it's quite safe. Statistically, of the thousands who go climbing every day: very few have accidents and even fewer die. Of course, when Robinson says climbing is safe, he isn't talking about free soloing, which is *actually* on the edge—sometimes over it.

Roped-up climbers have the luxury of a fear response to get that floaty feeling, but free soloist do not because they have to maintain strict focus and detachment to avoid the fear response, which could kill them.

ACCORDING TO ROBINSON, THE FEAR response is only triggered when a person has the ability to respond and a chance to survive. We see this in nearly all accounts of near-death experience: survivors report feeling a sense of calm detachment, an out-of-body experience as they describe it, a depersonalization where they get a glimpse of the Other.

When death is inevitable, as recounted by people who have fallen or suffered accidents in which they had no conceivable chance of survival and yet still survived, the experience is one of supreme calm rather than fear. Edward Whymper described the sensation of being "perfectly conscious" but "like a patient under chloroform" during his near-fatal fall on the Matterhorn in 1864. In *Deep Survival*, Laurence Gonzalez described his father's experience: The only survivor of a bomber crash during World War II, he watched with curious detachment as a German farmer aimed his pistol at him and pulled the trigger. He didn't feel anything resembling fear; he just calmly watched and expected to die. But he was lucky—the gun jammed.

It is a phenomenon also reported by free soloists, who lose themselves in the flow of such extremely focused climbing. They cling to the shimmering edge and move instinctively, almost without thought or volition; they do not climb, but rather the climbing happens through them. In this situation, panicking would awaken them to the horror of the reality—if you fall, you die—which would cause a fear response, bring the climber out of this trance, and send them plummeting to their death. This seems to turn the situation on its head; in most cases, you only panic if you have a chance of surviving, but if you panic while free soloing, you ruin your chances of survival.

Robinson thinks that some people panic too easily, while others—the survivors—display "nerves of steel." He proudly tells a story about his daughter learning to drive on the highway: a rabbit ran out in front of the car and she drove right over it without even flinching. A panicked person, on the other hand, might have swerved and caused an accident. He's not kidding. In 2019, a Spartanburg, South Carolina, school bus driver swerved to avoid hitting two squirrels that ran out into the road; the bus crossed the centerline, spun out, hit a tree, and crashed into the side of a house. Around the same time, an eighty-two-year-old woman driving in Traverse City, Michigan, swerved to avoid hitting a squirrel, hit a parked car instead, and flipped her vehicle. And a woman in Cairo, New York, saw a spider on the seat inside the car, panicked, and drove into a rock wall.

Statistically, driving a car is one of the most dangerous things people do. Unfortunately, many people take it lightly, becoming desensitized to the danger. "We have stopped being able to even see that risk," Robinson wrote, "because we slide so blithely into the driver's seat at our convenience and even whim." The same thing happens when you go climbing with a rope. At first it seems scary and dangerous. The thought of climbing high off the ground hanging on by your fingers and toes produces anxiety. But after a while, you realize it's not so scary; you develop skill and learn to trust in your ability to hang on, to not fall. You gain a sense of control, which gives you confidence. And even when you do fall, it's no big deal; you're roped up and on belay, so you usually only fall a few feet, and the rope catches you. From then on, climbing becomes routine; you become desensitized to the risk. Maybe you still get that little feeling in your gut before you start up a wall, that little tingle of fear that brings your mind into sharp focus and allows you to pull off the ground and climb upward despite the risk.

Or maybe you don't. Maybe you're one of those people whose amygdala is tired, who, to continue getting that feeling, needs to up the game by climbing longer or harder routes—routes with long runouts above poor protection—making first ascents in remote, inhospitable lands, or going up there without a rope. As Simon Robinson warns in *Sport and Spirituality*, this "can lead to a stress on the experience itself, and thus the danger of the experience becoming the end in itself. This leads to greater and greater efforts, to maintain the intensity of the experience, with dangers of addiction to the experience itself." According to an article, "Addiction in Extreme Sports," published in the *Journal of Behavior Addictions* in 2016, "Rock climbing athletes appear to experience withdrawal symptoms when abstinent from their sport comparable to individuals with substance and behavioral addictions."

Even Mihaly Csikszentmihalyi warns that the addictive power of flow can take over your life and turn you into a "flow junkie":

> *Any enjoyable activity can become addictive, a necessity that interferes with "real life." This dependence (the inability to pay attention to anything else) results in loss of control of the content of our consciousness, and we become hooked like heroin addicts. Our self becomes captive to this type of order (the flow state) and makes us unwilling or unable to cope with the ambiguities of life.*

Geoff Powter challenges that point, cautioning that while certain addictions are very real phenomena, feeling addicted to flow is not an addiction in the truest sense. "It's critically important from a clinical point of view to differentiate a drug addiction from the so-called addictions to habits and pleasures of choice," he says. "We hear about addictions to sex, or watching TV, or bad relationships as being the same as substance addictions, but that's pop psychology rather than science, and I'd put every form of climbing, including soloing, in the same category." He differentiates them from real addictions because they are all things we voluntarily choose to do. "Though it can sometimes feel like we suffer when we can't do them," he insists, "no one ever went through true physiological withdrawal from not getting out climbing. It's apples and friggin' hand grenades."

Robinson's theories, while mostly undisputed, have been called mechanistic because they don't consider the overall experience of climbing, only one component of it. "You need to look at it more holistically," Ed Mosshart believes. "Because it's true—you *do* have the chemical cocktail that goes off when you do these things, and that's probably an instinctive trigger when we put ourselves into those fight-or-flight situation[s], where we can control the urge to fight or flee, but at the same time that's just a part of it."

"I like Doug Robinson. He's always been this guru kind of guy from back in the sixties and seventies, you know, and he's always been on this path, that 'People take drugs for this, but they don't have to, man!' and 'They can get high just by going climbing, man,' which is true," Mosshart says. He thinks people make the mistake of "literalizing, becoming overly identified with one aspect of the phenomenon, like overly identified with this spiritual ecstatic experience and refusing the mechanistic experience, or . . . saying it's all just mechanistic, it's all just brain chemicals, and that's a delusion."

He believes the truth lies somewhere in the middle. "It's like both," he says. "It's all true, but [Robinson's theory] is somehow very unsatisfying in terms of an explanation or an understanding of what's going on, because I think there's so much more than that."

PART IV

Under the Influence

"Right now, there's some kid that just read about El Cap being soloed and he's like, 'What's bigger? What's cooler?'"
—Alex Honnold

"Stay on a rope, kids. You're not Alex Honnold."
—Peter Ward

One Thursday afternoon when I was in fifth grade, my class was herded into an adjacent classroom to watch an educational film. These weekly films were usually boring, but it was a break from routine and so we eagerly looked forward to them. Our teacher, Mr. Barcott, patiently threaded the 16 mm film into the Bell & Howell projector, turned off the lights, and flipped the switch. As the projector whirred to life, a scratchy trailer counted down to the start of the film. Sharp-peaked mountains filled the screen, then the title: *Solo.*

A solitary man appeared, hiking contemplatively through a forest lit by morning sunbeams. Soon, he arrived at the base of a granite cliff towering endlessly skyward. He climbed up effortlessly on sunlit gray

Alex Honnold chalks up for the camera during the filming of Valley Uprising *in 2014.* (Photo by Drew Kelly)

stone. The rock became steeper, then frighteningly vertical. Uncon-
cerned, he climbed higher and higher, to where the rock was so steep
it seemed he could go no higher. Instead of climbing down, he pulled
a rack of iron spikes out of his backpack, hammered one into a crack
in the rock, clipped a short rope ladder to it, stepped carefully up the
ladder, then pounded in another spike, then another, and another. He
stepped up, and then swung joyously, almost crazily across the rock
face, spinning, twirling through space like a madman, for no apparent
reason other than for the absolute fun of it.

Higher up the cliff, all solemnity restored, he tried to climb past a
horizontal overhang by whacking metal spikes into a tiny upside-down
crack and dangling from them, one after the other, until he reached
the lip of the overhang. He placed a spike in the crack and, as he went
to hammer it in, it slid out and fell seemingly forever through space,
hitting the rock face every few seconds—*ping . . . ping . . . ping*—quieter and quieter as the sound receded through empty air to the ground,
impossibly far below.

Then the spike he was hanging from pulled out and he fell suddenly
and swung uncontrollably, smashing into the wall below, to the gasps of
horror from the class. But he was okay; he just had a bloody nose. He
wiped the blood away with the back of his hand, then wiped the blood
on his pants, unperturbed by his seemingly near-death experience, and
calmly resumed his ascent.

Soon he was past the overhang and atop the rock cliff, dashing
unencumbered up snow and ice and rock high on a mountain ridge,
then pulling himself over a final overhang of rock seemingly miles
above the ground to reach the top of the mountain where he balanced
precariously and smiled joyously, arms lifted upward, radiant and sublime in his success at reaching the top of the impossible mountain.

The sheer beauty and magnitude of the climbing, the joy and grace
of moving on rock and ice, the idealism of one man challenging himself
and prevailing against nature—it was overwhelming. I was soon climbing everything in sight—trees, buildings, retaining walls—anything that
could be climbed. The best part was I could do it by myself, whenever I
wanted. Nobody could stop me.

MY LITTLE BROTHER, DAVID, AND I often went out exploring while visiting our grandmother's house. During one weekend visit, after scrambling up to the gravel road above the house, we came upon a road-cut, 30 feet high, dirty and overgrown. It looked impossible to climb, but that didn't stop us from trying. One side, where a slab intersected steeper rock that led to a ramp, seemed more feasible, so I scrambled up, only pausing slightly when the rock turned loose. It was exciting to be so high off the ground, clinging to the rock; I was not afraid of falling. Below me, my brother was not having quite as much fun. He got half-way up the ramp before he pulled on a bracken fern that uprooted and sent him scuffing down the slab 15 feet to the ground. He was unhurt but momentarily dazed.

After scrambling down to make sure he was okay, I went off to inspect the center of the cliff, a near-featureless buttress leading up to a rotten flake and rottener slab, 30 feet from base to peak. When I reached up, I found nothing but slight wrinkles and tenuous edges for purchase. I could scarcely pull myself off the ground. It seemed far too difficult to climb, and dangerous at that. I took it as a challenge.

"So," my dad asked when we got back to the house, "what have you two been up to?"

We looked at each other, and then proceeded to tell him exactly what we had been doing, although David left out the part about having fallen off the cliff. Naturally, my stepmother had a fit when she heard we had been climbing: "Climbing is dangerous! *You could have been killed!*" We hung our heads and dutifully promised that we would never, ever do something so foolish again.

The next weekend, we were right back up there. This time, we came equipped with an old yellow utility rope, slings tied from clothesline, three steel snap links, a rock hammer, and three railroad spikes. I could, I imagined, hammer the spikes straight into the rock, just like the guy in the *Solo* film. I tied the rope around my waist with a rudimentary knot and tried to climb up the wall. There was little to hold onto and no cracks to whack my improvised pitons into—an unexpected setback. I managed to free climb 10 feet up to a narrow ledge before I ran out of handholds.

After climbing back down, I scrambled up the ramp and tied the rope to a tree above the center of the cliff. Then I scrambled back to the base of the cliff and climbed, pulling myself up the rope hand-over-hand, stopping here and there to inspect the rock for holds.

On our next visit to the roadcut, I hung the rope through a snap link clipped to a braided cotton sling so I could try using a toprope, a technique I had looked up in a book in the school library. I was halfway up the cliff when my dad came hiking up the road.

"So," he said, "what are you fellas up to?"

We were sure he would tell us to pull down the rope and get back to the house. Instead, he offered to hold it while I climbed. With my dad pulling the rope in as I inched upward, I was able to climb right up the middle of the cliff without falling.

The next time we visited, I led up the cliff, protecting the whole 30 feet of steep rock with a railroad spike hammered into a rotten flake and a machine nut tied off with laundry cord. Then I climbed it without the rope. Even if it was only a grubby 30-foot roadcut, I felt proud of my accomplishment. I was a solo climber, just like that guy in the film.

CHAPTER 18

GoPro Heroes

Many climbers will only free solo when they are alone. They see it as highly personal and aren't seeking attention. They don't want recognition or to inspire anyone. They don't want anybody to see them fall should they make a mistake. And they definitely don't want to be photographed or filmed.

When these climbers get the twitch, they go off by themselves and climb; if another climber arrives, they go somewhere else. If someone asks to photograph or film them, they decline. But there are also many climbers—seemingly more today than at any other time in the history of the sport—who enjoy the attention and notoriety free soloing brings them. They are not only willing but sometimes eager to indulge a photographer or film crew.

In May 2017, a film called *The Art of Solo* was posted on YouTube, followed a year later by a film called *World of Free Solo Climbing*. Both films feature a South African climber named Matt Bush. They're overly dramatized, featuring slow, sweeping drone shots and treacly music that romanticize free soloing as a sort of rare, heroic art. The footage is thoughtful and sometimes stunning, showing the scale and exposure of the routes Bush is free soloing—especially *Casualties of War*, a 5.11b on Paarl Rock, a huge, weathered granite outcrop near Cape Town—while obsessively narrating.

"Every route is a choreography for me," Bush says in a hushed yet reverent tone as *The Art of Solo* begins. "A creation. I see myself as an artist, and I paint with movement on nature's canvas." Bush talks melodramatically about overcoming fear while he takes a short fall while roped, then returns to free solo the 200-foot wall without any hint of difficulty. Near the top, he stops, turns around, and stretches his arms out fatuously in the attitude of *Christ the Redeemer.*

When he reaches the top of Paarl Rock, Bush stands facing away from the camera, overlooking the landscape in a romantic pose reminiscent of Caspar David Friedrich's *Wanderer Above the Sea of Fog,* then he pumps both fists skyward as if in post hoc celebration of a great victory. The film is beautifully shot with interesting narration and, while perhaps the delivery is wonky, seems to honestly convey Bush's thoughts about his art.

The second film, *World of Free Solo Climbing,* is better, partly because there's more climbing footage and less narration, although it still self-indulgently describes Bush's motivation, approach, and experience. "I ask myself, 'what would I do if I lived my life without limits,'" he begins as a sweeping drone shot shows him standing on a ledge. "The answer is," Bush says, pausing for dramatic effect as the music begins to pump up, "'*free solo.*'" He stops talking for a while and just climbs, the best part of the film. "Imagine, you're hundreds of meters from the ground. Birds fly by. There's a cool breeze. I breathe in, and out. I make my moves calm and relaxed. This is the world of free-solo climbing," he finally says. "*My* world, where *I'm* free."

Although Bush comes across as somewhat overbearing in the films, he seems more genuine and humbler in other media. "What appeals to me in free-solo climbing is the focus, the presence, the clarity, and the simplicity," Bush said during an interview with EpicTV. "Fear is a big part of the free-solo experience," he added. "I've been asked, 'Were you born without fear?' 'Are you just wired differently?' I wouldn't say that I was born without fear. It's just that I'm learning through this experience as a free soloist to manage that fear."

Bush, who has free soloed routes as hard as 5.13d, knows what he has to be afraid of: he fell off of a route in Montagu, South Africa, called *My Route by the River,* an 8a+ (5.13c) that has a wild, dynamic move—where the climber launches upward, letting go with hands and feet, for a hold that's out of reach. Bush tried to solo the route one day and didn't catch the hold; he fell 30 feet, the kind of fall he admitted could end a climber's career, physically or mentally. Luckily, he landed on a sandbar below the cliff and was physically unhurt, but he had some mental reckoning to do. "I thought it might really affect my psyche if I walked away," Bush told the *Outdoor Journal.* He decided to try the route again, right after falling; this time, he pulled it off.

Of course, like many self-proclaimed artists, Bush sometimes sounds pretentious. "Free solo is a language," Bush is quoted as saying in a 2017 article for *The Red Bulletin*. "When you climb, you speak it. If you don't speak it, you don't understand it. It's that simple."

Bush had gone largely unnoticed outside of South Africa for years until clips showing his free solos surfaced in early 2015, after which he was approached by a production company who asked if they could film him. Bush arranged to meet them at Waterval Boven, a popular sport climbing area east of Pretoria with some picturesque climbs beside a waterfall. Filmmakers Ruan Kotze and Dawie Oberholzer had only seen free soloing on video before, and were astonished when Bush soloed up a wall to rig their lines for filming. "It was pretty epic to see it the first time," recalled Kotze. "My palms were sweating."

The resulting film showcased Bush free soloing some of the hard routes he'd done at Table Mountain, which Kotze described as "gnarly" and "insane." A clip featured on the Red Bull website in early 2015, accompanied by a brief article proclaimed, "Alone and without ropes, free solo climbers transcend fear and risk on their journey into the unknown. South Africa's Matt Bush is one of the world's best." It's all quick cuts of dramatic action—hurried movement, semi-lunges, swinging across the lip of a roof, dangling upside-down from an overhang—accompanied by energetic music, the kind of hyped-up radical-dude-style video that makes free soloing look dangerous and cool.

The media loves risk, and with the film came attention. Magazine articles about Bush started to appear in the US in early 2017. In March, Moja Gear published an interview with Bush, and the *Outdoor Journal* published an article about him that said, "While other free soloists—rock climbers who shun ropes and other safety gear—have parlayed their artform into major sponsorships and TV commercials, South African Matt Bush has largely flown under the radar." While Bush had been well known in his homeland, the media attention and videos brought him international acclaim and attention.

In the Moja Gear interview, Bush was asked what advice he had for other climbers interested in free soloing. "I prefer not to give advice for free soloing," he answered. "For me, it's a personal pursuit with no set recipe or formula. I do not encourage others to solo because it's complex and individualized. I don't want to put myself in the position of being responsible for others' actions." His comments, of course, ignore the fact that by making films that glorify free soloing as an exalted art form, he's encouraging others to do it.

WHEN I FIRST STARTED CLIMBING in the mid-1970s, there weren't a lot of climbing films, and the internet didn't yet exist. I saw Mike Hoover's 1974 film, *Solo*, at school; it was nominated for an Academy Award, but it didn't win and wasn't what you'd consider a commercial success. I remember seeing Henry Barber climbing English sea cliffs on ABC's *Wide World of Sports*, although it may have aired only once. In the late 1970s, George Willig starred in a few *Wide World of Sports* episodes, including a mostly solo climb of the Bastille Crack in Eldorado Canyon. But nobody was making a living on climbing films back then, unless they were getting paid to rig or film big-budget Hollywood blockbusters or doing stunt-like climbing for TV.

Back then, if you wanted to solo a route for attention, you would have a very limited audience. Mark Hudon recalled free soloing *Kamps Crack* in the Black Hills in 1979 in front of only four people: Max Jones and three impressionable young climbers sitting on a nearby boulder. One of those young climbers was Todd Skinner, a college student from Wyoming who would go on to claim the first free ascent of the *Salathé Wall* route on El Capitan (he later told Hudon he was inspired to become a good climber after watching Hudon's free-solo climb). Someone might take a random picture of a free-solo climber at Joshua Tree or in Yosemite and show it during their winter slide show, but nobody was going out free soloing with a photographer along for the sole purpose of taking photos.

Even so, there has always been an element of exhibitionism in free soloing. When John Bachar went on his free solo circuits around Hidden Valley Campground or on the Cookie Cliff, everybody watched, especially when he soloed harder routes. Free-solo climbers might seem as if they are in a Zen-like meditative trance focused entirely on climbing, but that isn't always so. The climber is probably well aware of being watched—they may even like it. Matt Bush told the cameramen he felt relaxed when they were around and sometimes even more focused and determined to execute a solo climb well. That's how I felt when I was being observed free soloing; I tried to look like I was in total control so that people watching would think, "Damn, that guy is good." But mostly, I didn't want to fuck up.

In 1991, Eric Perlman produced the first *Masters of Stone* video. Ostensibly a documentary about rock climbing in America—featuring Ron Kauk, Tony Yaniro, Todd Skinner, John Bachar, and Dan Osman, among others—it combined what UK Climbing described in April 2013 as "a pumping soundtrack, dramatic commentary and constant high-level action [that] raised viewer's heartbeats way above anything they'd seen before. The sweaty-palm era of climbing films had begun." The first video focused on rock climbing, and was so popular Perlman produced several more that spanned bouldering, big walls, hard sport climbs, free soloing, and more. Most of them featured Osman, and there was seemingly nothing he wouldn't do for the camera. For one installment, Osman free soloed a hard route in The Needles of Southern California, spectacularly but unnecessarily leaping for a hold mid-climb to thrill the audience. For another, he free soloed three hard routes, up to 5.12 in difficulty. In the fourth installment, Osman ratcheted up the heart-stopping action with an outrageous speed-solo on *Bear's Reach* at Lover's Leap.

Osman eventually started doing other stunts, including climbing a very wet, thundering waterfall with ice tools and taking long roped falls and swings off of bridges and cliffs. These clips were included in the series along with the usual rock-climbing fare. His later stunts were pure spectacle and helped transform *Masters of Stone* into a sort of extreme-sport thrill show. After Osman's death, the film producers took a hiatus of several years, but a sixth edition was released in 2014 that picked up right where they had left off, featuring Dean Potter and Alex Honnold free soloing in Yosemite, Steph Davis wingsuit jumping, and a stunt called speed free-solo racing, a reckless exercise involving two unroped climbers racing each other up a rock wall like lizards on steroids to see who will finish first.

DURING THE FIFTEEN-YEAR GAP BETWEEN the fifth and sixth *Masters of Stone* films, a new production company called Sender Films entered the market for hard-core, character-driven narratives about climbers pushing the edge, many of which it featured in its *Reel Rock* series. In 2009, Sender Films released a short film titled *Alone on the Wall*, featuring Alex Honnold free soloing *Moonlight Buttress* in Zion National Park and the *Regular Northwest Face* of Half Dome in Yosemite. The ad copy for the film was hyperbolic:

Twenty-three year old Alex Honnold is taking the high-stakes sport of free solo climbing to new heights. Climbing truly massive walls without a rope, and zero chance of survival if he falls, Alex is calm and fearless (except when it comes to girls). But attempting the 2000-foot wall of

Half Dome, the greatest free solo ever attempted, would finally teach
Alex the meaning of fear.

National Geographic released a teaser for *Alone on the Wall* showing clips
of Honnold soloing various hard-rock climbs around the world, including
Half Dome, and the ad copy was just as over the top:

Alex Honnold makes the first free solos of the largest walls in North Amer-
ica. He scales 2000 feet with only shoes and chalk bag—no rope, no safety,
and no room for error. Though he's a superhero on the walls, off the rock
Alex is a shy, self-effacing young guy living in his van.

The hyping of Alex Honnold as a humble-yet-badass, free-soloing superhero had begun, and it earned Honnold and Sender Films mainstream attention. In 2012, he was featured on *60 Minutes* free soloing the *Chouinard-*
Herbert route on Sentinel Rock in Yosemite. "Watching Alex move spider-like
up a sheer mountain face . . . is terrifying, even for some of our bravest reporters,"
said CBS on January 1, 2012. To film the "The Ascent of Alex Honnold," CBS
hired Sender Films, which positioned fourteen cameras to capture his ascent
of the 1400-foot, 5.11c route. They also snuck in a short video of Honnold free
soloing *The Phoenix*, a 5.13 in Yosemite, just to show you how out there he really
was. But what really seemed to astonish viewers, even climbers, was Honnold
climbing a thousand feet above the Valley floor, unroped on a sheer granite wall,
having such a good time that he could be heard whistling to himself.

The *60 Minutes* segment was a buildup to Honnold's eventual free-solo
ascent of El Capitan in 2017. But Honnold was not the only free-solo climber
getting media attention. In 2018, *Outside* online named Brad Gobright "Alex
Honnold's new nemesis," suggesting there was some sort of competition
between Gobright and Honnold to be the "top dog" of free soloing. Honnold
and Gobright were themselves good friends who climbed together sometimes, but they were also increasingly in competition as Gobright began making inroads into Honnold's media territory. He was even the subject of a short
film called *Safety Third*, released by Sender Films in 2017.

The film features Gobright alternately defying death by climbing unprotected routes, recovering in a hospital bed after taking a serious fall, and
then getting back on the rock and "overcoming his fears" while treading the

fine line between being bold and being a dumbass. He was well known as a sometimes-impulsive free soloist who would "go for it." Produced by Cedar Wright (who also wrote the 2018 *Outside* online article about Gobright), the film made the Mountainfilm selection in 2017 and was voted the audience favorite for best short film.

As reported in a 2019 *Outside* online article, Gobright's "willingness to take risk fueled some of his most notable successes." He'd free soloed the *North Face* of the Rostrum, *The Naked Edge* multiple times, and a 5.12 called *Hairstyles and Attitudes*, an exposed face pitch high on the Bastille in Eldorado Canyon, where a fall would certainly be fatal. Wright wrote that Gobright caught his attention because he "climbed ropeless in Eldorado Canyon with a boldness and fervor unlike anything I'd ever seen."

Gobright dialed back his free soloing after his accident and focused more on speed climbing. He eventually broke Honnold and Hans Florine's speed record for the *Nose* of El Capitan by four minutes, during which he climbed the final pitch by pulling himself from bolt to bolt using his middle fingers. "That's why I have the record, and you don't," he told Honnold and Tommy Caldwell (they reclaimed the record in 2018, posting a time of 1 hour, 59 minutes). Gobright and Honnold competed on other routes, including taking turns free soloing a 2000-foot 5.9 called *Epinephrine* in Red Rocks, Nevada, as fast as possible. Before Honnold free soloed El Capitan, Wright joked with him about Gobright beating him to it. "Dude," Alex responded in *Safety Third*, "if he were to go up there and solo El Cap, first of all I would be like, 'Whoa, that's scary,' but I would also be like . . . Respect. . . . Sometimes the bold man wins."

At El Potrero Chico, a popular rock-climbing area near Monterrey, in November 2019, with a rope and partner, Gobright climbed *El Sendero Luminoso*, a fifteen-pitch rock climb rated 5.12d that Honnold had free soloed in 2014. The climb went well, but while descending, the two climbers were rappelling simultaneously to save time when Gobright rappelled off the end of the rope and fell 600 feet to his death. He was thirty-one.

AS I FINISHED WRITING THIS book, Sender Films released a new film, *The Alpinist*, featuring Marc-André Leclerc, a cutting-edge alpinist and free soloist. People who knew him found it ironic that Leclerc was going to be the subject of a feature film, because he was shy and sought to avoid attention. Journalist Matt Skenazy spent a week with him in December 2012 and remarked that "he seemed more excited to have me around as a belayer than by the prospect of media coverage. He simply loved to climb."

As Skenazy later wrote, it was not only the difficulty and audacity of Leclerc's climbs but also his approach that made him unique. "He was, technically and athletically, on the same level as someone like Alex Honnold," Skenazy wrote. "Yet he largely flew under the radar." As Francis Sanzaro wrote in his review of the film published in *Climbing*, "The main thrust of the film is about getting to know the 'elusive' Leclerc."

Leclerc was born on Vancouver Island; his family moved to Agassiz, a small agriculture town in the Fraser Valley southeast of Vancouver, BC. He was a smart, introspective kid with a love for science and a hyperactive mind. His mom gave him a book about climbing when he was eight years old, and it opened his mind to a new realm. He climbed in a gym but preferred the outdoors. For his fifteenth birthday, he got a copy of Fred Beckey's *Cascade Alpine Guide* and was soon going wild in the mountains near his home.

At age twenty-one Leclerc gained attention after a one-day link-up in 2014 of three routes on Slesse Mountain, a towering 8002-foot peak in the Cascades of Southern Canada. He free soloed the *East Buttress Direct* (5.9), *Navigator Wall* (5.10+), and *Northeast Buttress* (5.9+), a total of more than 7000 feet of climbing in just over twelve hours. Earlier that year, he had soloed *The Corkscrew*, a link-up of several routes that go around and up the 10,262-foot Patagonian spire, involving 3900 feet of 5.10+ and A1 rock and 90-degree water ice. It was regarded as the hardest route ever soloed on Cerro Torre, and he did it on-sight, without having climbed it before. He described the experience on his blog: "You are questing up the mountain and figuring it out as it continues to unfold."

Two years later, Leclerc returned to Patagonia and soloed the *East Pillar* of 8809-foot Torre Egger, which was even harder, and then returned to Canada where he soloed an unprecedented three hard mixed routes on the Stanley Headwall, a 600-foot limestone wall with routes that combine vertical and overhanging rock with extreme water ice. He repeated the hard sections of one route, *Nightmare on Wolf Street*, for the camera. The footage of Leclerc working his way up the exposed rock face of the Stanley Headwall using the picks of his ice tools and points of his crampons is hard to watch.

"Marc wasn't a careless climber, quite the opposite," Sanzaro wrote, "but he rolled the dice and won a lot, so much so his risk tolerance only increased." For Leclerc, dangerous climbing was an adventure worthy of the risk. According to Drew Copeland, who wrote about him in *Climbing*, Leclerc was seeking "the raw experience of being in nature."

In March 2018, Leclerc joined Alaskan climber Ryan Johnson for an ascent of the unclimbed 2500-foot north face of the Main Mendenhall Tower near Juneau, Alaska. The morning of March 5, Leclerc texted his partner, Brette Harrington, who was climbing with friends in Tasmania. "Love, I'm at the summit!" he texted. "It was an incredible climb." Then Leclerc went silent.

After not hearing from him for a few days, Harrington contacted mountain rescue. When she heard that the pair had not returned to their skis, she rushed to Juneau. After several days of bad weather and helicopter searches, their rope was spotted in the bergschrund at the base of the mountain, and it was surmised that Leclerc and Johnson had fallen into a crevasse. Leclerc was twenty-five years old.

PETER MORTIMER, THE FOUNDER OF Sender Films and director of *The Alpinist*, made his first film, *Front Range Freaks*, in 2003, featuring a cast of several eccentric Boulder-area climbers including Derek Hersey and a dog named Biscuit. Since then, he and his crew have filmed a lot of climbers free soloing and doing other dangerous things, including Dean Potter and Alex Honnold. After Honnold free soloed *Moonlight Buttress* and Half Dome, he repeated several pitches for the camera, which resulted in the film *Alone on the Wall*. Mortimer has spent a lot of time behind the camera or directing others in the filming of free solo climbers.

"Free soloing is a little bit like big-wave surfing," he told me in an interview, explaining why it is so appealing to film producers and audiences. "You don't have to be a climber to understand the risk-reward calculation. . . . You watch and see someone up there with no rope in a perilous situation and you to get sucked into that." It's the simplicity of the story line: a lone climber, a simple goal, inherent conflict, inescapable tension, and ultimate resolution that make films about free soloing so riveting. As Mortimer says, "Here's this really soft-spoken, humble, internal individual who's doing this absolutely terrifying thing that would be most people's worst nightmare."

Like many climbing films, *The Alpinist* includes reenactments. It's common for a climber to go back up on a wall or rappel in and reclimb some of the more photogenic pitches for the camera. Hansjörg Auer did it on *Il Pesce*, Alex Honnold did it on Half Dome, and Leclerc did it on the Stanley Headwall. The film includes live-action footage of Leclerc, Mortimer points out. "We felt that the stuff he was actually climbing, what we captured [live], was so authentic, just purely about who this guy was," he says, but he admits that he did climb some routes a second time for the cameras. "If Marc or Alex or anyone is out there soloing something and you're out there filming them with the cameras, you have this incredible fear of affecting that experience, whether by moving or just being there," he told me.

But Mortimer says, the decision is entirely up to the climber, not the film crew. "Even if we had suggested [to Honnold] going back up there and doing [the hard pitches on Half Dome again], he would have quickly set parameters, like 'This is how I want to do it.' With Alex, Marc, or Dean, those guys are kind of in charge. . . . They're going to tell you."

Still, Mortimer acknowledges that filming a free soloist can be scary. "We'd just showed up in the Valley to do the *60 Minutes* shoot," he recalls. "Alex was like, 'Hey, man, do you want to get up with me at five in the morning? Let's go over and do *The Phoenix*.'" Honnold rappelled in to the base of the overhanging 5.13a finger crack and had Mortimer pull up his rope and harness. He rappelled into position beside the route to film it, and wasn't sure he wanted to be there. "That is one of the most terrifying things I've ever been a part of," Mortimer admitted.

Mortimer acknowledges feeling a sense of responsibility simply by being present when another climber is risking his life in front of the camera. "Honestly, if you're involved in filming it, no matter what the scenario, if something—God forbid—happens while you're filming, it's going to ruin your life," he says. "I'm not aching to go make another film about another soloist. . . . There is responsibility, and whatever your relationship is, you're intertwined with this experience," he continues. It's a constant recalibration, how you feel in that moment. What was comfortable for me years ago very well may not be comfortable for me now."

Mortimer acknowledges that media influences people's decisions to free solo, but he says, "A lot of climbers are motivated with or without media, but every sport is evolving," he says. "To me, what's so appealing about Marc as a climber and a person is his pure motivation, his personal motivation, his deeply thought-out vision of what he wanted to do with climbing."

Although Mortimer knows he'd feel responsible if he was filming a climber who fell and died, he doesn't think that would necessarily stop him or someone else from doing it. "I think that line is completely about your trust in that person, in your relationship with that person. Your decisions are going to grow based on your relationship with that person, what they're doing, and your calculations."

"INCREASINGLY, WHAT WE DO OUTSIDE is less about enjoying the activity itself as an intrinsic good," wrote Marc Peruzzi for *Outside* in 2018, "and more about planning ways to go bigger, faster, and farther, often for our selfie-stick-mounted cameras." A climber who is not shy about publicizing their free-solo climbs on social media and films is more likely to get the attention of sponsors who view free soloing as sexy, cool, almost irresistible. Some climbers even earn six-figure annual incomes from their sponsorships. But these videos can also normalize and even glamorize risk.

Nina Williams is a climber who excels at highball bouldering, a form of free soloing closer to the ground. These climbs—which can end up more than 30 feet off the ground—were once thought of as free-solo climbs. This was true of John Gill's 1960 ascent of the Thimble, a 30-foot pinnacle in the Black Hills of South Dakota that he climbed via a 5.12 face, where a fall would have meant landing on a potentially fatal guard rail. Modern highball boulderers increase their chances of walking away from long falls by employing spotters and placing foam pads at the base to cushion falls from sometimes as high as 50 feet off the ground. These days the Thimble and other highball problems are climbed regularly by boulderers who stack pads at the base for protection, allowing them to fall off multiple times like pole vaulters landing in a foam pit.

According to a 2019 *Daily Camera* article by Chris Weidner, when Williams sees a big, tall boulder, she feels an impulse to be up there without a rope, even if it's 50 feet high. "Maybe it has something to do with this feeling like I shouldn't be up there," she told Weidner. "It makes me want to be up there even more." While Williams uses a lot of crash pads, boulderers have been seriously injured even while using pads. The sense of safety the pads offer may encourage them to push their limits. They're taking more long falls, which increases the odds that they'll land awkwardly or miss the pads. Some even begin to blur the line between highball bouldering and free soloing.

On the hardest and highest boulders, Williams rehearses with a toprope. When Weidner asked her why she feels the need to risk injury by taking away the rope after she's successfully climbed the problem, she told him, "Being on a rope takes away the 'I'm-not-supposed-to-be-up-there' kinda thing." Without the element of risk, even carefully calculated risk minimized by relentless rehearsal of the moves and a stack of foam pads and cadre of spotters, the climb would have little value for her. She also might not get the same attention.

Williams is the subject of a short film released in 2019 called *The High Road*, which features her making the first female ascent of a highball boulder problem near Bishop, California, called *Too Big to Flail*. The film shows her working the route with a toprope until she has it dialed in, then focuses on her mental process when she climbs it with only pads for protection. The stakes are higher when she climbs without a rope. As Weidner wrote, "Above the halfway point of the boulder the pads become almost irrelevant; if she falls, her legs will snap like twigs." He describes Williams's climb as "absolutely terrifying—and moving—to watch."

While Williams see her motivation as rooted in security and confidence she feels when she succeeds, it's her risk-taking that is irresistible to sponsors. (As of the writing of this book, Williams lists The North Face, Scarpa, Organic Climbing, and Black Diamond as her sponsors.)

Weidner's article predictably sparked a series of debates as to whether publicizing the exploits of climbers like Nina Williams could encourage young climbers and those new to the sport to imitate highball bouldering and free soloing. "I do think it's an issue worth acknowledging, and we should be careful how we present it to the masses," Weidner told me. "That said, I think it's worth honoring people like Alex and Nina who do dangerous climbs in a very calculated, non-reckless way."

Weidner thinks the climbing media should report on everything noteworthy or record breaking, such as Honnold's free solo of El Capitan, even if it is, as he puts it, "near suicidal." He cited *Safety Third*, a film featuring Brad Gobright free soloing a route called *Hairstyles and Attitudes* in Eldorado Canyon, as an example of the latter. The route, rated solid 5.12, is up an exposed face high on the Bastille, where a fall would certainly be fatal. (Bob Dergay fell from close to this spot while free soloing an easier route in 2019, with the predictable result.) Gobright's free-solo ascent was groundbreaking, according to Weidner, and thus sufficiently noteworthy to be included in Wright's film, but perhaps just barely. "Even Brad himself says he should not have soloed it that day," Weidner told me. "It's scary to watch because he appears out of control. If anything, I think this film would convince the audience *not* to free solo."

THERE'S A THIN LINE BETWEEN highball bouldering and free soloing, a line that Isamer Bilog crossed in September 2016. Dan Krauss was photographing Bilog on his attempted first ascent of a boulder problem in the San Jacinto Mountains above Palm Springs. "I'd really consider it a free solo," Krauss says of the overhanging 25-foot wedge of rock above a steep hillside. "It was wild and reckless."

Bilog was stoked to be climbing with his friends there photographing and filming him. "I thought I was putting them in a pretty exciting position," Bilog said afterward. "I was like, 'Cool, you get to see something crazy go down.'"

"Dude, I don't feel comfortable with this," Krauss told Bilog. "You're not going to walk out of this if you fall."

But Bilog wasn't concerned. "I was willing to risk it all," he says on film.

Everything went fine until the last move, when his foot slipped off and he fell, landing on his head and tumbling like a ragdoll down the boulder-strewn hillside. Krauss and another climber scrambled down the slope and found Bilog face down, his feet twitching. "I thought he was dead, but luckily he wasn't," Krauss told me. Bilog was airlifted to a hospital, with multiple head injuries including a fractured skull and severe brain swelling. The rescuers didn't have high hopes for his survival, Krauss recalls, but after emergency surgery and several days in a coma, he pulled through.

"To put those three guys . . . in that position never even crossed my mind," Bilog says in the film. "I didn't think I would have such a big effect on so many people. . . . Going through that experience helped me . . . realize that everyone is struggling with something and everyone has problems," he explains.

Witnessing his friend's nearly fatal fall caused Krauss, a professional photographer (whose photo of Brad Gobright appears on the cover of this book), to reconsider photographing free solo climbers. "That really damaged me mentally," Krauss told me. "But I still photographed Brad soloing after that."

But he wonders whether photographing a free soloist is morally justified. "On one hand, it's witnessing something great and incredible. It seems almost silly to not have a photograph of it if [they're] already doing it. On the other hand, why are they doing it? Is it for fame, the photo, or recognition?"

Whatever it was that motivated Bilog, his accident didn't stop him. He returned two years later to make the first ascent, but this time, they rigged a safety net—and he wore a helmet, just in case. He was lucky; not everyone gets a second chance.

IN 2002, NICK WOODMAN CREATED a camera that could capture close-up footage of him surfing in Australia. His invention, the GoPro camera, quickly revolutionized the extreme-sports video industry. The internet was soon flooded with thousands of short videos showing people performing all kinds of dangerous stunts. In his 2014 *New Yorker* article titled "We Are a Camera," Nick Paumgarten called it "a perfect instrument for the look-at-me age." "Its charm lies perhaps in its sublimated conveyance of self, its sneaky tolerable narcissism," Paumgarten wrote. He also noted that the presence of a camera can lead people to take greater risks as they attempt to go viral—the old "Kodak courage" reborn as "GoPro guts." "It may not be fair to say the camera is the reason people attempt to brush the ground while flying past an outcrop in a wingsuit," he wrote, "but perhaps seeing it done on film inspires other people to try."

If there's such a thing as a GoPro antihero, it's Kyle Walker. He was climbing alone in Colorado in April 2019 and posted the resulting GoPro video on YouTube. As reported in an article in *Climbing* titled "The Fallen Soloist," Walker fell off of a route called *North Crack*, a two-pitch 5.9+ on the Second Flatiron in Boulder, Colorado. "Climbing the Second Flatiron as he has '100 times before' according to his now-deleted YouTube comment and having climbed '5.10 in hiking boots,' according to another YouTube comment," the article said, "he had decided to try the route free solo."

Walker often went on trail runs in the Flatirons and started scrambling on them after seeing others doing it. Climbers and scramblers often solo the easy routes up the Flatirons, sometimes in their trail shoes. One day Walker followed a barefoot climber up the Second Flatiron, figuring if she could do it barefoot, his running shoes would stick to the rock just fine. He had no climbing experience at the time. "Zero," he told *Climbing*. "I knew I could do a bunch of pull-ups." At first, he was just climbing up and down, working on controlling his fear of heights.

Eventually, he was intrigued by the real climbers he saw on the Flatirons. Walker met a climber who suggested if he could climb 5.13, he could free solo the steep side of the Second Flatiron. He'd looked up 5.13 on the internet and found out it was "a climb without a lot of holds." He also saw a video of a climber free soloing a wall and doing a human flag at the top, a stunt that made him think free soloing was just another extreme sport like BMX racing or mountain biking, two sports he was familiar with, where he could push his limits without real consequences. One day he was looking up at a wall and saw a route that he thought looked easy and decided to climb it. He told his girlfriend, "Hey, I'm gonna go. I'm gonna turn it up a little bit and do some crazier stuff." And he brought along his GoPro.

"It was an easy climb up the slab," Walker said, recalling the incident. But at the top of the slab, which involved 5.2 climbing, he started having doubts. "Maybe [I'm] getting in over my head," he thought. "But you know what? Just keep pushing." Eventually, the rock started to overhang, and he decided that maybe he wasn't supposed to be there. He was wearing Saucony running shoes he'd bought specially for climbing, had no chalk, and was getting tired and starting to panic. Trying to calm himself down, he shifted his weight onto his feet to rest his arms.

The YouTube video posted online begins as Walker starts to panic. He's breathing hard and struggling to maintain his composure. You see his hands groping for a good hold on the chunky rock, the camera bumping into a big patch of yellow lichen, then he stops. "What have you done?" you hear him mutter under his breath. Then he starts downclimbing. Taking a step down, he moves his hands to different holds, and then suddenly there's a tumult of rock and sky and the top of Walker's head as he sails down the cliff back first. He hits the ground, and tumbles several times before coming to a stop, laying there nearly motionless for a long time.

The video goes on for several minutes after the fall, after Walker has crawled out of frame, recording the ground, a tree, and the sky from an odd, almost surreal angle. If you didn't know better, you might think Walker had died there at the base of the Second Flatiron, leaving his GoPro to record the void he'd left behind.

WALKER'S FALL WENT VIRAL, EVEN making the national news, and he became something of an unlikely celebrity. He attributed his poor decision to free solo *North Crack* to the Dunning-Kruger effect. "You think that you know enough about something to be an expert in it, but really your knowledge is nothing. You don't know enough to know to know more."

But the GoPro played a role, as well. "I was gonna show this badass video of me climbing this crazy rock," Walker said. He isn't alone. There are innumerable similar posts on social media meant to show how rad a climber is. These climbers hope to be featured for taking the "Whipper of the Week," or maybe they plan to piece together a short film that might be accepted for the next *Reel Rock*, giving them the cred they need to land a sponsorship deal. And there's always YouTube, where free-solo videos have been viewed hundreds of thousands of times, some even millions of times. A trio of short films featuring Alex Honnold alone has collected more than fifteen million views.

But high risk doesn't always lead to high reward. In 2017, after the release of the film *Valley Uprising*, Clif Bar announced that it was terminating its sponsorship of Alex Honnold and Dean Potter, among others, because they believed those climbers were taking too many risks. The company recognized that by sponsoring these extreme athletes, it was promoting and, in effect, glorifying dangerous activities that others might emulate.

They are sponsoring other climbers now, including Ashima Shiraishi, a twenty-one-year-old national champion boulderer and sport climber from New York and the first woman to climb a V15 boulder problem, who Honnold described as "one of the best climbers in the country, hands down." Another climber sponsored by Clif Bar, Kai Lightner is a twenty-three-year-old former youth world champion sport climber from North Carolina who has climbed 5.14d and is a strong advocate for diversity in the sport. They are emblematic of a new generation of young climbers who pursue difficulty over risk and vow, like many of their peers, to never, ever free solo.

CHAPTER 19

I'm Lucky to Have This as My Job

The short film *Free Flow*, featuring Hazel Findlay free soloing a trio of routes in north Wales, was posted on YouTube in May 2019. The impetus for the film came in 2014, according to director Paul Diffley, when he saw another filmmaker's short had been well received. "I guess naturally as a climbing filmmaker my brain went into the process of whatever could I make about climbing that would resonate with a wider audience," Diffley told UK Climbing. "It got me to start thinking about what made [the other filmmaker's] videos so sharable and what I could make that would have the same effect." He eventually connected with Findlay, an accomplished rock climber who, among other things, has free climbed El Capitan by four different routes and repeated *Magic Line* (5.14b), one of the hardest traditional leads in Yosemite.

Like Matt Bush's films, *Free Flow* doesn't really have a plot. It follows along with Findlay who is having a stonking day out running and climbing by herself among the crags of Snowdonia. The film originally was supposed to have an environmental theme about living simply and not using plastics, but that message didn't resonate with early audiences as well as the solo climbing sequences, so it was recut to focus just on Findlay climbing and sharing her philosophy about free soloing.

"The film came about because my friend and filmmaker wanted to make a film about simplicity and low-impact living and how you don't need much to have an adventure," Findlay told me, "but once we had the footage he decided to make it more about my psychology when I climb."

While talking to me, Findlay twice referred to being filmed free soloing as her job. "I agreed to do it because it's my job as a professional climber to be in films and it sounded like a fun project," she said at one point. "I feel pretty lucky that I get to do stuff like this as my job," she said later, adding, "I feel even luckier that the bulk of my climbing is done with friends or alone and only a small proportion of my climbing time is spent in front of a camera." As Diffley had hoped, the film got a positive response from most people, and generated plenty of discussion on YouTube.

"Great video and an inspiring young woman," one comment said. "However, I think solo climbing is an irresponsible sport." Another comment said "Your poor mother!"

"My mum doesn't like it," Findlay admits. "She's not a climber so she thinks black and white: ropes is safe, no-ropes in unsafe. My dad doesn't care at all."

IF YOU'VE SEEN FREE SOLO, you know how it turns out. On his first attempt to solo *Freerider*, Honnold didn't feel solid and bailed early. "I don't know if I can try with everybody watching," he said. "It's too scary. I don't know if I can try for real." It was scary for the people watching too. "I'm scared," said Mikey Schaefer, a member of the film crew, "because I don't want to see anything happen to him."

Jimmy Chin also acknowledged his conflicted feelings: "It's so dangerous," he said. "It's hard not to imagine your friend, Alex, soloing something that's extremely dangerous and you're making a film about it which may put undue pressure on him to do something and him falling through the frame to his death. And we have to work through that," he added, "and understand that it's something we can live with even in the worst-case scenario."

Chin also talked about the camera adding extra pressure on Honnold. "Our being there is always going to change things," Chin tells Honnold. To which Honnold replies, "I know I could just walk away but, you know, I don't want to." The next time, he tried for real and succeeded. If it bothered him that people were watching him, it didn't show. He even smiled at the camera after pulling through the hardest pitch. He was having fun.

"I WOULD NOT PRESUME TO tell any of these people that they're not soloing or that there's a purer way to do it," Henry Barber says. That's a bit hypocritical coming from a man who used to free solo for the camera, who soloed routes not because he wanted to but because he'd agreed to do it and felt he had no other choice. But he also free soloed big walls and big mountains without any publicity. Barber has issues with the way climbers approach free soloing these days, with photographers and film crews following them around. That's not what he calls soloing. "You know, really what soloing is," Barber says, "it isn't going up there with a camera crew showing what you are doing. It's really going up there alone, whether it's with a rope or not.

"Look at people who are being filmed, expert photographers rapping down to take pictures of people," he says. "There's an opportunity for someone to swing over on a rope and say, 'Here, grab it.' It takes an element of danger, of risk, out of it."

But he also sees how the danger in what they are doing can compound with each climb. "I wonder why a lot of people who are free soloing are doing it," Barber says. He gives as an example Alain Robert, the French climber who calls himself the "human spider." In addition to free soloing difficult rock routes, Robert has made a career of climbing skyscrapers around the world with only rock shoes and a chalk bag. "I worry about guys like him," says Barber.

He worries about Alex Honnold, too, in part because he's been in Honnold's position, feeling pressured into free soloing a climb because he had a camera crew waiting. "Obviously, Honnold on *Freerider* could call his crew in and rap off. In fact, he did it. But," he adds, "obviously the likelihood of him being saved on the crux traverse, that ain't gonna happen."

He's not the only one who sees the danger in having risky climbing as your job. Sharon Wood, who became the first woman from the Americas to summit Mount Everest, points to Alison Hargreaves, the British climber who died on the summit of K2 in 1986. Hargreaves had felt she had to keep climbing harder and more dangerous mountains to earn a living as a professional climber. "I was on a panel with her at the Banff festival a thousand years ago now, and she called herself a professional climber," Wood remembers. "She had just done all those solos in the Alps, and the media was following her, and she was a fast-rising star, and she obviously had a high-risk threshold, and she was a talented climber, but unfortunately, she was a bit trapped." She couldn't back down, Wood believes, because climbing was her profession. "She didn't *have* to do it. Nobody *has* to do it. It's a choice," Wood says. "But if you choose solo climbing as your profession, I just think that it's a dangerous combination, a really dangerous combination."

BARBER ISN'T WORRIED ABOUT THE fact that people are doing big free solos, but rather that they're glamorizing them. "Some of the things that people have done are truly huge feats," he says. He points to Hansjörg Auer's free solo of *Via Attraverso il Pesce* on the Marmolada as an example. "He did it once, then three or four years later, he goes back, raps down, susses it out, then goes back the next day and solos the whole route. Insane."

"That to me really is more what solo climbing's about," Barber continues. "He didn't wire the whole thing and it wasn't a party trick; he hadn't been practicing it. I certainly don't want to denigrate what Alex has done," Barber adds. "I'm not intending to cast any aspersions on his accomplishment. That's in a whole other realm. But to me, Auer's solo of the *Fish*, people should know about that climb. I mean, *holy shit!*"

BORN IN 1984, HANSJÖRG AUER climbed his first mountain, a 9800-foot peak, at age six with his older brother Matthias. The third of five children, Auer lived on his family's farm in the Tyrol region of the Austrian Dolomites. Surrounded by mountains, climbing was a natural activity, and Auer later described his first summit as "a very common hiking mountain" on his website. A few years later, he climbed the Hemrachkogel with his brothers Jakob and Matthias and their father.

"My father showed us the Strahlkogel, the highest elevation in Umhausen, back then," he recalled. "This summit drops steeply on all sides. At that time, I was far from being able to climb it, yet I looked over at it with a longing that has not let go of me for many years."

In the summer of 2000, Hans and Matthias made a first ascent of the direct north wall of the Strahlkogel. Although the route was not as difficult as they'd anticipated—they summited after only a few hours of climbing— the route held a special place in Auer's memory, and he returned to climb it often. "When I see this north face today, I always think back to the hours I spent climbing it in winter, summer, alone or with my friends," he wrote. "And I think about what it would have been like if our father hadn't climbed the Hemrachkogel with us boys that day."

Although he was far from athletic growing up, and struggled with anorexia, Auer found a talent and passion for climbing and made it his life's pursuit. He became a certified teacher of mathematics and sports, teaching secondary school for several years before becoming a mountain guide and eventually a professional climber in 2009.

In 2006, Auer free soloed *Tempi Moderni* (*Modern Times*), a twenty-seven-pitch 6c+ (on the French scale, 5.11c on YDS) route on the south face of the Marmolada d'Ombretta, a slabby 3000-foot limestone wall in the Dolomites, which gained him some notoriety. (It was not the first free solo of the route—Italian climber Maurizio Giordani and Czech climber Tomo Česen had done it previously.) Then in 2007, Auer free soloed *Via Attraverso il Pesce*, a thirty-seven-pitch route rated 5.12c on a 3000-foot limestone wall, despite having never successfully free climbed the route without falling.

Named for a fish-shaped alcove halfway up the route where many climbers bivouac, *il Pesce* is considered a serious route with sustained free climbing, including eight particularly hard pitches bracketing the niche. It's as unlikely a free-solo climb as any route you can imagine. Auer, after a day of rappelling in from the top to inspect and practice the crux pitches, simply hiked up to the base of the wall and started climbing. Giordani had soloed much of the route in 1990 but used a rope to belay himself on the hardest pitches. Auer's ropeless ascent was masterful and quick; he completed the route in just 2 hours, 55 minutes. If he'd expected to be alone on the wall, he may have been disappointed by the two German climbers he encountered halfway to the top, who watched, astonished, as the lone climber approached and then passed them.

Auer's free-solo ascent of *il Pesce* was a surprise to nearly everyone, and many climbers didn't at first believe he had done it. Nearly everyone who climbed it fell off at least once, usually more than once, and often lost the route. "*Il Pesce* is quite dangerous, mostly because the routefinding is so challenging and the slabby moves are hard to reverse when you're 50 feet run-out in the wrong direction," Andrew Bisharat, publisher of *Evening Sends*, wrote following his attempt to free climb the route. "Many chuckleheads think that they're up to the challenge of *il Pesce*, and crawl away with broken legs."

Several pitches are notorious for their difficulty and commitment. There's the Open Dihedral pitch, rated 7b (5.12a), which involves precise, sequential moves that would be difficult to reverse. The route is mostly slab climbing up to the eponymous alcove, then rears back to near vertical, requiring keen route-finding skills as it weaves along the line of least resistance. Then climbers encounter the Boulder pitch, rated 7b+ (5.12c), a tricky sequence with widely spaced, sloping footholds and mono pockets to a big reach across to a small crimp. Many succeed on the Boulder pitch only to fail on the Pendulum pitch. Although it's only rated 7a (5.11d), this pitch assumes climbers will swing across on the rope instead of free climbing the blank slab, which involves intuitive friction moves interspersed with single-digit finger pockets.

Auer didn't have a photographer or film crew along; in fact, only his parents and brother knew what he had planned to do that day. Fortunately, one of the German climbers snapped a few photographs of Auer soloing past, which provided proof of his ascent. "I keep thinking about what would have happened had the Zander couple not photographed me during my most difficult free solo ascent at the end of April 2007," Auer wrote on his website. What would have happened is that nobody would have believed him.

As is typical when someone does a groundbreaking free solo, Auer was besieged by photographers to go back up on *il Pesce* for photographs or to film it. Auer resisted the urging of many photographers but did invite his brother Matthias and friend Heiko Wilhelm back onto the wall to photograph him reenacting some of the sections of his free solo climb. In a way, they're beautiful; and in a way, they're horrifying, showing Auer moving across steep, blank slabs, fingering tiny edges and pockets, a thousand feet or more above the ground. The position is reminiscent of Alex Honnold on the Boulder Problem pitch on *Freerider*, where the holds are so small and the moves so subtle that one slip would lead to a fall—not a free fall through open air here though, but a long, tumbling fall like a ragdoll down an endless slab.

Auer's free-solo ascent of *il Pesce* and the resulting publicity helped him to become a full-time professional climber. Auer climbed routes as hard as 8c+ (5.14c) and had a reputation for fighting to the finish. As he told Planet Mountain in 2007:

> *The fascinating thing about soloing is living total freedom and lightness of movement. . . . At the start of the route you somehow immerge yourself*

into another world which belongs to you only and you play with it with your body movements. . . . It seems as if it's pre-programmed, like in a film. There's no fear and your head almost explodes with self-confidence. . . . When I'm at the start of the route I let my thoughts drift up high, so that it isn't fear which overcomes me but the joy of feeling complete concentration and that I'm about to make a dream come true. One waits for moments like this for a long time.

Auer completed many first ascents in the Alps, Alaska, and Himalayas, including the first ascents of the 22,982-meter Gimmigela East with Austrian climber Alex Blümel, and, the next year, of 23,481-meter Lupghar Sar West. He climbed solo on Lupghar Sar West, an ascent that would garner him alpinism's most prestigious prize, the Piolet d'Or, in 2019.

"Climbing and mountaineering on the borderline of possible is a game—a risky game . . . but one that I cannot live without," Auer wrote on his website.

The game is simple, the rules always the same. The present moment counts for everything. I want to do things that push me. With all my heart or not at all. The more intense it is, the more enriching it is, and the stronger the feeling that I am heading in the right direction. I do however begin to ponder. Especially when I am injured or after a close call. I think about my friends. I think about what it would be like if one day I didn't return, if I had to pay the price for the mountains. And yet I cannot resist to take on the challenge time after time. I will never stop searching because what I find fascinates me every time I head out.

In April 2019, Auer, thirty-five, joined David Lama, twenty-eight, and Jess Roskelley, thirty-six, for an ascent of Howse Peak, a 10,800-foot peak in Alberta, Canada. They hoped to make the second ascent of a route on the mountain's 3000-foot east face called *M16*, established more than twenty years earlier by Steve Howse, Barry Blanchard, and Scott Backes, and considered one of the most difficult and dangerous mixed climbs in the world.

The three climbers, all members of The North Face climbing team, reached the summit on April 16, 2019, but were caught in an avalanche during the descent and swept off the mountain. Their bodies were recovered several days later.

CHAPTER 20

Taking Up the Challenge

Over the course of one month in Yosemite in 1985, I got into the habit of free soloing regularly. Among other routes, there was a 5.8 I went to each afternoon and climbed over and over until it got dark. I usually waited until other climbers had rappelled off and headed to camp so I could have the route to myself. One evening, as I neared a small ledge, 150 feet off the ground, I encountered two climbers anchored to the wall, preparing to climb the second pitch, a thin crack that split the broad granite slab. My timing was perfect. If I'd arrived a few minutes later, they would already be climbing and I'd have to wait, try a risky variation to get around them, or climb down. Where they were, I could make a few moves on easy ground to pass them and keep climbing. They were there first, though. I had to ask permission.

"Mind if I pass?" I asked, standing on a small ledge just below the two climbers. They gave me a startled look.

"Sure," one of them said after a pause. "Go ahead."

"Thanks," I said. I moved quickly past them and started up the crack. I stopped a few feet above them and looked down. They were looking right at me, silently watching my every move. Based on their response, it occurred to me that they had never encountered a solo climber before. If so, I didn't want to disappoint them. It was showtime.

I'd seen John Bachar free soloing enough times to be able to imitate him—his smooth, precise movements, Zen-like focus, thousand-mile stare. I started climbing like that. I cruised up the crack like it was nothing, flowing like water up the steep slab. Before long, they were far below me, out of sight and mind. I didn't think about them again until many years later.

I NEVER MET MICHAEL YBARRA, but I enjoyed reading his articles about climbing, like one published in the *Wall Street Journal* in 2009 titled "Climbing Alone, Risking It All," about Ybarra's first exposure to free soloing. He and a partner had been climbing in Yosemite in 1985 and were passed by a solo climber who appeared out of nowhere, asked permission to climb through, and continued above them on a 5.8 he made look as easy as walking on a sidewalk.

Ybarra eventually took up free soloing himself, although he admitted he didn't think it was the best idea, like the time he was free soloing what he thought was a 5.8 only to find out later—after he'd gotten scared and barely managed to climb down—that he was on the wrong route and would have faced 5.11 climbing if he'd continued. "Almost every time I free solo something scary," he wrote, "I promise myself I'll never do it again." It was nice to read about free soloing from the perspective of someone who had the twitch, who didn't couch it in terms of recklessness, irresponsibility, and suicidal ideation. The article continued:

> It's hard to explain free soloing, let alone justify it. . . . Everything in life is a risk of some sort. . . . Most people exist so swaddled against danger, measuring out their lives with coffee spoons, that those who reckon by a different calculation of risk and reward appear insane. Yet to survive a perilous situation is to love life more than the average person can imagine.

Ybarra died while solo climbing in Yosemite in 2012. In his obituary, the *Wall Street Journal* wrote: "His passion for the outdoors was evident not only in his writing . . . but in the way he lived."

He'd gone on what was supposed to be a two-day traverse of Sawtooth Ridge, a rugged subrange composed of sharp-edge granite ridges and tooth-like peaks in a remote area along the park's northern remote boundary. The traverse, first climbed in 1984 and later climbed solo by Peter Croft, is airy and consistently exposed, with a full day's worth of exposed rock climbing up to

5.8 in difficulty, in addition to some airy rappels. It isn't all that difficult and is considered "casual" by experienced climbers if you bring a rope to rappel down the steepest drops. Although Ybarra was climbing solo, he brought a rope, but probably wouldn't have used it except to rappel.

When he failed to return on Sunday night, he was reported missing. A search was convened and his body was located on the south side of the ridge. He had signed the summit register for 12,279-foot Matterhorn Peak, the highest summit on Sawtooth Ridge, and was traversing west along the ridge when he fell. They found his rope, still coiled, several hundred feet above him. He may have tried downclimbing a steep section instead of rappelling, but he could just as easily have simply slipped or fallen due to a hold breaking on easier ground. He was forty-five years old.

A LOT OF PEOPLE FREE soloed in Yosemite in 1985; the climber Ybarra wrote about in the *Wall Street Journal* could have been any number of people. But I've always wondered if perhaps it was me. I'd like to think it wasn't.

"I've thought about this a lot. It kind of disturbs me, people seeing other people soloing," Henry Barber told me. What worries him is that people might be influenced to solo if they see someone else do it, and they might get hurt. He has a reason to be concerned. One day at the Gunks, he was soloing a route when a small group of climbers appeared and watched him from below. He climbed down and went off to solo another route. When he returned, he heard someone yell, "Ahh!" He ran toward the sound and found one of the climbers from the group lying on the ground. He'd been up soloing where Barber had just been and had fallen and landed badly. Barber tried to help and comfort the fallen climber, but it was too late. "He was dead. He died right in my hands."

Although it's rare for a nonclimber to be inspired to free solo a difficult route after watching an experienced climber, it definitely makes an impression. The impression is even stronger for someone who has some experience climbing, thinks highly of their ability or invulnerability, is susceptible to impulsivity, sees someone free soloing and thinks "I can do that," and then does it. That's how I got started free soloing. I'd already been climbing for several years when I saw John Bachar solo a hard route at Joshua Tree. The next day, I went out and tried it myself. I'd done some easier climbs unroped before that, but seeing Bachar in person inspired me to really go for it. Because of that, I've sometimes wondered if my own free soloing ever inspired someone else to do it. I hope it didn't, or, if it did, that nobody got hurt.

Often the factors that influence someone to take up free soloing are more immediate and organic, a subtle form of peer pressure, when someone free solos a route on the spur of the moment and others get caught up in it. Russ Clune remembers climbing one day with an acquaintance who joined him on an ascent of a 5.5 at the Gunks called *Frog's Head*. When Clune announced that he was going to free solo the route, his companion didn't flinch. He started right up after Clune. They soloed up the route easily, but near the top, 200 feet off the ground, Clune took a detour. "At the very top of the cliff there's a variation that you can do," he told me. "You go through an overhang. It's like 5.6 or 5.7 and it's on less-than-positive holds. It's a little bit tricky." Clune impulsively took the tricky variation, soloed easily through the overhang, and reached the top of the cliff.

He turned to watch the other climber, who had decided to follow him up the overhang, but suddenly stalled. "I could see he was going to blow it," Clune told me, recalling one of the scariest moments of his climbing career. "Just be calm," he told the other climber. "You're cool. Just grab this hold over here." The other climber made it through, but it was a close call. "I just about shit my pants watching that," Clune recalls. "If he'd fallen, he would have died. It definitely made me be much more aware about the casualness of just saying, 'Hey man, let's go.'"

"Did I put pressure on him to do it because I suggested it, not thinking it was any big deal?" Clune wonders. "I still think about that."

I told Clune that his article about free soloing in the Gunks, and his free solo of *Supercrack*, had influenced my decision to free solo the 5.12 where I nearly fell. That I had a competitive streak, too, and that his 5.12 solo climb had given me the green light to go for it.

"It was never my intention to influence anybody to go do something stupid," he said. "And if I did, then I'm sad that's the case."

ALEX HONNOLD GAVE A PRESENTATION at the FICO World tech conference in February 2019 in front of an audience of about five thousand people. He was talking about his free-solo climbs of Half Dome and El Capitan when he turned and asked the audience, "How many of you have climbed the cables to the top of Half Dome?" About ten people raised their hands. "How many of you have been to Yosemite?" Maybe fifteen people raised their hands. "How many people here are from California?" Quite a few hands went up. Alex looked out at the audience in disbelief. "You people need to go to Yosemite," he chided them. "You need to hike up the cables to the top of Half Dome. It's right there!"

Audience member Ryan Jurkowski, a cybersecurity professional who analyzes risk for a living, felt like he'd been scolded. He lived in California but had never been to Yosemite, had never been climbing. "I was kind of embarrassed," he told me. After hearing Honnold, he decided he had to check it out. He went to the base of El Capitan to see what Honnold had been talking about. Standing below the huge cliff, watching climbers working their way upward, he felt the twitch. On the drive home from Yosemite, he listened to podcasts of famous climbers talking about the sport and was hooked. When he returned home, he went to his local climbing gym, took a belay lesson, and began to execute his new four-year plan.

Although Jurkowski enjoys gym climbing, he views it as a means to an end. "I think the social aspect is cool," he says. "I love the physical nature of it, the complex puzzle solving." But he's more focused on learning and experiencing every aspect of climbing as quickly as possible. "I'm climbing El Cap in four years," he insists. "I need to do everything possible at every moment to make sure that I can achieve this goal." Within a few weeks of first setting foot in the gym, he was climbing outdoors. By the end of that year, he was leading moderate, multipitch trad routes. Soon after, he was making plans to climb *Freeblast* on El Cap, the first part of the route Honnold free soloed, to build experience and prepare for his eventual ascent of El Capitan. "I know time is of the essence, and I wanted to get crackin' as soon as possible," he says. "I'm not getting any younger."

When Jurkowski says he is going to do everything possible to reach his goal, he means it. In June 2020, barely a year after he first stepped into a climbing gym, Jurkowski tried free soloing for the first time, climbing an 800-foot route on Tahquitz Rock called *White Maiden's Walkway*, alone, without a rope or protection, a route he'd climbed for the first time only a few weeks earlier. He had been planning to meet a couple friends at Tahquitz Rock but decided to sleep in and arrived late. On the drive there, he formulated the plan. "You know what?" he said to himself. "It's been a year since I first climbed on Tahquitz. Let's make this a special day. I feel really confident."

Things went well until the crux of the route, which involved a step-across move 600 feet off the ground. "It wasn't a big deal," he says, "but it was very relieving after completing that move for sure. It would be a bad spot to fall."

He caught up to his friends, who were surprised to see him. "I intentionally didn't want to make any social media posts until I had at least passed the crux," Jurkowski says. As he approached the wall, one of his friends called down, "So what's your plan?"

"Solo!" he called up.

"He wasn't too happy about it," Jurkowski admits. "It made those partners feel a bit uncomfortable, they shared with me later, but I hadn't sought out anybody's approval or checked in with anybody."

Like many free soloists, Jurkowski realizes his impulse to solo comes partly from not wanting to be burdened by such nuisances as ropes and partners or waiting for others to teach him when he can just go climbing and gain experience himself. "I'm going to go and do this stuff, because time is of the essence," he says.

Jurkowski doesn't blame Honnold for inspiring him to start free soloing but acknowledges that he's at least indirectly responsible. He even saw *Free Solo* the day before the tech conference (although he says it had no impact on his decision to start climbing). "It's a funny thing about that *Free Solo* movie," he says, "he's done the route about fifty or sixty times, he knows all the moves, he writes it all in a journal, he's a physical specimen, so it's not a big deal. He even says it's no big deal."

But Jurkowski isn't sure. "The more you get into climbing, you realize how unbelievable it is. It's really wild, a kind of weird oscillating ride of 'that's not a big deal' to 'that *is* a big deal.'"

Although he doesn't feel Honnold directly influenced his decision to free solo, Jurkowski knows he had *some* influence. "It's cool to get to the point where I feel comfortable on something even pedestrian," he says. "I can kind of feel what he's feeling, in that sense, even though it isn't anywhere near the same difficulty."

Jurkowski thinks it's a natural progression. "People are going to try soloing when they feel confident, and in that regard, I think Alex is probably one of the best examples, and one of the best role models for that, because he is so well prepared," he says. "He's so strong, and he's so mentally tight that if anyone's going to go and solo something like that, he's a good example of how overprepared you should be."

He also sees free soloing as about assessing and accepting risk, an essential part of Jurkowski's job. "No one can eliminate all risk in a company, so these companies are trying to ascertain what their risk is and then push the boundaries of that risk as far as comfortable so that they can stay competitive.

"If you don't take on any risk, your company's not going to survive." He believes that same philosophy may apply to climbing, but of course, he admits, "With free soloing, obviously there's some heavy risk."

CHAPTER 21

Jumping the Strid

Alex Honnold has insisted that no kid will be influenced by him to free solo; that any kid who did would get 12 feet off the ground, get scared, and never try it again. He forgets that when he was a kid, he climbed up playground equipment, trees, onto the roof, ignoring his mother's insistence that he get down. He's not the only kid who was like that; there are a lot of kids who are inquisitive and adventuresome by nature, who explore their environment and test their limits, doing things that would horrify their parents if they only knew. Alex's own mother, Dierdre Wolownick, was once a kid like that.

"When I was little, we used to go to Pennsylvania to see my grandparents," Wolownick told me. She mentioned two huge rock formations on the outskirts of the town. "King Rock and Queen Rock, they called them. And all the kids played on King Rock and Queen Rock, and they were several stories tall, and all of us free soloed all over the place," she recalls. "We didn't know the terms; we didn't know that climbing was a sport. We were just out there having fun. . . . And I *loved* it! I wasn't supposed to go climbing; I was supposed to wear dresses, be a nice little girl."

Wolownick wasn't influenced by a film or article she saw about a free-solo climber. It was simpler than that: She was a kid and there were some big rocks in the park near her grandparents' house. All the other kids were climbing up and around them, so she did too. And she wasn't afraid, she says—not at all.

"Kids are *taught* to be afraid. Oh, goodness, kids are taught to be afraid," she says. "Their natural instinct is to have fun and explore and find out what they can do."

"ADOLESCENCE IS A TIME WHEN there is a peak in sensation-seeking," Beatriz Luna, director of the Laboratory of Neurocognitive Development at the University of Pittsburgh, said during a presentation at Stanford in 2013. "This is evident across societies and across species." Although it can lead to risk-taking, which can threaten survival, exploratory behavior and novelty-seeking are normal and necessary parts of adolescent development.

According to Luna, the brain is going through substantial transformations during adolescence. "The gross morphology is already available," she says, "but hasn't been fine-tuned." This includes not just the prefrontal cortex, but also areas throughout the neocortex—areas responsible for language, executive control, and attention. At the same time, the availability of dopamine is peaking. "We have a brain that is very driven toward sensation-seeking," she says. "It's a very impulsive system aimed at getting a reward." But the adolescent brain can't maintain cognitive control as well as an adult. The dorsal anterior cingulate cortex—the part of the brain that monitors what we do, its "alarm system"—is dramatically changing during adolescence.

"Whenever we commit an error, it lights up," she says. "This should inform subsequent behavior. That is still not there in adolescence, and continues to improve into the twenties." As Luna explains, "The brain is experimenting, turning the volume of various regions up and down, till it finds its optimal performance range. This is a crucial part of development . . . that allows the brain to really adapt itself to its environment. Risk-taking might be an adaptive mechanism that allows the individual to go out, veer into the environment [and] gain the independence skills needed to make them into a successful adult."

"Saying that one studies the adolescent brain is often met with comic skepticism and feigned relief that adolescents do indeed have a brain," says BJ Casey, director of the Fundamentals of the Adolescent Brain lab at Yale University. Casey's research, including her 2013 study "The Teenage Brain: Self Control," has dispelled some of the myths that attempt to explain impulsivity and risk-taking by teens and young adults, such as that their behavior is irrational or deviant, that they are incapable of making rational decisions because of their immature prefrontal cortex, and that the Sturm und Drang adolescents experience during their journey to adulthood results in poor self-control and predisposes them toward risk-taking behavior.

"This description pathologizes an important phase of normal development that allows individuals to learn how to function relatively independently in society," Casey wrote. "Clearly, the prefrontal cortex is not the only part of the brain that changes during this developmental period." Casey believes the spikes in risky and emotive behavior during adolescence are not solely the result of an underdeveloped or immature prefrontal cortex but are "part of a developing circuitry that is fine-tuned with experience during this time."

According to a 2010 study about brain development in adolescence, published in the *Journal of Physiology-Paris*, exploratory behavior, including risk-taking by adolescents, is normal, even necessary from a philosophical perspective, during this period of "redefinition of the self and the quest for self-affirmation." It also asserts that adolescents are prone to taking immediate action in response to conflict.

Action serves as a major testing ground for the process of self-definition. Adolescence is the first time that an individual's sense of him- or herself as a sexual being is principally measured by what he or she does, rather than simply wishes to do, and not just by what his or her parents say or how they react. Both the quality of their emotional experiences . . . and the judgments of their peers contribute to the fine-tuning of adolescents' actions and values. This process of self-definition through action ultimately makes an important contribution to the relatively stable self-representations of adulthood.

Accordingly, the study suggests, the need to experience—even though it leads to increased risk-taking—is a healthy and vital part of growing up.

ENGLISH CLIMBER MARK RADTKE WAS seven or eight years old and on a family day trip in the late 1960s the first time he visited the Strid, a scenic spot on the River Wharfe where the river is funneled through a cleft of rock just narrow enough to tempt many visitors to leap across. In his memoir, *A Canvas of Rock*, Radtke recalls his mother warning against trying to make the leap. According to legend, the Boy of Egremont had drowned there in 1128 while attempting to jump across the gorge. Although the Strid was narrow, it was also deep; although the water flowed gently at the surface, it was fast-moving and turbulent below. Falling into the Strid, his mother knew, meant certain death, and she made sure her son knew it too.

Radtke returned to the Strid at age thirteen, on a camping trip with his friend Adrian Ledgway. "It was a spontaneous decision to attempt the jump, but it wasn't a reckless act," he told me. "It was coupled with intelligent and calculated assessment. Inwardly, I could feel anticipated excitement as we carefully chose our takeoff and landing points and talked through the jump tactics."

Ledgway went first and executed a perfect leap. He'd broken the mental barrier; it could be done. Now Radtke had to summon the nerve to follow.

"I was sort of committed now and had to suppress any self-doubts," Radtke recalls. "I made the jump."

Their excitement at their success was short-lived. Now they had to get back to the other side, which presented a new problem. They couldn't reverse the leap they'd just made; it had been from a higher ledge to a lower one, easy one way but not the other. They searched up and down the Strid and found another spot that looked promising; it was a little wider and not as secure but seemed to be the best option. "It looked like a tough leap," Radtke recalls, "but we'd already had the taste of success."

With a second jump under their belts, they spent the rest of the day jumping the Strid. "It was basic thrill-seeking, but it was all wrapped up with challenge and risk," Radtke recalled. "It gave us a real buzz. We decided that we'd be back for more the following day—it was addictive."

On reflection, Radtke believes a number of factors were in play that influenced his decision and drive to make the leap, factors that also influence his decision to free solo. "The macabre, romantic tales from the past about previous fatalities were a stark warning of the dangers of the place, yet I had an overriding urge to challenge this sense of fear," he told me. "There was an element of friendly rivalry between Ledge and I, but more importantly when Ledge went first he demonstrated that the jump was possible." Once his friend had done it, Radtke had to follow. He made the leap. "Then there was the sheer emotional exhilaration as everything came together in success and this was a powerful chemical cocktail," he recalled.

He views his experience of jumping the Strid as evidence that he is wired to look for possibilities over obstacles, and to take risks because he thinks he can, rather than avoiding them out of a fear of failure. "Over time, I became a person who if someone said 'It can't be done,' my mind immediately said 'Why not?'" he told me. "I became—and still am—a bit of a rule breaker. I still take pleasure in flouting what I consider to be rules and regulations that demean intelligent thought."

This perspective manifested itself in Radtke's approach to rock climbing—he took on many new routes that others had dismissed as being impossible, too loose, or too dangerous. As he wrote in his memoir:

> In today's society some people seem to hold the belief that somehow hazards and risk shouldn't exist. You turn the TV on and advertisements from law firms suggest that if you have some mishap or other, then someone else is to blame. . . . We need to accept that the environment we live in does have hazards. . . . Risk assessment should be an intrinsic and well-developed mental process, something that becomes an instinctive or intuitive part of our cognition.

Radtke thinks we may actually be safer when in the presence of a hazard, because it forces us to focus on and manage the risk, that being afraid, having that queasy feeling in our gut, teaches us to make appropriate decisions. "We manage the stress and fear rather than letting the fear dictate our path," he wrote. "There is a paradox with this of course. If we are to be acutely tuned in to danger, we also need to experience it first-hand." People who haven't experienced and learned to manage fear are susceptible to what Radtke calls "amygdala hijack," overresponding to a perceived threat, which can lead to a bad outcome, like swerving to avoid hitting a squirrel and crashing into a tree instead. The benefit of free soloing, Radtke believes, is that it exposes you to danger and teaches you that you can manage the risk through concentration, focus, preparation, and action. "We all get shit scared," he says. "The key attribute is developing the ability to channel the fear in the right direction, at the right time, to get the right result."

Radtke thinks this ability to channel fear in the right direction to get the right result is what allowed him to jump the Strid, but he knows it could have gone very wrong. "I sometimes look back and shudder at the thought of what could have happened," he admits.

ONE DAY IN 1952, FOUR schoolboys from Keswick, England, were wandering about the hillsides of Borrowdale Valley looking for bird eggs. Bird nesting was a hobby, something adventuresome for the lads to do. Usually they'd climb trees to find nests and take just one egg for the sport of it. But they'd heard that jackdaws, small gray-headed crows, nested on the cliffs that dotted the valley hillsides, so they rode their bikes there and hiked up to the base of a promising-looking cliff. There they saw scratch marks on the rock that seemed to indicate people had climbed there before, and so they started up the blocky slab, one after the other.

"About halfway up we heard shouts from our left," one of the boys, Paul Ross, recalled in an interview published on the *Footless Crow* blog. It was two "real" climbers trying to warn the lads that they were endangering themselves and should turn back. They kept climbing. "None of us had been on rock before, but we were all enthusiastic tree climbers so we were quite unfazed," Ross said. They climbed to the top of the 130-foot crag, then climbed back down the way they'd come. "I think we all thought this was great fun," Ross recalled. "The bird nesting was now forgotten."

The group had unwittingly free soloed a Very Difficult (5.4) route called *Brown Slabs Direct*, up and down, and then had wandered to the area of the wall called Chamonix, a 200-foot cliff capped by a 40-foot overhanging headwall. As they walked along the base of the crag, they found more scratch marks. Three of the group were still game to climb and started up. At the halfway point, they arrived at a ledge. Two of the group traversed left, following easier-looking ground that would bypass the headwall, while a third member had already scrambled to the top an easier way. Ross, a clean-cut lad in an Oxford shirt and shorts and leather dress sandals, continued up the steep headwall, alone. He cruised along thin flakes nearly 200 feet above the ground, feeling quite pleased. Despite the intimidating aspect of the headwall, Ross found good cracks and edges to grab onto and was soon pulling over the top.

Ross had just free soloed a route called *Little Chamonix* that, although not appreciably more difficult than *Brown Slabs Direct*, was much steeper and more exposed. He had no rock-climbing experience.

From his innocent beginnings on Shepherds Crag, Ross would go on to become a leading British climber, establishing hundreds of new routes in the Lake District in the 1950s and 1960s, often bold, difficult leads done in the traditional ground-up style (although Ross was considered controversial at the time because he used pitons as protection). He was also part of the team, with Don Whillans, Hamish MacInnes, and Chris Bonington, that made the first British ascent of the *Bonatti Route* on the Dru in the Alps. Ross had a fast-paced lifestyle of bold climbing and motorcycle riding that caught up with him in the sixties; climbing falls and a motorbike crash (he hit a flock of sheep at 70 miles per hour) landed him in the hospital with a back injury. In the late sixties, Ross moved to New Hampshire where he worked as a climbing instructor, and in 1973 participated in the first British ascent of the *Salathé Wall* route on El Capitan. He went on to complete hundreds of first ascents on desert walls and towers in Colorado and Utah.

Ross is back in England, living in a small two-story row house in Keswick, just a few miles from Shepherds Crag. He mostly rides his mountain bike around the Lake District now. (When I visited him in November 2019, he took me for a "wee bike ride" of 20 miles.) He doesn't climb much anymore, but when he does, it's usually *Little Chamonix*. In 2017, to celebrate his eightieth birthday, he climbed the route wearing boxing gloves and roller skates. In 2019, at the age of eighty-two, he free soloed it.

BUT RISK-TAKING BY ADOLESCENTS IS not without, well, risk. Mortality rates are more than triple for fifteen- to twenty-four-year-olds compared to younger adolescents, according to the 2013 study, "Adolescents: Which Risks for Their Life and Health?" Although studies have found little difference between decision-making patterns in this age group and older adults, the fifteen- to twenty-four-year-olds were more likely to engage in dangerous behaviors despite being aware of the risks, especially in emotionally charged situations where complex feelings came into play—like wanting to look cool and fearing peer rejection.

"It is generally held that adolescents take risks to test and define themselves, as risk-taking can be both beneficial and harmful," the researchers reported. "The proclivity for risk-taking behavior plays a significant role in adolescent development, rendering this a period of time for both accomplishing their full potential and vulnerability."

The study also cites exposure to mass media as an influence on adolescents. They are bombarded with emotionally arousing media imagery that encourages the risky, addictive, and life-threatening activities that their developing brains may be powerless to resist.

SNOW CANYON STATE PARK IS not among the popular climbing destinations of southern Utah. More jets fly over, bound for Las Vegas and Los Angeles, than there are climbers challenging themselves on its sandstone walls. The park has several established routes on its steep slabs and buttresses, including petrified sand dunes that alternate in color from white to gold to red and consistency from bullet-hard to crumbly soft. Although rock climbers tend to head to Red Rocks or Zion, a few stray climbers visit the park. It's not the greatest place to climb, they'll tell you; the rock is solid in places, but it is well known for its friability. The park is more popular with picnickers, hikers, and sightseers, who enjoy exploring the rock slabs and buttresses that angle up from a desert floor dotted by drab sage, piñon pine, and golden dunes, and who also sometimes go off trail and get into trouble.

According to news reports, thirteen-year-old Elijah Baldwin and his younger brothers, ages eleven and nine, were visiting Snow Canyon in March 2019 with their mother to take a hike and explore. The family had started hiking together on the Pioneer Names Trail, a "short and fun little hike" according to an online guide, that passes below sandstone cliffs where early Mormon settlers had written their names in wagon-axle grease. The trail itself is mostly flat and sandy, but the boys would sometimes take detours, scrambling up the slabby walls here and there, exploring ledges and caves, having fun as kids do, while their mother watched carefully from the trail below.

At one point, Baldwin started climbing up a sandstone slab; his brothers followed him at first, but soon lost interest and scrambled back down to the trail to look for lizards. While they and their mother continued hiking on the trail, Baldwin kept climbing. He eventually reached the top of the 300-foot-high formation called Island in the Sky.

"This thirteen-year-old was in a more advanced area, I would guess," Lieutenant Regan Wilson, a Utah State Parks spokesman, told ABC News.

A lot of the climbing on the lower part of the formation is merely slabby scrambling, easy enough that climbers normally wouldn't rope up, but the upper walls are steeper and more difficult. The original route on the wall, one of several, follows one of the obvious lines of least resistance and is rated 5.5. "He did make it to the top," Wilson reported. "On the way down, I think, is where the difficulty came."

Elijah's mother, minding the two younger boys, did her best to keep an eye on things, but eventually lost sight of him. Fearing something was wrong, she ran to the ranger station to report that her son had disappeared, leaving the two younger boys to watch for him. While she was returning from the ranger station, one of Baldwin's younger brothers yelled "I can see him!" According to news reports, his mother looked and saw him falling briefly before disappearing behind a brushy ledge.

Washington County Sheriff's Sergeant Darrell Cashin, who leads most search-and-rescue efforts in the area, told the *St. George News* that Baldwin had probably been climbing down one of the gullies or chimneys before falling 75 to 100 feet onto the ledge. He surmised the boy had possibly slipped or lost his grip, but a block of sandstone near his body suggested a broken hold may have caused his fall. It's a fair guess; if you read accident reports, there's almost always a broken rock involved when someone falls in Snow Canyon. A thirteen-year-old boy visiting from out of state would be unlikely to consider this danger before climbing up the wall.

According to a news report, Baldwin's mother had told authorities that her son loved to climb, and that they had planned to rock climb in Zion National Park later that week. While Cashin saw Baldwin as merely a "curious thirteen-year-old that was climbing along the rocks and probably had no idea the danger he was in," there is no question that Baldwin was free soloing—rock climbing without a rope or protective equipment, like Paul Ross and his mates on Shepherds Crag—even if he wasn't aware of the risk. Right up until the moment he found himself in a difficult spot, he was likely having a blast, climbing to the top of the huge rock slab then climbing down. If he'd picked a different way down, he might have had no difficulty or encountered no loose rock. His family would have gone rock climbing at Zion later in the week, and he would have had great stories to tell. But he went the wrong way, a rock broke, and he fell.

It would be easy to criticize Elijah Baldwin's mom for allowing him to climb on the rocks, just as people criticized Alex Honnold's mom when she allowed him to explore his limits, but by all accounts, everything was going fine right up until it wasn't. Baldwin may have simply chosen a way down that looked easier than it was, or maybe he was on easy terrain after all and just had bad luck. That's how the sheriff's sergeant saw it.

"Sometimes, accidents just happen," Cashin said. "But you know, sometimes . . . a rock breaks loose. I'm not going to criticize."

CHAPTER 22

How Do You Talk to Your Kids about Free Soloing?

When I went to see the film *Free Solo* for a second time, I invited my friend August Welch, a young father who had done some hairy free soloing in his youth. He brought his seven-year-old son, Archer. Afterward, Welch told me the film made him uncomfortable. "It made my hands sweat like no film that I've ever watched before," he said, "not so much because of the footage, or that the film itself was scary, but because I know as a climber how difficult the route was."

I asked Welch how he felt about bringing his son to watch a film he found terrifying. "You know, as far as Archer goes, I didn't really have much thought or squeamishness," he answered. "It was the first exposure he had [to] seeing this guy climbing; he doesn't really know how hard the route is. It certainly looks climbable, it's all there, and I just let him watch it."

"It does look *really* hard," Archer interrupted.

"What did you think when you saw the movie?" I asked him.

"Uh, it's insane," he said.

"Why is it insane?"

"Because he's like fifty million feet in the air with no rope or support, and if he falls, he's dead."

In a way, even though he thought it was insane, seeing the film inspired Archer. After watching it, he became more interested in climbing and started going to the climbing gym with his dad. At first, he got scared when he made it 20 feet up a wall. He'd stop climbing, look around, say "Okay, I'm good here," and ask to be lowered down. But the more he climbed, the more comfortable he got with it. "Now I don't care," he says, "as long as I have a rope and a belay."

Like me, Welch is a former "rock rat" who spent most of his free time as a teen and young adult hanging out at the University of Washington practice rock, trying to find and create an identity for himself through hard bouldering and badass rock climbing. Like most of the other rock rats, this inevitably included free soloing. According to Welch, that's how he got the twitch: peer pressure.

"It was the day I went up the tower," he says, referring to the 30-foot fin of concrete and granite at the center of the practice rock that provides a sort of litmus test for aspiring hard climbers. "I'd watched my friends go up the tower. They were a couple of years older than me, and I wanted—needed—to be cool. I knew if I wasn't able to go up it, I really wasn't going to be cool."

Welch did a lot of free soloing, including climbs in Joshua Tree and Yosemite. But his perspective changed after a day where he attempted *Spider Line*. Welch was leading the route, roped up and placing protection, but then he got too far above his protection. That's when he fell. He remembers falling, smashing into the ground, then waking up after blacking out and realizing, "*Holy shit!* I just hit the ground." His friend described the impact. "Your body looked like a water balloon that you dropped onto the ground, but it didn't pop. All four of your extremities shot out, arms and legs shot out, and then snapped back."

Welch survived his fall without apparent serious injury, but it eventually caused a curvature in his spine and a rotation in his pelvis that affects his ability to maintain physical strength. He has to train consistently to ward off further deterioration.

Now that Archer's seen Honnold's film and has started climbing, Welch has thought about the best way to talk to his son about free soloing. "I think the best way for me to approach this is to use a kind of cliché thing from my middle school days," he told me. "If you don't talk to your kids about drugs, who will? I think that by talking about it and talking about what I did and why I did it, it sort of helps solidify the sense of what's real and what's fantasyland."

This is one of the ways of combatting what he refers to as the "Alex Honnold effect."

"I started him very early on with some of the video games that he plays, and he's very keen at recognizing, 'This is a game. It isn't real. It's different from the real world that we live in,'" he says. "And that's kind of how I approach how I talk about free soloing, because it's not a game."

Welch came from a background of depression and alienation, something else he talked openly about in front of Archer. "I was definitely there," he told me. "There was definitely a darkness and a depression that was going on with me and the struggles of growing up and trying to find out who I was, what I was doing on this planet . . . doing these really badass solos gave [me] something, it did pull me out of some dark holes."

Even though the rock-rat tribe was part of how Welch got through those dark years, he thinks that the antidote to depression, for Archer and the next generation, is a healthy self-concept, so they don't feel that bottomless pit of despair and like they have to do something dangerous to gain self-esteem and self-actualization. He's trying to raise Archer so he doesn't feel the need risk his life to feel good about himself. "Maybe I'm taking credit for something I don't deserve," Welch says, "but I think there's some truth to it. Maybe I kind of have built in a certain level of base common sense from the time he was very young."

IN 2018, I INTERVIEWED DREW RUANA, an eighteen-year-old from a suburb east of Seattle, who had been climbing 5.14 since the age of thirteen. He had just finished competing in a bouldering competition and I met him, along with his parents, afterward at a nearby coffee shop. Climbing for Drew, I found out, is a family affair. His parents met while climbing at Smith Rock, in Oregon. They went on a three-month road trip together that they refer to as their first date.

"I did a lot of crazy stuff," Drew's father, Rudy, admits. "Call it that eighteen- to twenty-five-year-old thing. I look back and I'm just like, 'Jesus. What was I thinking?' And I think males are probably more prone to that." Like any parent of a young climber, he worried that Drew might do crazy stuff, too, like free soloing.

So did Drew's mother, Chris. "It seemed like every couple of years, some soloer died, like Michael Reardon and John Bachar," she told me. "It seemed like it was just a matter of time for just about anybody that pushed those type of limits." She continued, "So when we were raising our own kids, and especially when Drew really took off on the climbing, we often had talks about safe ways to process things—ways to manage the risk, because if something happens, it's just over. You're done. And it's not worth it."

"Don't do what I did," Rudy told Drew. "It was dumb."

"I would be murdered if I did that," Drew says, looking at his mom, smiling.

Instead of risk, Drew has focused on difficulty, which makes his parents happy, although they know sport climbing and bouldering aren't without risks. "You climb long enough and even with your rope, you get yourself into pickles," Rudy admits. "You don't bring the right piece of gear, all of a sudden, you're in a ground fall situation. I mean, stuff like that happens." Like the time Drew, just twelve years old, climbed a sport route in Canada that hadn't been fully bolted and got into the "no-fall zone." He unwittingly made the first ascent of the 5.13 route, but his father concedes, he would have died if he hadn't pulled it off. "He thought it was just a bolted sport route," Rudy says. "He didn't realize it was a project that was not done yet and not fully bolted, and I think that scared the bejeebers out of him."

Drew's parents have been in similar situations. Rudy remembers a close call on an offwidth crack in Canada where he brought the wrong-size gear and had no protection. He barely pulled it off. Chris's happened in Yosemite, when all of her protection pulled out when she was 70 feet off the ground at the crux of a climb. They know climbing has unavoidable risks, that things happen sometimes, but think there's enough risk already that it's foolish to add more. "There's risk in just living life," Rudy says, "but there's no reason to accelerate the demise."

Rudy is a vocal critic of the glorification of free soloing in the media. During a climbing trip, he confronted a group of young men who were discussing the film *Free Solo*. Rudy recalls, "You could tell they were out of college and working but they didn't have families, they didn't have a bunch of disposable income, and they were climbing, and they were fit, young, strong people, and they were talking about how amazing this thing with Honnold was. The thing that tipped us off was them talking about 'What's gonna be next?'"

He and Jim Herson, a Yosemite veteran who also has kids that excel at climbing (in 2018, his fifteen-year-old son, Connor, free climbed the *Nose* of El Capitan in a day with his proud dad belaying), engaged the group, expressing the opinion that the film had glorified free soloing, even sought to influence others to think about it in terms of taking it to the next level. Rudy thinks that is terrifying. "You know, what he did, that is not necessarily something that should ever be upped, or will ever be upped," they told the younger climbers. "Maybe it will be upped, but it's going to take another person like Honnold, with that very unique circuitry to be able to do it. He is borderline at the limit of human performance to be able to keep it together on insecure hard climbing."

MATT ROBERTSON AND MAREN NELSON are the parents of two sons, Gavin and Brighton, both of whom climb at high levels and have been competing for a number of years. They're friends of the Ruanas, and the two families often climbed together when their kids were growing up. I'd climbed with Matt before and had even been scolded by him for free soloing.

"When *Free Solo* came out, the boys were old enough that they'd been hearing this message for a lot of years, and I don't think we even had to talk with them much about it," Maren told me. "Gavin has refused to see the movie." She explained, "He knows Alex survived, but he said it's just too stressful for him to watch that because he understands the objective danger that's there."

"Gavin had talked with Connor Herson about things like that and he was very aware of free soloing and what that meant," Matt added. "Neither one of them came away thinking 'Oooh, that's rad.' Both of them were like, 'Wow, that's pretty ballsy to do something like that.' They understand that it was a super-high-risk thing to do."

"One of the things which we've always talked with the boys about from the very beginning, and which their coaches have also emphasized, is safety," said Maren. "It doesn't matter whether you're in the gym, out in the mountains, climbing a mountain, on rock. The idea that you need to stay safe is built into the fundamentals of what we're doing with climbing."

"Both of them have bouldered some highball problems," Matt says. "They have [a] real good understanding about the risks that they're taking when they're doing something like that. And they're very measured in their approach to doing an unroped climb."

"I would also say, because of their skill and confidence, that they're probably more comfortable with free soloing than I'm comfortable with them doing it." He cites the time Gavin "scrambled" up to get to the base of a climb at Smith Rock when he was eleven or twelve, essentially free soloing a 5.4 pitch. "He just started climbing it," Matt says. "He didn't even think twice about it. And I just had my back turned because I was getting out the rope. . . . By the time I turned around he was already at the belay station up above me."

Both parents acknowledge that peer pressure could influence their kids to take unnecessary risks, not necessarily in the form of free soloing, but in the form of climbing an approach pitch unroped. Matt mentioned the story of a young rock climber who died while scrambling up to the base of a climb in France.

"Normally what people do because of the exposure is they clip in, and they go along their butt," Matt says. "A peer pressure attitude for high-level climbers would be 'We don't slip on stuff like this,' and she did, and she fell to her death." The family had a conversation around the dinner table that night, "Super-good climbers like this have accidents too," they told their boys.

"Peer pressure is definitely a concern," Maren added. "All you have to do is look at *Accidents in North American Climbing* and there's examples of people exceeding abilities, regardless of whether it's rock climbing, snow travel, hiking, scrambling, any of those types of things. If you get in over your head, a lot of times, that's because of peer pressure." She hasn't experienced peer pressure issues as much as Matt has. She thinks she knows why.

"They say that if you have more than two women in a party, you're more likely to not get caught in an avalanche because the women actually talk about and voice the concerns," she told me. "We're less concerned about being seen as weak or spoiling the fun, or for whatever reason." She is more likely to admit that she's not comfortable, she says, than the men seem to be. "So, I think that's definitely an issue. I just don't know that it's unique to rock climbing."

"I remember when both the boys were really little and we were just starting to climb outside," Matt says. Someone had mentioned something about free soloing, he explains, and both boys responded, "Oh, I'm never gonna free solo. I would never do that. Way too dangerous."

"We sat down and had a conversation immediately after that and I told them, no that's not true at all," Matt recalls. "Everybody free solos; you just free solo on different stuff. If you take it to absurd levels, we free solo when we walk out to get the mail."

They responded, "Well, that's not climbing."

"True, it's not, but if you're doing second- or third-class stuff, do you need to rope up on that?" Matt asked.

"Well, no."

"Okay, then you're free soloing."

"But that's easy."

"Exactly. So for 5.13 climbers, 5.8 is pretty easy."

The boys were looking at it from the perspective of "I can't possibly fall." That's a mistake, I told them. "You know, if I fall going out to get the mail, I bang up my knee. But if I fall because a hold breaks or I reach into a deep pocket that's full of yellow jackets, and I'm on a 5.8 without a rope, now the consequences are way, way more severe," Matt says.

I can sympathize with Matt's boys, listening to their dad explain the risks of free soloing. I was the recipient of one of Matt's lectures on the subject myself. We'd gone rock climbing together, roping up, clipping bolts, when in between climbs I'd wandered off and free soloed a 5.6. Matt had just had a close call in the mountains, when a slip on snow nearly sent him sliding over a cliff.

"When I came home from that, I really rethought what I wanted to do with climbing," Matt says. "At that point, Brighton and Gavin were really young, and I realized 'I've got kids; I should not be willing to take risks like that.'" Matt knew I had kids, too, and told me I was foolish for free soloing, even on an easy route. "I bet that's one of the things that caused me to say what I did to you," he says.

After listening to Matt's lecture, I told him I appreciated his concern for me. "No, I'm concerned about your kids, and I'm concerned about hauling you out," he said. "You're third on my priority list."

CHAPTER 23

How Could I Have Stopped You?

In the fall of 1986, a local TV show called *Front Runners* aired a segment that featured me climbing Castle Rock, a 600-foot granite cliff near Leavenworth, Washington. The program showcased up-and-coming athletes but with a Pacific Northwest bias for outdoor adventure sports like mountain biking, trail running, and mountain climbing.

I'd contacted them a few months earlier, hoping they could feature Hugh Herr, the amputee rock climber who was flying out from the East Coast to climb *City Park*, a 5.13d at Index Town Walls. They were interested but couldn't fit him into their schedule. "Could he come back in September?" they asked. "We could do it then." He couldn't, I told them; Hugh was scheduled to start classes at MIT in the fall.

"We'd love to do a climbing story," they said. "Do you know of any other climbers we might do a story on?" "Maybe," I told them. "How about a climber who climbs without ropes?" The show's producers thought that sounded great. We set a date in early September to film the segment. It was a perfect day.

We arrived early and hiked up to the base of the cliff. The film crew shot some B-roll first, then it was showtime. I tightened my laces, chalked up, and started climbing, swinging out over 300 feet of open air on a 5.8 I'd chosen because it wasn't that hard but would look badass. The film crew was kind of clueless about what I was doing. When I was halfway up the pitch, they asked me to downclimb so they could film a sequence again. I obliged. They asked me to climb the upper 300 feet of the wall three times so they could film me from below, the side, and above. No problem. They asked me if I could climb a particular wall because the light was good. There wasn't an actual route there, but I was able to traverse into a position they liked.

But when they asked me to wear a microphone and provide a running narrative of what was going through my mind as I climbed, I refused. "I need to focus on what I'm doing," I told them. "If I'm talking while I'm climbing, I could lose my concentration and fall off." They weren't happy about that, but gave in. They'd interview me when I got to the top then dub over the climbing footage.

I soloed the wall once, ran down the trail, and soloed it again while they filmed, then helped rig a rope for the cameraman to rappel down. He lowered himself carefully to a ledge 10 feet below the top and declared it far enough. I ran down the trail and waved up to signal I was ready. The cameraman waved back. I started climbing.

When I reached the top and sat down for an interview, I told them, "Before I start, I think about how dangerous it is, but once I'm on, I don't think about it at all. Everything's out of my mind except what I'm doing. And that's part of what's fun about climbing, the total commitment, the total concentration on what you're doing. Everything else just takes a back seat. You don't worry about when the rent's due . . . you're just climbing, concentrating entirely on what you're doing."

When the segment aired a few weeks later, I watched it with my mother, who was proud that her son was going to be on TV. I hadn't really told her what I was doing on TV, just that they'd filmed me climbing. She knew I went climbing nearly every weekend and took climbing trips every spring and summer, but aside from that she was fairly ignorant about what that entailed. She assumed I was climbing with other people, which for the most part I was. I didn't really talk to my mom about free soloing. I didn't want to worry her.

The host of *Front Runners*, a local weatherman named Steve Pool, broke the news to my mom. During the show's opening, he described me as "a guy on the way up." Then he said, "Every time he practices his hobby, he shakes hands with death." A concerned look came across my mom's face. "He *what*?" she seemed to be asking. It got worse.

"I don't think climbing unroped is as dangerous as people might see it," I said in the voiceover as I climbed alone and unroped nearly 600 feet above the highway. "The routes I climb unroped are usually not so hard that I would be afraid of falling. Sometimes they are. Sometimes I get a little crazy and do something I shouldn't," I admitted at the end of the segment. I was being shown on the wall from far below, a tiny speck clinging impossibly far above the shadows. "But so far I've come out of it okay."

"Well," I said to my mom when a commercial came on, "what did you think?" The shock was written all over her face.

"You *do* that?" she asked, wide eyed. "You climb *without a rope*?"

"Yeah," I said. "I've been doing it for years."

"Are you *crazy*?" she asked.

I wish I could have talked to my mom while writing this book, to ask her how she felt learning via a TV show that her only son risked his life climbing rocks without a rope. Unfortunately, she passed away in 2013. So, I turned to the next best person I could think of, someone else who might understand what my mom had felt: Alex Honnold's mom.

"Well, it wasn't quite as black and white as your mom's experience," Dierdre Wolownick told me about the first time she saw film of her son free soloing. "I had seen photos of him in magazines . . . but my brain didn't really process what the photos meant. But the first time I actually watched a video of a free solo that he did . . . you know the name *Moonlight Buttress*? *Moonlight Buttress* is a horribly scary thing to watch."

Honnold had free soloed *Moonlight Buttress*, an 800-foot route in Zion rated 5.12d, on April 1, 2008. He told only a few friends who thought it must be an April Fools' joke. Later he went back and free soloed several pitches for the camera. When the footage was shown as part of the *Reel Rock* film tour later that year, people realized it was not a joke.

"It's terrifying to watch, for anybody, and it still is for me today," Wolownick says. "There are two climbs of his that I have trouble watching, and that's one of them. And that's the first one I watched. And I watched it in public."

Wolownick had attended a film festival in Nevada City that year with her son. When Honnold went up to the podium to receive an award, they showed the film. She watched quietly, trying to maintain her composure.

"One of the ladies sitting in front of me turned around during the movie and stage whispered to her friend right next to me, 'How would you like to be that kid's mother?'" Wolownick recalls. "I'll never forget that. And so, I told them that I was his mother . . . they were both mothers, you know."

Watching it in a crowded room wasn't easy. "I had to kind of keep it together," she recalls. "I turned it all off at the beginning. My brain didn't really allow me to process what free soloing was. I kept saying to myself, 'Nah, I must be understanding this wrong.'" Then she saw the movie and started thinking, "Huh? Huh? . . . Okay, I've got to figure this out."

"That was just like the beginning of the process," she continued. "It took years to really come to terms with what he does and how I deal with it. So, I really felt for your poor mother. That was not the way to do it. That was not the way to introduce her to what you do."

During my interview, Wolownick turned the tables and started asking me about my mother, what she knew about my climbing, and what she would say when I left to go climbing.

"All along, I'd say 'I'm going climbing,'" I told her. "She'd say, 'Okay, be safe.' But after she saw me free soloing on TV, she was like, 'What? *That's* what you do?'"

"And what did she say after that?" Wolownick asked me.

"Well," I answered, "she said, 'You shouldn't do that. You're going to fall off. You're going to die.'"

"But in the ensuing months and years, did she get on your case about it?" Wolownick asked.

"No," I said, "but I think when she said 'Be safe' it was with a little more urgency."

"Ha!" Wolownick said. "A *lot* more."

Wolownick has seen a lot of films now of her son free soloing, including *Free Solo*, which she's seen many times. The first time she watched it, her feeling was not the same as when she saw *Alone on the Wall*, the film that featured Honnold's climb of *Moonlight Buttress*, although there were similarities.

"I was in a crowd, and I had to take control," she says. "It was really hard to watch." She knew he was fine, that he'd survived; he was sitting there with everyone. "But that doesn't change the experience at all because your mind flashes to 'What if . . . What could have . . .'"

"I've conditioned myself to not react viscerally, if you will, to watch these free solos," she says. "It still makes my innards clench, and it makes my heart

race, but it probably always will because we all know the god-awful consequences, you know? It's a constant battle, but so far, I've managed to win it."

In her book, *The Sharp End of Life*, Wolownick wrote about her first multipitch climb. Although she was securely anchored to the rock wall, she was
still scared. Then two climbers suddenly appeared and free soloed past her.

"I'll never forget that," she told me. "They free soloed right past me. . . . I
was climbing with Alex that day and . . . and all of a sudden, I turned around
and there's this guy, not attached to anything, not wearing a harness even. I
was like, 'Holy . . . !'" She grabbed on harder and said, "Go ahead! Just don't
fall on me."

"Good thing their mothers can't see them," she remembers thinking.
"When I said that, I was thinking of your average mother who doesn't know
anything about climbing," she told me. "Most mothers could not deal with that
as level-headedly, if you put it that way, as I have learned to do," she added. "But
it took years to get to this point. It wasn't a sudden thing. I remember thinking
that. Yeah, most mothers are not trained year after year to deal with this."

Although she's learned to deal with her feelings about watching her son free
solo on film, it is only because she watches these films with him sitting beside
her, and she knows he's okay. Watching him in real time would be different.

"I've never watched him free solo," Wolownick says. "He doesn't want me
to know beforehand. We've never talked about it, but he's always made that
decision and I've always appreciated it."

In her book, Wolownick wrote that, as a mom, her main job had been
to anticipate all the bad things that could happen to her kids and protect
against them, a response she had to turn off to be able to deal with the idea
of Honnold free soloing, although she concedes she can't really turn it off,
not completely.

"You can't turn it off if you're a mother," she says. "That's who you are; it's
what you are. But you can teach yourself little by little to not let it show."

Like my mother, Wolownick's first reaction to hearing that her son had
free soloed Half Dome was, "That's crazy!" She didn't mean crazy, she says—
not exactly.

IN 2018, ALEX HONNOLD LED his mom up the *Nose* of El Capitan. (They
climbed El Cap again in 2021 to celebrate her seventieth birthday.) Wolownick

trained, practiced jumaring, got into shape; she didn't want to be the reason they got stuck on the route after dark. She and Honnold made relatively quick work of the climb, with him leading and her jumaring up each pitch after him. The experience of climbing El Capitan herself allowed her to begin to understand what free soloing the wall had meant to her son, and what it had required for him to do it.

"First, total commitment," she says, "110 percent commitment. Second, intense training. . . . And the third thing, which is the most important, is complete mind control. And that's what Alex excels at, and most other people don't." A lot of climbers have the commitment and training—the desire and physical ability—to free solo a route like *Freerider*, Wolownick believes, but they don't have the main ingredient—the ability to focus so intently, to completely control their minds, and be able to squeeze all sense of fear and doubt out of the equation and actually do it. "And I think you have to be born that way. I don't think you can learn that."

It isn't a real surprise to Wolownick that Honnold didn't tell her before he free soloed El Capitan. She's never talked with him about free soloing on anything more than a superficial level, and she doesn't think she'd want to. "I don't want to add to the press deluge," she continues. "He gets requests every day to talk about this, you know."

"I don't want to put him in the position of having to defend who he is," she adds. "He is the person he is, and that person seeks perfection and gets immense satisfaction from the challenge of that. And that's enough. I love who he is; I understand who he is, and I don't need him to defend it for me, you know?"

In the film, Wolownick says she would be happy if Honnold didn't free solo, but she won't say she's unhappy that he does. "It's an integral part of him and a part that gives him the most joy, and the most satisfaction, the high that everybody seeks out there," she says. "It's what completes him as a human being, if you will. How can you deny your child the most profound part of what completes him? So, I've made my peace with it."

NOT ALL MOTHERS ARE LIKE my mother or Alex Honnold's mom. Some moms, like Rowena Fletcher-Wood, who were already climbers before they had kids, seem to have a different view. Fletcher-Wood isn't discouraging her daughter, Robin, from climbing onto the roof; she's taking her up there herself.

"I've already taken my five-month-old out with us when we're climbing," Fletcher-Wood told me. "I've climbed onto the roof of our house and our neighbor's shed 'babywearing' with a sling. You can't conceal something like climbing from them—their exposure to their parents' addiction is inevitable."

Fletcher-Wood, who's originally from Sheffield, England, grew up walking in the Peak District and doing what she describes as "weaseling on the grit." "I come from a single-parent family," she told me. "Although my mum was never interested in sport and didn't encourage me in it, I fell in love with the outdoors, the rocks, the heather, and the turbulent and unpredictable fogs."

She did her first rappel at age five with Woodcraft Folk, an organization that fosters growth and learning for children, and later did some climbing with the Scouts, which got her interested in it. Her school math department ran a climbing club for a short time, until the teacher leading the program got pregnant. It wasn't until she went to university that she had the opportunity to climb regularly. She became so keen on climbing that when she found out her boyfriend (now husband) used to climb, she insisted that he get back into it. Even her pregnancy didn't stop her climbing; in fact, she climbed up to thirty-nine weeks before finally taking a break.

"I grant a lot of credit for the healthy pregnancy and delivery to fitness," Fletcher-Wood says, "and the role climbing played in my physical and mental well-being, not only preparing my body, but also teaching me focus, concentration, breathing, and being in the moment, which are amazing techniques for managing pain."

She was back climbing soon after her daughter was born and is not hesitant about introducing her daughter or any future children to the sport. "I like to feel that I would imbue common sense and good safety assessment skills in my daughter," she says. "It's tempting as a parent to teach your children what you want them to be or do, but you can only really teach them how to think and problem solve."

"I've made it my career to teach people how to think and learn," she adds, "so I'm optimistic that if my daughter decides to climb and even free solo she will ease into it slowly, learn skills from the people around her, and make sure she is kick-ass awesome at it before she takes those chances."

MOST OF THE PARENTS I talked to while writing this book were unwilling to intrude too much on their children's experience. They know if their kids are doing something like free soloing, unless they're doing it for dumb reasons, that it's what makes them feel alive. These parents felt they couldn't really say, "you can't ever do that; I forbid you to do that," because, for one, it wouldn't have any effect (their kids would do it anyway because they're kids), and two, they just couldn't take away something that gives their kids so much joy, even if they know it might harm them. This is especially true of parents who used to free solo themselves—like Sharon Wood and August Welch—as well as my dad.

"I have a thirty-year-old son now, Hank," Wood told me. "He discovered soloing in his early twenties, and it terrified me, because I knew exactly what he'd discovered, and what hooked him, right? And he would go off and solo hard things, on the sea cliffs near Vancouver and Mount Assiniboine, and around Canmore, and I just felt helpless to stop where he was going."

Wood was concerned about her son soloing because she knew how good it felt and how addictive it could be. She felt helpless to say anything to Hank because she used to solo herself. "He calls me a hypocrite, right?" she says. "As soon as I open my mouth to say anything, he says, 'You can't, Mom; I know your story.'"

Wood first found out her son was soloing after he'd climbed Mount Assiniboine, the highest mountain in Banff National Park, which has easy but loose Class 5 rock climbing. Hank had secretly headed off on his bike at midnight, ridden to the trailhead, summited the peak by five in the morning, and ridden home. He didn't tell his mom for some time, but eventually did. "It was such a highlight for him," Wood says. Then she discovered he'd done other solo climbs and didn't know quite how to respond.

"It's funny. I thought I was out of the woods because neither one of my kids liked alpine climbing, right? But both of them got into sport climbing in their late teens, when it became the cool thing to do, and their friends were doing it," she recalls. "So, I guess I felt this sense of resignation and dread, and paradoxically also some . . . not pride, but a sense of, oh, he knows what that's like, he's found that joy."

"It's kind of strange," she admits. "It wasn't cut and dry for me, my reaction."

Although she knows her son's motives for soloing were personal, Wood has concerns about others who might be solo climbing for the wrong reasons, because of social media or the fear of missing out. "The place where I would draw the line is when it comes to social media, or who do you have to tell? Who do you want to know about this?" she says.

I think social media has brought in some dangerous investors to what I think is a pretty pure practice," she adds. "As soon as you invite anybody else into this thing that you're doing, it mars the purity of it. It's almost like you're inviting an investor that's going to compromise your motives or your decisions."

She wonders what's motivating the need to share. "Are you doing it for your ego? Are you doing it for money?" she asks. "People are going to treat you differently, right? They're going to respect you more, you're going to climb a few notches up the ladder, towards being the alpha dog or the alpha climber, and you're going to get this respect.

"I just think that's not the right reason to be doing it," she says. "And I think it's dangerous."

She also worries that the proliferation of risky climbing, including free soloing, on social media is, in a sense, immoral. "It's a bit hardass, I know, but it's sad," she says. "But if they're doing it for a living, if they're doing it for social media, if they're doing it for their ego, then that's where the morality comes in for me." She doesn't think that's right. "I think that you have a social responsibility to not entice young warriors to do that themselves to become the next Alex Honnold."

"I hope these young guys who want to be the next Alex Honnold know that they're never going to have a mind like Alex Honnold. There's a lot of young warriors out there that don't have that mind and don't have that experience," she adds, "and won't have that experience, but want to be the top dog. And it's going to hurt a lot of people."

Fortunately, her son, Hank, wasn't interested in that. "He didn't tell anybody. He wasn't doing it for his ego; he was doing it for that state of mind. I can't argue with that. . . . He's alive now and he's over it, he says," she adds, clearly relieved to have dodged that bullet, although the way she says "he says" betrays a lingering unease.

FATHERS DON'T SEEM TO ALWAYS share the same feelings as mothers when it comes to their children taking risks. Mark Synnott's father didn't seem too concerned when he dropped off his son and his friend, Jeff Chapman, both fifteen, at the base of Cathedral Ledge one day. As Synnott tells the story, he and Chapman were standing there with a utility rope, planning to climb the 500-foot granite cliff, when Synnott's dad asked, "Hey, what are you guys planning to do here?" "Nothing much," they assured him. As Synnott wrote in *The Impossible Climb*, "My dad gave the scene a good hard look, then delivered the wood-paneled door two hard slaps. 'Okay,' he said. 'You boys have fun.'"

Hearing Synnott tell the story made me think of the day my dad wandered up the road and caught me and my little brother, David, dangling from a yellow utility rope halfway up the side of a cliff. "What are you fellas up to?" he'd asked us, a rhetorical question since he could see precisely what we were up to. Instead of freaking out like my stepmother would have done, he'd offered to belay.

When I asked him about coming upon that scene, he laughed. "When I saw you up there, I thought you weren't up so high that you could get paralyzed or killed if you fell off," he remembered. "Maybe I was wrong. But you went for the rocks. Whatever it was, you were climbing it. It was apparent you were really serious about it. You were taking risks but being safe. You were learning, challenging yourself."

My dad's reaction to watching me free solo on TV was also different than my mom's—quite different.

"I thought it was cool," he told me. "It made a good story. The way they filmed it, and the way you were climbing, I thought maybe you were just a few feet off the ground, and they were trying to make it look high up."

"The wall was actually 600 feet high," I assured him. "I was way off the ground."

"*Holy macaroni!*" he said. "Geez. I guess it would have bothered me a lot more if I had known that."

Despite the revelation that I'd been climbing far above the ground during filming, he still wasn't all that bothered.

"It's your life," he said. "You knew what you wanted and what you were doing. It wouldn't have done any good to say 'Don't do that! Are you crazy?!' It wouldn't have been fair to say you can't do that just because I couldn't understand it," he told me. "You'd done enough climbing and were smart enough that I knew you weren't going to go out and get killed. At least, I didn't think so."

"How could I have stopped you anyway?" he wondered. "It would be like trying to convince someone to stop smoking. They're not going to do it. In fact, with kids, if you tell them not to do something, they'll just go do it," he added. "So, tell you to quit climbing because it's dangerous? *Come on!*"

He continued, "You had enough brains to figure out if it was too hard or too high up. You weren't going to go out and say, 'Oh, well!' and climb something stupid. You knew when to back off."

I'M NOT AS TRUSTING AS my dad was. While working on a rock-climbing guidebook one summer, I took my son, Loren, age nine, along. A popular hiking trail coincidentally passed close to a popular rock-climbing crag, a perfect opportunity for some father-son time. We could go for a hike and make a stop at the climb, where I could scramble up to take photos, count bolts, and draw the topography of the cliff. It would take five minutes, and we could continue up the trail.

A climbers' trail forked off and led to a broad, flat ledge at the base of the cliff. From there, a Class 3 traverse led to another ledge where several new sport routes had been developed. It wasn't difficult climbing, but it was exposed. A handful of climbers had slipped off and been injured, and quite a few dogs had fallen off the ledge and died.

"You wait here," I told Loren. "It will only take a minute. I'll be right back."

"Okay," he said.

I traversed the ledge to the upper part of the cliff and busied myself with guidebook work, hurrying to take a few photos and hastily sketch the cliff outline and bolt locations—not wanting to leave Loren alone too long. Once I'd finished, I tucked my camera and notepad into my rucksack and started down. And there was Loren, halfway across the traverse.

"*Stop!*" I yelled. "*What are you doing?*"

"Coming to find you," he said, looking up at me, clinging casually to the rock 30 feet above the boulders below.

"Wait there," I said, and hurried across to where he was to help guide him back to the ledge. It was a useless gesture; he didn't need my help. He moved confidently across the traverse and arrived safely back on the ledge.

"I told you to stay here," I said. "Why didn't you wait for me?"

"You were taking too long," Loren said. "I got scared."

"You scared the heck out of me," I told him. "It's dangerous out there. You could have fallen and gotten hurt. Even killed. Your mom would kill me if something happened to you. Didn't you think about that?"

"No," he said.

"Weren't you scared?"

"No."

I felt a surge of pride in that moment—my kid was badass—but it wasn't strong enough to overcome my sense of panic and fear, which I expressed as anger.

"I'm never taking you climbing again," I told him. "You don't respect the rock."

It was a lie, of course. I took Loren climbing again, but he never became very interested in it. And honestly, I don't mind. If he liked climbing, he might have turned out like me.

PART V

We'll Quit When
We're Dead

*Between clinging and letting go, I feel a terrific struggle. This
is a fine chance to let go, to "win life by losing it," which means
not recklessness but acceptance, not passivity but nonattach-
ment. If given the chance to turn back, I would not take it.
Therefore the decision to go ahead is my own responsibility,
to be accepted with a whole heart.*
—Peter Matthiessen, *The Snow Leopard*

The night before a friend's wedding in Leavenworth, Washington, I got
the twitch. Looking up at the mountains in the evening light, I realized
there was still time to get in a climb. I was married then, and my wife
sensed my restlessness. "Go ahead," she said.

I drove up the canyon road and hiked quickly to the base of a
100-foot-high buttress. The area had been overflowing with climbers
earlier in the day, but now, with darkness falling and the katabatic winds
howling, it was empty. I put on my rock shoes, chalked up, and started
climbing, linking crack systems up the buttress, my hair and T-shirt
blowing wildly in the wind. Several times a sudden gust threatened to
blow me off the wall; I tightened my grip and held on.

John Bachar free soloing Shithooks (5.10b), *Tuolumne Meadows, Yosemite* (Photo by
Phil Bard)

The next day, after the ceremony, my wife wanted to visit the faux-Bavarian shops in town. "You can do the tourist thing," I told her. "Just drop me off somewhere." She drove me to the nearest cliff and told me she'd be back in about an hour.

I ran up to the base of the wall and started climbing. A hundred feet off the ground, as I picked my way across a delicate traverse, I encountered two climbers rappelling down the wall. They gave me a concerned look. "Do you want to tie in?" they asked. "No thanks," I said. "This isn't very hard." I passed them on the ledge and continued to the top, down-climbed off the back, and hurried to the base of the cliff to climb again.

I'd climbed several pitches, over 1000 feet of rock, which must have taken an hour, I guessed. Sure enough, I looked down and saw the car pull up. I finished my climb, changed into my trail shoes, and dashed down the switchbacks.

"What were you doing up there?" my wife asked in a mildly accusatory tone.

"Nothing," I said, amused that she didn't seem a bit concerned that I'd been climbing without a rope hundreds of feet off the ground for more than an hour, only miffed that I'd interrupted her shopping. "Just climbing."

CHAPTER 24

Broken Promises

Dave MacLeod started climbing at Dumbarton Rock, a basalt crag near Glasgow, Scotland, in 1993, at age fifteen. He worked his way quickly through the area's boulder problems and, within three years, was climbing new routes rated as hard as E7 (5.13) and repeating many of the hardest routes in Scotland and the Peak District. MacLeod studied sport science, which he applied to his training for climbing. He improved quickly. By 2002, he had established Scotland's first E9 route and was on-sighting E7s. Like other climbers, MacLeod had experimented with soloing, but a bad accident while soloing an E8 on gritstone in England, when he was nineteen, put him off soloing for a long time. His decision was also influenced by his wife, Claire, who'd asked him to stop free soloing.

"I agreed with Claire to stick to roped climbing in an effort to limit my exposure to risk a bit," MacLeod told me. "I was quite happy with this and from my point of view it made sense. Breaking holds is one thing," he added, "but I was starting to realize that I was not really experienced enough to make good judgments in climbing and given my eagerness to push my limits, some sort of external brake with an arbitrary rule was probably a good idea."

MacLeod didn't stick to his self-imposed no-soloing rule religiously. He bent the rules, including with the 8b (5.13d) route called *Hurlyburly* he'd established at Newtyle Quarry in central Scotland in 2003, which he returned to free solo in 2005. "I was really solid on it on redpoint and just decided to solo it," he said. "I was particularly jealous of Alex Huber's solo of *Brandler Hasse* in the Dolomites. The pictures had my eyes on stalks and, having climbed on the same face before, I pictured myself up there."

He had promised Claire he wouldn't free solo, but he asked if he could free solo *Hurlyburly* anyway. "Surprisingly for him and probably more surprising to me, I agreed," Claire wrote in her blog. "He must have caught me in a really good mood." Not only that, she also agreed to belay him while he climbed the route again to dial it in, and eventually filmed him when he free soloed it. What MacLeod didn't tell his wife was that, despite his expressed confidence in his ability to free solo the route, he was having doubts.

A few days later, MacLeod and Claire arrived at Newtyle Quarry. MacLeod's plan wasn't to free solo the route straight off; instead, he would climb the route a few times and see how he felt. On his first go, he climbed the route and lowered to the ground.

"I think I'll try and redpoint it again," he said, stalling. "That'll be good for today."

"Why bother?" Claire said. "You know you're going to do it, don't you? Why bother with the rope? You might as well just finish it now."

"One half of me couldn't believe what my wife was saying!" MacLeod recalled. "To the other half, the words reinforced what I was feeling myself but was too scared to act upon."

He took a deep breath and removed his harness, then stood quietly below the route for a few minutes, emptying his head. Claire picked up a video camera and switched it on. MacLeod chalked up and pulled onto the rock.

DESPITE HIS SUCCESS ON *HURLYBURLY*, free soloing didn't go to MacLeod's head. At least, not too much. His promise not to free solo still held, but he conceded his self-imposed rules were arbitrary. The routes he was working on tended to have long runouts on difficult terrain with poor protection. The consequences of a fall on these were serious, sometimes deadly. MacLeod had already taken several long falls on *Rhapsody*, a technically difficult route he established by linking the hardest sections of other routes directly up the Requiem Wall at Dumbarton Rock, which, at E11 7a (5.14c), was the hardest trad route in Scotland at the time. Some of those falls had been 70 feet, with only a thin brass nut slotted in a crack to save him from falling to his death.

His next project was a hard, desperately runout climb on Ben Nevis's Tower Ridge called *Echo Wall*. The second pitch of the route climbed a 230-foot arête that had barely any natural protection, and what it did have would be difficult to place given the sustained, technical nature of the climbing. He'd been working on it ever since he'd completed *Rhapsody*, including spending eight days in 2006 trying to toprope it, eventually returning after he'd advanced to climbing 5.14d.

On many sport climbs, the first bolt might be 20 or more feet off the ground. Unless you clip it with a cheat stick, you're risking a ground fall until you've soloed up to the first bolt. And there are sometimes long runouts between bolts where, if you blew the clip and your belayer wasn't paying attention, you could deck. The prospect of a long, dangerous fall is amplified on a trad climb, when you're placing your own gear where the rock allows it, which is sometimes far apart in insecure placements. Ground-fall runouts are part of the trad-climbing game, and if your gear isn't good, it's likely to pull out and send you plummeting.

And so, claiming he needed to solo something hard to get his mind prepared for leading Echo Wall, MacLeod decided to solo *Darwin Dixit*, an 8c (5.14b), with his wife there to film it.

SOLOING A ROUTE RATED 8C was barely thinkable, although in 2004 Alexander Huber had come close. Huber, who, with his brother, Thomas, had made the first ascent of the *Freerider* route on El Capitan in 1998, was already an accomplished free soloist. In 2002, he'd free soloed *Brandler-Hasse Direttissima*, a 1500-foot 7c (5.12a) route on the Cima Grande, and in 2003, he'd free soloed an 8b (5.13d) route called *Opportunist*, the hardest free-solo climb yet done at that time. The next year, he upped the game.

One April morning, he hiked up to Schleierwasserfall in Austria, intending to free solo *Kommunist*, an overhanging 70-foot face route rated 8b+ (5.14a). Pleased to have the crag to himself, Huber did some bouldering as a warmup. As he prepared for the climb, a hiker arrived, breaking the solitude. Instead of abandoning his attempt, Huber recruited the hiker to film him. He handed the video camera he'd brought to record himself to the hiker to keep him occupied, Huber said, so he wouldn't break the spell.

When Huber was mentally prepared, he started climbing, moving up the first half of the route quickly and easily. Twenty feet off the ground, he paused, chalked up, and then launched into the crux, a technical sequence above a large boulder that made falling off "unthinkable" according to Huber. "Three finger pocket, two finger pocket, undercling, crimp—it's only a couple moves, the decisive five meters," Huber wrote on the Huberbuam website, describing the sequence. "The long reaches require powerful climbing, there is no room for thought—and no memory of any thought remains." Once past the crux, Huber rested again, then continued climbing, making quick work of the 5.12d moves to the top.

"I was consciously searching for the limit in what I could achieve in climbing," Huber wrote about his decision to free solo *Kommunist*. "I knew that by free soloing the *Opportunist*, I had not yet reached the limit." Just thirty-six years old, he was already feeling pressure to push hard while he still could. "I knew that I only had a short time left to reach the apex," he wrote. "I obviously was not getting younger."

Huber's motive in free soloing *Kommunist* may have been similar to MacLeod's in soloing *Darwin Dixit*: he was mentally training for something bigger. Huber had designs on free soloing El Capitan. In fact, he went to California in 2004 with that goal firmly in mind. However, he realized it would take a huge commitment to pull it off, including years of living in Yosemite, going up on the wall, practicing the moves, wiring each pitch, until he felt confident to put them all together. He couldn't afford it, and so he abandoned the idea.

Huber conceded that at the time of his free solo of *Kommunist*, his climbing ability was not much higher than 5.14a, and that his margin for error was extremely thin.

MACLEOD WAS ALSO SEARCHING FOR his limit. He was aware that, if he pulled it off, his free solo of *Darwin Dixit* would be the hardest free solo yet done. He wasn't egotistical about it, though. Doing the most demanding free solo ever wasn't his goal. He was doing it to develop the focus and mental control he would need to climb even harder routes that would involve potentially long falls.

Even though it was rated 8c, a grade no one had ever free soloed before, and despite his promise to Claire, MacLeod kept thinking of the crux of *Darwin Dixit*. "I remember thinking as I was doing the move, 'I could be soloing here.'" The thought stuck in his mind. Just like on *Hurlyburly*, instead of climbing it again to dial it in, he decided to just do it right then. "I didn't want to over practice it," he wrote afterward in his blog, "to make sure I felt fresh on the solo."

He didn't ask Claire this time, but he told her he needed to do it as training for the hard route on the Ben. Claire didn't say no.

The Laboratori wall at Margalef swells outward in a sweeping curve like the underside of a clamshell strafed with bullet holes. The routes are short but powerful, climbing out of the cave at the base of the cliff following bolts that define the imaginary lines connecting flakes, edges, and solution pockets in the hard limestone. In the film, MacLeod spends several minutes mentally preparing, visualizing before he starts climbing. He does the initial moves with his feet dangling, pulling himself up the tiny holds using arm strength alone, then sets his feet on the rock and extends almost horizontally along a flake, clinging to small edges, toes edging to maintain balance, or sometimes cutting loose and hooking in pockets. Then comes the first all-or-nothing move, a deadpoint lunge to a flake beyond reach; he has to throw for it, but in a balanced way.

MacLeod catches the hold with his right hand and his feet come loose and swing. He then does a dead hang from his right hand, sets his feet on the barest of edges, and pulls through with his left hand to a solution hole that accepts only his middle finger up to the middle joint. He stuffs it in until it's locked in the hole, then pulls up, grimacing. Two fingers of his right hand fit in the next pocket, but only about an inch. Clinging to the overhanging limestone by three fingers, MacLeod brings his left foot up to a hold and then reaches far to the left for another pocket. He looks solid now, reaching right to a slot, then bringing his left hand up to what counts as a huge hold, a pocket that he can get three fingers into. From there, it's relatively easy.

When he reaches the ledge at the end of the route, he stands there, breathing, looking out into space and then down at the route, something like a dazed grin on his face. By the time he's scrambled down and is walking back to the base of the route, the dazed look is gone. He's grinning now, full on.

"I feel in my head I could do 8c, to put it in control, knowing I wasn't going to fall," MacLeod explains at the end of the film. "I wanted to test that, soloing, that was the idea. I think it worked. I feel like I had a little bit of control in there."

"It's a bit extreme, is it not?" Claire asks, off camera.

"A bit extreme way to test it?" MacLeod asks.

"Uh-huh," Claire answers.

"Well," MacLeod says, smiling and looking up at the route. "Got to."

"Watching him solo this, I was surprisingly unemotional about it," Claire revealed on her blog after Dave's 8c free solo. "Maybe it was because I was detached from what was going on as I was watching it on a screen." She shares that she has unwavering confidence in him, "If he tells me that he thinks he can do this, then I have to believe him. He's been right so far, after all."

CHAPTER 25

The Largeness of the Price

There's a photo on the Mountain Project website of Michael Reardon free solo-ing a route called *Potholes* at Stoney Point, a popular bouldering area in South-ern California that has a few steep sandstone cliffs high enough for toproping and lead climbing. The photo of Reardon is a hero shot; he's striking a pose near the top of the route, leaning back, arms extended, long hair flowing, as he climbs through the crux, "the moment of truth" move according to the route description, "which, surprisingly, can be finessed rather than brute forced."

Because it's only 50 feet high and a "mere" 5.9, *Potholes* is a popular free solo, and the photo of Reardon no doubt adds to its attraction. But the route is also awkward and leans back. From Reardon's photo, it's clear that if you were to fall off from where he is clinging, you'd land on a hard, flat rock.

A longtime fixture of the Southern California climbing scene, Michael Flood grew up with his parents and older sister in the West Hills area of Los Angeles County. Flood started climbing for real as a teenager in the mid-seventies with his middle-school classmate, David Katz, and never stopped. In 1973, the pair, then thirteen years old, rode the bus to Point Dume, a sea cliff near Malibu, and made the first ascent of a 5.8 up the middle of the main slab, placing three protection bolts. Over the next forty-plus years, Flood pioneered many new routes throughout the state, even making a solo ascent of the *Nose* on El Cap. He also spent a lot of time bouldering and climbing at Stoney Point, a sandstone outcrop near his home in Woodland Hills.

Three days after his fifty-eighth birthday, Flood decided to go to Stoney Point to climb. It was a sunny day in the low eighties, a little windy but good weather for bouldering. He went alone, which was not unusual—after decades of climbing at Stoney Point, he was considered a regular. He hadn't been climbing in a while but felt confident enough to free solo *Potholes*, a route he'd soloed many times.

One of the climbers there reported seeing Flood struggling near the top of the route, at the last big pothole about 40 feet above the ground. He ran around some bushes trying to get to the base of the route to spot Flood in case he fell, but it was too late. He heard a thud and arrived to find Flood lying unconscious on a rock. Other climbers rushed to the scene to help while someone called 911. Medics arrived and airlifted him to nearby Northridge Hospital.

Flood arrived at the hospital in critical condition. As his sister, Leslie, reported on Facebook that day, he had "bleeding on the brain, a fractured spine and other broken bones, bleeding in his gut, etc." By the end of the first week, he'd had multiple surgeries to control internal bleeding and remove necrosis. After a roller coaster of improvements and setbacks, Flood was upgraded to stable condition and got out of the ICU.

Flood's daughter, Miranda, had left to do her medical residency at the University of Tennessee the week before his accident. Flood was also estranged from his wife. Neither of his parents were living. After the accident it fell to Leslie to assume the role of sole caretaker.

When I heard about Flood's accident, it hit close to home. I was just a few weeks older than him and still climbed and sometimes free soloed. As I read the details of his injuries, and listened to what his sister, Leslie, told me, I imagined a grim picture. *So this is what happens,* I thought. For Leslie Flood, it was something she had never even imagined and thrust her into a role she was unprepared to assume.

"He does wake up," Leslie told me over the phone a few weeks after his accident. "He will open his eyes, he will track people with his eyes, but when they do the formal commands like, 'Michael, open your eyes really wide,' or 'squeeze my hand,' he's not responding to those.

"I never really paid attention to Mike's climbing," she continued. "I had no idea of his reputation." One of Mike's friends made a comment about free soloing, explaining how it is a personal choice, but she doesn't know or understand the logic behind that. "It's so dangerous," she says. "As time has progressed since his accident, my feeling is that I understand why people graduate to that, but at the same time, there is always this danger, always . . . anything could happen.

"If he gets into the condition where he can climb again, is it fair for me to say, 'I don't want you doing this'?" she wonders. "How can I tell him that? If he chooses to do that, then it's his choice, and I can't take away what he loves."

"If he wants to do that, then it's his choice to do that," she concedes. "But I also know this side of it: the pain, the stress. I'm dealing with the hospital and all of his bills, I'm taking care of his house. I'm trying to figure out whether I need legal advice . . . and I'm alone in this."

"And my own stuff is . . . " Leslie pauses, as if trying to conjure up an image of the long-lost world of life before Mike's accident. "My own stuff?" she continues. "I'm not even looking or thinking about it, you know?"

When I talked with Mike Flood more than a year after his accident, he told he had been completely comatose for thirty days. He had had ten surgeries but had recovered—mostly. "I was very fortunate to live through it," he said. "I'm kind of a miracle case."

His surgeon saved his life several times, he says, but Flood injured one of his feet so badly it had to be amputated. "It is what it is," he told me. "I've had to recover my life several times over. I have wonderful support from my new wife and my sister, and from the climbing community."

Although he has some lingering memory issues from his accident, he remembers that day well. He'd found himself with a couple of hours to kill, and had his rock shoes and chalk bag, so he drove over to Stoney Point and started climbing. It was no big deal, he thought. He'd been climbing there since his early days, when John Yablonsky was his mentor and they'd spent hours there bouldering, soloing, and training for the big walls they aspired to climb. He knew all the routes and was confident in his ability, even though he hadn't been climbing in a while and was a little out of shape.

"Stoney Point *is* a very delicate place to climb because holds break," he told me. There was speculation that a hold may have broken or that a wind gust caught him and caused him to fall. But he says he fell because of a mental error. "I was showing off," he says. "A couple of people came up behind me, and the next thing I knew my foot slipped and I couldn't recover." He pushed himself away from the rock, hoping to avoid a bad landing, but pushed too hard and landed in some boulders.

"I always tell my students 'don't show off,'" he says. "I broke my own rule. I'm disappointed in myself, but I have a new life now."

Despite his injuries and setbacks, Flood is remarkably upbeat. He fell, he lived, and life goes on. He's not letting it get him down. A CNC machinist by trade with research and development experience, he's already thinking about designing a prosthetic foot that's adapted to his style of climbing.

JOSHUA OURADA WAS INTRODUCED TO climbing in his early twenties while serving in the US Marines at Camp Pendleton. "I was quickly consumed by climbing and knew that it was something I wanted to do for the rest of my life," he told me. After his discharge, Ourada moved to San Jose so he could continue climbing, starting out bouldering and working his way up to leading 5.12. By age thirty-two, he had completed an ascent of El Capitan. Climbing unroped had become second nature to him, so even when he began climbing longer routes—traditional free climbs and big walls—using ropes and protection, he still felt comfortable free soloing easier routes when the mood struck him.

One Sunday morning in April 2021, Joshua Ourada decided to free solo *The Nutcracker Suite*, a 500-foot 5.8 in Yosemite. The route is one of the most popular free climbs in the Valley because of its short approach, moderate difficulty, and airy climbing up clean granite cracks that are at a relatively low angle. These qualities also make it a very popular free-solo climb.

Ourada had free soloed *The Nutcracker Suite* before—even at night, using a headlamp—and had no difficulty. He felt comfortable with his choice to free solo that morning, cruising up to a boulder-strewn ledge at the top of the second pitch. There he encountered other climbers, but after asking and receiving permission to continue above them, he continued up the wall, following a long, narrow crack up the steep slab. About a rope length above the ledge, some 400 feet off the ground, the slab briefly reared back to vertical at a bulge. It's an exposed spot, but relatively secure. Ourada had his hands jammed in the crack, his feet firmly on holds, and was moving confidently upward.

And then, suddenly, he wasn't. One second he was cruising up the crack, the next he was falling. He doesn't remember exactly what was going through his mind at that moment, other than "Fuck, this is happening and I need to do whatever I can *not* to die." After a short free fall, he hit the wall below him, a steep slab, and started sliding downward. He had flipped around into a sliding position, facing outward, and tried to dig in the heels of his hands and feet and use his thighs and butt to slow his fall. His efforts seemed futile, although they probably slowed him down sufficiently, allowing him to maintain his body position long enough to ultimately save his life.

During the fall, Ourada could see the ledge he had just passed, more than 150 feet below him. He aimed for it. "My biggest focus was trying to figure out where I was going to land and make sure I didn't hit anyone," he told me. "I also was pretty focused on landing on the ledge and not going even farther." Cole Ramey, one of the climbers he had just passed, was still on the ledge and saw him coming, jumping out of the way to avoid being hit by Ourada.

That Ourada landed on the ledge and didn't keep falling is a minor miracle. If he'd been tumbling out of control—head over heels like Rick Cashner when he fell off *Darth Vader's Revenge*—he would likely have fallen another 200 feet to the ground. If he hadn't been able to maintain his body position during the fall and fallen a few feet to the left or right, he would have missed the ledge completely.

"I don't know if it's a miracle," Ourada told me. "I remember actively trying to aim for the ledge when falling." However it happened, by dumb luck, incredible skill, or divine intervention, Ourada landed heels-first and collapsed onto the ledge, and Ramey was right there to grab him and prevent him from falling the rest of the way to the ground. Another climber called 911, and a rescue was summoned. After several hours, Ourada was finally airlifted off the ledge.

"I was conscious the entire fall," Ourada posted on Instagram after the accident, "clawing and scraping at anything to catch myself or slow down." His injuries included a compound open fracture of his right heel, large laceration of his left foot, fractured pelvis in two places, an exploded L1, two fractured ribs, fractured sternum, collapsed lung, and a broken left thumb. "I still can't feel or move my toes and feet nor my groin/butt area," he says.

Ourada has permanent injuries and depends on a wheelchair for daily activities, but he is optimistic about his recovery. "I am doing pretty good all things considered," Ourada told me. "All my broken or fractured bones are healed now." Looking forward, he says, "I'm currently working on learning how to walk with forearm crutches and hiking poles and will hopefully be able to start walking around outside by the end of the year." According to his posts on Instagram, Ourada is making progress; he was walking and even went on a short hike the following fall.

Ourada's fall generated the usual questions about his sanity and moral responsibility, especially since he had nearly fallen on another climber, and the impact his accident had on the other climbers on the wall, the rescuers, and his family. Along with the expressions of sympathy and wishes for a speedy recovery posted on Facebook in response to the *Climbing* article covering the incident were the typical negative comments calling him foolish and irresponsible—comments that he in some ways agrees with.

After the accident, Ourada expressed regret that he almost fell on another climber and that he put others through a lot of trauma. He was conscious of the climbers below him during his climb, and even after he realized he couldn't stop his fall, he still tried to avoid landing on and injuring them. "Before the accident, I never really thought twice about soloing around others," Ourada admitted. "When I soloed, there was no doubt in my mind that I would do the routes without any problems." But now, despite his conscientiousness in asking permission to climb through and his efforts to avoid landing on other climbers, he can't justify his decision to free solo with others on the route. And having reflected on his accident, he can't justify his decision to free solo *The Nutcracker Suite* that day.

"I don't think I was in a good headspace that day," he told me, recalling that he was sleep deprived after his recent ascent of El Capitan. "I have struggled with depression for many years and think it played a role in my fall. . . . The night before I fell, I was writing in my journal and just having a pretty bad time with some negative emotions that were pretty overwhelming."

When Ourada woke up the next morning, it was late and his friends were gone. He went to meet them for breakfast but there was no parking. That's when he got the idea to solo *The Nutcracker Suite*. "Soloing has always provided me with an outlet to help me deal with my depression," he says. "It seemed like a good way to start the day."

Falling and nearly dying hasn't diminished Ourada's obsession with climbing. He plans to start again as soon as he's able. For now, he's focusing on grad school and physical therapy, hoping to walk again soon, and then will see about climbing. Even if he doesn't fully recover from his injuries, he knows he can still climb, perhaps not at the same level as before, but he knows a lot of people with disabilities—blind people, paraplegics, amputees—still enjoy being up on the walls, climbing at their level of ability. As for free soloing, though, he says he's through.

CHAPTER 26

A Bit Like Cocaine

"I came into solo climbing from, I think, a very different direction than a lot of people," Sharon Wood told me. I'd met Wood, a Canadian, at the Banff Mountain Film Festival in 2019. She was promoting a book she'd written about her historic 1986 Everest climb, titled *Rising*, and we had been scheduled to sign our books at the same time. I arrived early to find a line of eager fans, books clutched firmly in hand, stretched out the door and down the hallway. The trouble was, they were all there to meet Wood. I soon discovered that Sharon Wood was a national hero.

"Your line is longer than Reinhold Messner's," I told her when she arrived.

"I'm so sorry," she said.

As Wood told me when I interviewed her later, she started teaching climbing at eighteen years old, before guide certification was mandatory in Canada, as part of a group of young climbers based in the Canadian Rockies near Canmore, Alberta. "I remember the teaching," she says. "We started teaching leading courses, which involved soloing around our leaders. We'd solo and check their gear because we were concerned about the risks that *they* were taking." It was common practice, Sharon told me, for the instructors to solo on multipitch climbs, climbing up and down to check on gear and provide instruction while unroped, sometimes hundreds of feet off the ground. For the most part, nothing bad happened, except that one time.

In 1991, a Canadian guide named Niccy Code was working as a climbing instructor in Leavenworth, Washington. On October 27, she was teaching a group of students on the *Saber* route on Castle Rock, a popular wall with several easy and moderate routes that went as high as 600 feet above the highway. Code was shepherding students on two pitches of the route that started from a ledge 300 feet above the ground; it was massively exposed but relatively easy, only 5.4 in difficulty, making it a popular beginner's route and free-solo climb. Code had set a belay anchor for a student on Saber Ledge, a broad ledge at the end of the first pitch, then untied from the rope and started soloing to supervise two students higher up. About 100 feet up the pitch, she fell, bounced off two ledges, and disappeared into the shadows. In all, she fell more than 450 feet. Code died of massive head injuries, only thirty-two years old.

According to an analysis of the accident in the 1992 edition of *Accidents in North American Mountaineering*, Code "decided to climb unroped for a number of possible reasons," possibly to save time or because she felt protecting the climb was unnecessary or would be impractical. The author of the report didn't understand that this was just the way she and other Canadian guides of her generation did things.

"Niccy Code came from that culture," Wood remembers. "When she fell that day . . . that kind of put us all in check." Soloing on their own climbs wasn't unusual for Wood and her contemporaries. It was expected in the Canadian Rockies that you'd climb unroped sometimes to cover ground quickly, to move fast and light.

"Even if you did have gear in, there was sort of a no-falling-allowed kind of rule because that gear might not hold," Wood told me. "I grew up with this approach, that it was okay to climb without protection, without ropes. . . . The other factor was, of course, we were in our twenties. We were immortal, right?"

One of those fallen climbers was a young man named Akihira Tawara, who Wood found dead at the base of Yamnuska, a 900-foot limestone wall near Canmore, in 2011. She was guiding a client when she made the gruesome discovery. "I was the first one to come upon him, along with the client," Wood says. "He must have augered into the ground from, I don't know, five, six, seven pitches above."

ALTHOUGH WOOD IS BEST KNOWN as the first woman from the Americas to climb Mount Everest, she did a lot of other impressive climbing, including two alpine solos in the Peruvian Andes that inspired her earliest writing. "It was mostly ice with a small section of rock, but it was my first alpine solo in Peru . . . really my first alpine solo," Wood says of her 1986 ascent of the west face of 19,797-foot Tocllaraju. "There were all kinds of circumstances that led up to me soloing that route. One of them was an unusually high snow year."

She'd already been in Peru for a month but hadn't summited anything because of the avalanche hazard. Then she saw the west face of Tocllaraju on the approach hike and felt the urge to solo it. "I was planning on just hanging out at base camp and maybe doing a few acclimatization hikes . . . but as soon as I saw that face, it set me back on my haunches and I sat down and I looked at it for a long while. . . . Within a few minutes, I was determined to climb it on my own the next day. There was this incredibly strong pull to do it."

She describes the urge as reckless and impulsive, but irresistible. "I wouldn't consider myself an impulsive person, but the strength of the pull that I felt to go climb that route was unlike anything else I'd experienced. So, I ran with it."

She started up the face early the next morning, alone, and had one of the best climbing experiences of her life. "I had never felt more alive than when I was climbing that morning," she recalls. "All my senses were fully engaged, and I felt like I was firing on all cylinders, which I think we rarely do in this day and age. . . . But to climb without a rope turns everything up another notch and inspires a level of performance that I don't usually realize."

Tocllaraju came close to being her worst climbing experience. After climbing 1000 feet of perfect, steep ice, she triggered an avalanche near the summit while trying a snow ramp that had looked easier than climbing directly up the face. She finished up the direct route, which was difficult and exposed, but still enjoyable. She summited and started down, planning to descend by the regular route, which had been climbed by a group the previous day and, she thought, would be a veritable trail down the mountain compared to the west face. When she could not find their tracks, Wood realized that a large amount of snow had accumulated overnight, making her planned descent route a death trap. Her only option was to downclimb the west face, something she briefly thought was impossible.

"The anticipatory angst of descending that route was horrendous," Wood remembers, but adds, "the anticipatory angst is almost always worse than the real thing. So, as soon as I started downclimbing I realized, 'okay, okay, okay, I can do this.'" She climbed carefully, taking her time, on high alert. "It was something that I didn't think was possible just a few minutes before, but I had absolutely no regrets about that experience," she says. "I may have made some mistakes in my judgment, but to me it was an essential step in my development as an alpine climber."

Two days later, Wood soloed the north face of 20,217-foot Ranrapalca. "Because I wanted more," she says. "Which is funny because, at the end of that first day I said, 'I'll never do that again.' Well, two days later, there I am at three o'clock in the morning and I'm approaching the north face of Ranrapalca. A bit like cocaine, I'd say." Addictive? "Oh, totally. Yeah."

Wood describes her motivation to do extreme climbs, especially solo climbs, as achieving self-mastery. "I believed that every climb I did in my early days was an investment towards mastery in my sport," she told me. "So, if I could find that kind of control, master my mind, my responses, under fire, in scary places, I would be a better climber. And that was very appealing to me.

"I was most interested in exploration of my potential, which I thought was boundless," she added. "I thought that at times I stopped a lot sooner than my ability would have taken me. You know, my head stopped me before my capability, or my capacity stopped me."

"I was always kind of looking for that line, and I found it that day," she says of her solo climb of Tocllaraju. "In alpine climbing, we did a lot of soloing, to move over ground quickly, and if your crampon comes off, or you break a tool, or a hold comes off, you're pretty dead pretty fast."

"It's not very forgiving," she adds. So, I wanted that head space and I knew I was in denial. I was, I think, immortal, and I just felt so good about myself."

"I suffered from depression through those years," Wood admits. "Chronic depression. Bouts of depression, and soloing . . . I became my best friend, my own best friend. I got along *really* well with myself. And proved myself to myself and so that was also a motivation. I knew that it would make me feel better. 'Good drugs,' as Doug Robinson says."

"I came down from that solo on Tocllaraju noticing everything was in vivid color," Woods told me. "Every conversation was richer, everything was turned up. And I sought that state more and more often for a while, and I sought the drugs that I got in doing that."

"I've never felt more alive than when I was soloing, like fully engaged, experiencing all my senses," Wood says. "And it took me a very long time to wean myself off of that state, I would say."

CHAPTER 27

He Shakes Hands with Death

In 1983, Mark Twight was just a regular guy who rented a room in Dan Lepeska's basement in Seattle's Wedgwood neighborhood and hung out at the University of Washington practice rock most evenings. He was a good climber, "a skinny, intense kid" who "moved easily between rage and humor, contempt and the need to be recognized as superior," as James Martin described him in a profile published on *MountainZone*. Twight *was* kind of competitive. If you showed him a hard boulder problem, he'd do it or fight like hell trying. If he couldn't, he'd do something you couldn't—or wouldn't dare. With Twight, there was always an element of one-upmanship, and if he couldn't beat you at your game, he'd change the game.

There was something fierce about him, you could tell by the piercing look he'd give you sometimes, the religiosity of his winter pull-up regime, and the times he'd go quiet and climb with an internal focus and intensity that made you afraid to say anything. It wasn't all that surprising when Twight later disappeared from the Seattle climbing scene and reemerged as Dr. Doom. But back when he lived in Lepeska's basement, he was just Mark Twight, and we went climbing together sometimes.

I remember once in Leavenworth when we had started off the day by attempting the first ascent of a 5.11, a seam I'd spotted on an otherwise blank wall that looked like it might go. As a magnanimous gesture, I allowed Twight to try it first. He fell. We swapped places and I pulled it off. Twight succeeded on his second try, but he seemed bothered that I'd succeeded where he had failed. He soon upped the game.

While I was coiling the rope, Twight disappeared. Next thing I knew, he was halfway up the wall, free soloing an adjacent 5.10. I dropped the rope and followed him up the wall. We were like that, competitive with each other. It was never an overt competition, but it occurred to me later that we had started playing a game, committing to bolder and bolder free-solo climbs, tacitly daring the other to follow. It happened more than once that I would solo a route and Twight would immediately solo something harder, which would spur me to do the same, maybe not that day, but next time. If Twight was around, I felt obliged to engage him, even passive-aggressively. At the practice rock, we were always trying to one-up each other, so this was nothing new, except the scale—and risk—was magnified. If we fell off, we wouldn't land in a gravel crash pit. There would be blood.

One afternoon in the fall of 1983 stands out in my mind. We had somehow ended up at Givler's Dome in Icicle Creek Canyon, also near Leavenworth, where Todd Skinner was working on a new 5.13. We were taking our turns trying to thrash our way up the obscenely overhanging crack. I'd become bored and had impulsively free soloed a 5.10a route. I hadn't done it before because it had a reputation for being poorly protected, a consideration that made no difference now since I wasn't roped up. I scrambled down and hung out with the assembled group, pleased with myself.

A few minutes later, I hiked around the corner to have a look at a 5.10b, a perfectly vertical, wafer-thin flake splitting a slightly overhanging 80-foot wall. I'd never climbed it before but was amped up now and thought I might give it a go. I was sitting on a boulder contemplating a free-solo ascent of the route when Twight came down the trail, pointedly ignoring me, and started up the wall. He climbed up the initial easy corner, chalked up, then pulled through the crux face section easily. Once he had a hold on the flake, he moved up quickly and effortlessly, flowing from hold to hold, hanging off his arms over open air. Twight pulled over the top of the wall and disappeared. I didn't follow. He had won that round.

Another day, we both ended up at a different crag, a small, gritstone-like buttress with several short, difficult routes that people mostly toproped. Given that the wall was only 40 feet high, I was in the habit of dispensing with the rope on every route except one 5.11 face climb that had a tenuous friction crux 30 feet off a hard rock ledge. With a toprope, it was reasonable, but it seemed too thin and sequential to try without a rope. A fall would break your ankles for sure, worse if you hit your head or tumbled off the ledge into the boulders, so we stuck to toproping that one—at least, until that day, when I bouldered partway up the face.

If the mood had taken me, I might have gone for it, but it didn't. The climbing was thin and hard, the consequences of falling off too great. It wasn't worth the risk. I reversed the moves, which I found surprisingly difficult. I consoled myself by free soloing a less committing route nearby.

Then Twight stepped up and started climbing the slab. He picked his way up the thin edges and smears to a good edge and chalked up, then took a few deep breaths and continued upward, clinging to the little knife-edged holds, palming on ripples in the granite, edging in on tiny quartz crystals with his feet, 15, 20, 25 feet off the ground. Everybody stopped and watched. It was mesmerizing and also a little horrifying, knowing how little Twight was holding onto, knowing what was coming next. He reached up and fingered a shallow depression in the rock the size and shape of a teaspoon. He'd have to crank on this flared cup of rock, palm down with his other hand, bring his feet up to a slight undulation, then pull up and grab a sloping edge an inch wide and mantel onto it. Although it was only 5.11a, it was a low-percentage sequence; most people who tried it, even good climbers, fell off at least once before they figured it out. And once you reached up and grabbed the edge, you were committed. From there, climbing down was not an option, although realistically, climbing down from Twight's position seemed just as unlikely.

Twight reached up and fingered the divot, then hesitated. He repositioned his feet and reached up again, palmed down and walked his feet higher, and paused there for a second, as if mentally preparing himself to let go with his left hand and reach for the edge. And then he started down. Watching him reverse the moves was just as gripping. He seemed constantly on the verge of falling off, fingers straining, grimacing, cursing under his breath. He was in a fight, not for his life exactly, although a fall from that high up would not have gone unpunished. Move by move, he hung on, until finally he stepped down onto the ledge and, disgusted with himself, walked away.

I didn't see much of Twight after that. Winter came and we retreated indoors to escape the rain, doing pull-ups in our basements to train for the next season. We'd go to the practice rock on sunny days, but after a while Twight stopped coming by. I'd see him at Lepeska's house once in a while, but he was hanging out with a different, more extreme crowd. Apparently, he was also soloing some hard, scary shit. I was concerned for him. I was sure he was going to die.

"INHERENT PEER PRESSURE EXISTS BETWEEN climbers," Twight wrote in his memoir, *Kiss or Kill: Confessions of a Serial Climber*, which he described as documenting his journey toward maturity. It explained, finally, why he'd turned into such an asshole.

"I surrounded myself with wannabes, pretend-to-bes, has-beens, and never-will-bes," he wrote.

> *I met people who wasted their talent or were afraid of it. They taught me why I hadn't become a good climber. Like them, I was afraid to succeed, scared to commit. I didn't want to be any better than anyone else. Eventually, I sickened of people, myself included, who don't think enough of themselves to make something of themselves—people who did only what they had to and never what they could have done. . . . The young punks and the music generated in me such a vehement intolerance of stupidity and mediocrity that extremism became my solution.*

When I read Twight's book, I took that passage a little personally. *Did he think of me as being mediocre and stupid?* We'd been friends, equals, I had thought, but Twight had decided one day to turn it up a notch, seek out a new level of extremism that bordered on suicide, and leave me and all the other losers behind. When a journalist interviewed me for an article he was writing about Twight, I told him I thought Twight was suicidal and was intentionally alienating himself so nobody would feel sorry for him when he died. At the time, I didn't realize Twight really was suffering from depression and contemplating suicide, which he wrote about in his book, although in retrospect the signs were there.

"I soloed a lot," Twight wrote, "risking everything to feel terribly alive." This feeling, he explained, centered on those clarifying moments in which an immediate risk of death required that he fight with every ounce of will and energy he possessed to survive—a hard free solo on Cathedral Ledge, with water running down the crux pitch; a close call on the Grands Charmoz, racing a storm to the summit, the ice breaking away beneath his feet, clinging to a single ice tool. "If you're convinced that once you die, it is all over, you'll fight with every last calorie to keep hold of what you have now," he wrote. "You'll do whatever it takes to stay alive—alive in the present."

He wasn't only soloing, of course. In 1988, with Randy Rackliff, he made the first and only ascent to date of a frozen waterfall in the Canadian Rockies called *The Reality Bath*, which the guidebook described as so dangerous (because it is below an ice cliff that regularly avalanches down the wall) that it has "little value except to those suicidally inclined." Other climbers saw Twight's ascent of what is considered the most dangerous route in Canada as evidence that he was suicidal. "That was not untrue," he admitted to *Gripped* magazine, "but I kept failing at it."

That same year, he was part of one of the most epic survival stories in Himalayan mountaineering while attempting to climb the Rupal Face of Nanga Parbat, one of the most dangerous mountains in the world. After his team endured an avalanche that nearly wiped them off the mountain, they accidentally dropped their ropes. Stranded high on the face, the team realized they likely could not climb down, but having nothing to lose, they were prepared to try anyway. That's when they discovered a cache of old ropes and pitons left behind by a Japanese team years earlier.

While his team had made a potentially fatal error on Nanga Parbat, Twight was increasingly making decisions on his solo climbs that seemed to border on suicidal. One example was his decision to time his 1988 free solo ascent of *Slipstream*, a 3000-foot frozen waterfall in the Canadian Rockies, which he made in 2 hours, 4 minutes, a speed record that still stands. He regrets timing himself. "It was driven by ego," Twight told *Gripped* magazine thirty years later, "which is a useful tool . . . and a way to communicate competence but unnecessary in the larger scheme of living and dying."

I didn't see Twight again myself for almost thirty years, until he received the Robert and Miriam Underhill Award at the American Alpine Club annual meeting in Seattle in 2017. When I approached him, I wasn't sure how he'd respond, or if he'd even acknowledge me, but he recognized me instantly and gave me a hug.

Two years later, at the Banff Mountain Film Festival, he made an emotional presentation about how quitting extreme climbing had affected him, which he also describes in his book *Refuge*, as being about "coming down . . . from the mountains . . . to discover meaning in what appeared so trivial when viewed from up there." I got to see the more human side of Dr. Doom, who was now, like me, approaching sixty, down from the mountains, but still missing life up there.

"Human experience is a quest for understanding of self," Twight said during a panel discussion. "I used climbing to annihilate the 'I' and get to the 'we.' Soloing was an environment to explore my inner self."

What did he find? In a world where most people are afraid to admit their weakness, Twight is remarkably candid. "I'm fucked up," he told the crowd. "I'm mentally ill."

He described his habit of soloing and extreme alpinism as an addiction, the addiction being "the presence of mind required to do it, to be less distracted, more present." He acknowledged that people can have those experiences doing different things, but that, for him, things without immediate life-and-death consequences didn't measure up, that he had required the consequences to hold himself to a higher standard of performance. His addiction was strong. "I was willing to die for the game. There was no question of stopping because I couldn't stop."

Twight was able to quit when he had taken extreme climbing "to its logical conclusions, gotten everything out of it that I needed." But quitting left a void. "Up there I'm not necessarily Nietzsche's superman, but I excise the disharmony caused by struggling against domestication," Twight wrote in *Kiss or Kill*. "I do things of an uncommonly high order. While these may not make me a better man, on the days when my ego soars I feel superior. No wonder it's so hard to fit in when I come down from the mountains."

IT'S OBVIOUS WHY GEOFF POWTER was selected as a panelist to discuss love and loss at the Banff Festival. As a clinical psychologist, he was the perfect choice to accompany Twight, an admitted risk addict with suicidal tendencies, and Margot Talbot, a former depressed drug addict who found an outlet in climbing. It was like a group therapy session open to a curious public.

Twight is unusual because, unlike a lot of other free soloists, he tells you what he's thinking, lets you look inside his skull, admits he's a self-centered asshole, and confesses that he had an egotistical or impure motive to free solo. Ego is the part of the personality that mediates the demands of the id, the superego, and reality. The id is what urges people to fulfill their most primal needs, while the superego is the moralistic part of an individual's personality. The ego is what many people call their value system, rejecting any opinions, beliefs, or behaviors of the self or others that lead to a disconnect between their personal narrative and objective reality. According to Ryan Holiday in *Ego Is the Enemy*:

> *The ego we see most commonly goes by a more casual definition: an unhealthy belief in our own importance. Arrogance. Self-centered ambition. It can manifest itself in a variety of ways: mocking or putting down others to make ourselves feel better, blaming others for our own short-comings or mistakes, competing with others to prove our worthiness, and taking risks to gain attention or recognition.*

If you're free soloing for wrongheaded reasons, trying to impress and get external recognition and peer approval, you can get into trouble. You're likely to rush things, underprepare, roll the dice, and go for it, compromising your safety—even your life—for the sake of being noticed, to be somebody.

I was curious what Powter thought about Twight's and Talbot's reflections on addiction and suicide, especially Twight's admission that he sometimes didn't care, as he put it, whether he lived or died when he was soloing, and in fact, if he died, that was okay. I knew from my own experience that accepting that you might die is part of the deal; you have to accept that before you can really step off the ground. But what Twight was describing sounded like a step beyond that, more of a welcoming of death as a possible outcome than merely acknowledging or accepting it.

"I think there's a continuum between 'I *accept* that I might die'; 'I *probably could* die'; 'I'm *willing* to die for the experience'; 'I *want* to die—that would solve my problems,'" Powter told me.

"I don't think there was any question in reading Johnny Waterman's diaries that he went to Denali to finish his story," he added. "Or when Maurice Wilson went back on Everest, he knew he was not coming back down. That was the final chapter of his story."

"What about Twight?" I wondered. "What I heard Mark say on the panel in Banff was that he was *willing* to die for the climb; that it would somehow be romantically worth it, perhaps in the same way that a samurai might be willing to die for his noble code," Powter told me. "But that's very different—even in Mark's case—from saying I *intend* to die doing this. That's *very* different from saying, 'I accept that I might,' [or] 'I'm willing to do this today because of how this makes me feel, I'm willing to take that chance, but I sure as hell don't *want* to die'."

Something that's always interested Powter is that of the notable free soloists who have committed suicide, most did so by more conventional means. That is, they didn't climb up a rock wall and let go on purpose, as if to avoid validating the image of free soloists as being suicidal. Powter wonders if perhaps that's a continuation of the romantic ideal: the soloing was a testing ground that these people traveled through to sort out the meaning of their lives—but once they found that soloing didn't sort out their demons, they didn't sully the sacred ground by killing themselves on it. It's possible that some climbers who free solo don't have a death wish, exactly, but are at a point in the continuum where they don't care if they live or die, and for better or worse, they are exploring that boundary. But then, through soloing, they become repossessed of their will to live.

Many people who've attempted suicide and survived have said that at the moment they made their attempt, they suddenly came back to their senses, and wanted to live. The same thing could be true, Powter agrees, of a free soloist who might be borderline suicidal or cavalier about whether they lived or died until they get on a climb, get gripped, and suddenly become highly focused on hanging on, on surviving. "They experience the life-affirmingness of the act rather than the life destruction of the act," he says, "though I don't think there is much life destruction in the act of climbing."

"There's some good evidence in people who have made serious attempts to suicide that what those people were really attempting to do in their attempt was to end the *life* that they currently *have*, not end themselves as a thinking being." Though, he acknowledges, it doesn't make sense given the real consequences of attempting suicide. "It's almost like they're trying to strike a bargain that says 'I'm going to do this and everything's going to change, but then I'm going to be okay, and I'm going to come back and resurrect my life in a different kind of way.'" He explains, "It's not, then, about killing *self*, but rather about killing the story, of maintaining self and coming back as the person you always wanted to be."

Powter recognizes that lacking a positive sense of self—a positive self-narrative even—leads to a sense of lack of control, purpose, a place in the world. Not everyone responds to this lack by attempting suicide, but some do. Others have an experience—whether through surviving cancer, having a heart attack, living through a suicide attempt, or going solo climbing—that tells them they *want* to be here and a sense of why. "That kind of journey—to find purpose and personal power—is essentially what therapy is," Powter says, "and if you can get to that place by going out and soloing something—as long as you fit all the criteria of knowing yourself, your limitations, your abilities, and all the reasons you're starting up the climb—all the more power to you."

"Ultimately, the only truly profoundly important choice we have in our lives is to live or die," Powter continues. "So, if you can appreciate that, and then engage that, that's you affirming life. And that's really an amazing thing to be able to do."

CHAPTER 28

The Naked Edge

When I visited Boulder in the summer of 1986, it was with the intention of climbing *The Naked Edge*. I'd been inspired by Robert Godfrey and Dudley Chelton's 1977 photo essay on the history of rock climbing in Colorado. Among the pictures of free climbers pushing the limits of difficulty and ethical climbing was a dramatic route climbing an exposed, overhanging prow on Redgarden Wall in Eldorado Canyon.

I was also inspired by Jim Erickson, one of the pioneering free climbers of the 1970s who shared his stories in *Climb!*, whose climbing style I admired, and his account of his first free ascent of the route in 1971. "Strenuous, overhanging finger-laybacking leads around a corner," he wrote. "A severely overhanging hand-crack pierces the prow leading upward thirty feet and out of sight. My forearms feel like silly putty as I struggle to rest, shaking first one arm, then the other, light years of emptiness beneath. I have but strength for one attempt." But Erickson's stories about free-solo climbing were even more gripping than that. Those made my palms sweat.

Unfortunately, it took some time to find someone willing to climb *The Naked Edge* with me. My intended climbing partner went off with his friends every morning, leaving me to hang out in Eldorado Canyon alone. Most days, I'd boulder a while to kill time, then start soloing easy pitches along the base of the Bastille, Whale's Tail, and Redgarden Wall. When a couple of climbers showed up, I latched onto them, and made plans to climb with them the next morning. But when I arrived on time and ready to climb, I found they'd ditched me and were already on the route. That night, at the Wendy's in Boulder, I met a guy named Milt Stickler, who claimed he'd spent the previous six months in a Buddhist monastery, and we agreed to climb *The Naked Edge* together.

For all the anxiety I'd felt about facing the several difficult, exposed 5.11 pitches, it wasn't that bad. In fact, it was pretty damn great. Our climb was, for both of us, as close to perfection as we might have hoped to achieve. None of the pitches seemed very hard. I'd led two of the 5.11 pitches cleanly, and had climbed the much-feared 5.11 chimney pitch without a problem. I hadn't come close to falling anywhere on the route. As I sat on a narrow ledge 700 feet above the canyon floor, belaying Stickler up the final difficult pitch, looking down over Eldorado Canyon, a thought entered my mind: *You could solo that.* I shuddered. *No way!*

JIM ERICKSON STARTED ROCK CLIMBING at the age of eight. He had been fascinated with caving, but found he liked the climbing part more than the actual caves. By age fourteen, he was climbing regularly with his brother, Dave, at Devil's Lake, Wisconsin. He progressed quickly and within three years was leading 5.10s at Devil's Lake and the Shawangunks. After graduating high school, he enrolled at the University of Colorado to study classical music. The university's proximity to some of the country's best rock climbing may well have played a role in luring him away from his aspirations of being a classical musician.

Initially, Erickson had a difficult time finding someone to climb with; he admitted to a reporter for the Denver-based *Westword* that after he arrived in Boulder, he took a lot of drugs and hung out looking for partners. Then, when he managed to find a partner, he had a difficult time adjusting to the rock, struggling to climb routes as easy as 5.7 and 5.8. Part of his problem was that he sometimes got off route and ended up on more difficult variations; another was that some of the climbs he tried were much harder than the guidebook rating indicated. Getting off route on a 5.7 and unintentionally attempting the first free ascent of a 5.10 will do that to you.

Despite his early setbacks, Erickson stuck with it, and eventually succeeded in making free ascents of some former aid routes that he found easier than expected. One of those routes was *The Naked Edge*. Although his free ascent of the route with Duncan Ferguson in 1971 was considered a breakthrough, Erickson felt that because he had fallen several times, he had, in a sense, diminished his accomplishment. He felt that if you fell and were held by the rope and a piton, you had crossed the line between free and aid climbing. Afterward, Erickson adopted a very strict moral approach to free climbing: "You fall, you fail."

He began to free solo more, even free soloing new routes. One of these was of a 5.10a crack on the Bastille he named *Blind Faith* that he just walked up to and climbed without any prior knowledge of the route. He also free soloed routes that had only been climbed previously using direct aid, including *Sooberb*, a long route over a roof 200 feet off the ground that Erickson rated 5.10b after he had free soloed it. Before long, Erickson became addicted to unroped climbing. He didn't need a partner; he'd just ride his bike to Eldorado Canyon with a pair of rock shoes and climb whatever he felt like climbing.

"I wanted to do something that epitomized the thing I was into—complete control climbing—which is what solo climbing is all about," Erickson told Godfrey and Chelton. "I guess in a sense I was trying to emulate the myths that I had heard about John Gill."

Even in the 1970s, Gill, a math professor and gymnast who is considered the father of American bouldering, was already a legendary figure. Although he mostly climbed routes close to the ground, where a fall is unlikely to be fatal, Gill almost always climbed them on-sight and without a rope, trying to achieve as pure an ascent as possible. Inspired by Gill, Erickson became so focused on free soloing—what he believed to be the purest form of "natural climbing"—that he began to view ropes and hardware as cheating. "All other things being equal, the closer I approximate nude solo climbing, the better," Erickson said. "I am more likely to depend on my own resources in a crux situation, and therefore, the experience is more meaningful."

Erickson's approach was as calculated as it was impulsive. He claimed not to have any fear once he'd committed himself to free soloing a route, and even if he wasn't sure what would happen, he'd still go for it. Even so, Erickson didn't define himself as a thrill-seeker; he disliked the myth that solo climbers were adrenaline-junkies. He climbed carefully and deliberately, often going up and down a pitch several times before committing to the crux. In this way, he could be confident that he could reverse the moves all the way to the ground if the climbing proved too difficult or dangerous to solo.

"I backed down from as many [solo climbs] as I completed," Erickson told *Westword*. "Most macho types would push it. That's a good way to die, and yeah, climbing is mostly very exhilarating because [if you fall] you're potentially dead—but I never liked the cheap thrill of it."

Despite the great care and deliberation he exercised when free soloing, Erickson had a close call in 1973. Fit from a trip to Yosemite, where he'd tried to free climb the *Regular Northwest Face* of Half Dome, he got back into his usual routine, but with a sort of cavalier attitude, and he soloed routes perfunctorily without really mentally focusing. While climbing a thin, overhanging crack behind the Fourth Flatiron on a hot day, his hands came out of the crack and he fell 30 feet onto a rocky slope. Erickson was knocked unconscious.

When he came to, he realized he had broken both legs and a wrist and was bleeding badly. He crawled toward the trail and was able to yell to a passing hiker who summoned a rescue. "Eventually the rangers found me, and I told them I fell while hiking," Erickson admitted. "I was too embarrassed to tell them the truth."

The truth was that Erickson had been what he described as "sort of . . . emotionally distraught" at the time, where he "didn't care that much" about dying. But he hadn't wanted to die. Before the fall, he had looked down and saw a stump in his fall line. He'd started thinking about how he'd be impaled on the stump if he fell, which interrupted his focus. Climbing down, he had moved the stump out of the way so he wouldn't fall on it, then had climbed back up and immediately fallen off—landing exactly where the stump had been. Afterward, he realized he should have just called it a day.

His accident put him off climbing for a while, but he eventually got back into it and continued free soloing, but never at the same level as before, especially after he had kids. "Not till I had children did I even think about it," he told *Westword*. "Your friends die . . . but you don't think it's gonna happen to you."

"I used to be able to say to myself, 'Well, if you get killed doing this, it doesn't matter very much,'" Erickson said. But after his accident, he lost the twitch. "These days I seem to value my life more."

IN 1979, MOUNTAIN MAGAZINE REPORTED that Jim Collins had free soloed *The Naked Edge*. Despite being one of the most significant ascents of the seventies, Collins doesn't talk about it much. This is surprising, given how much Collins talks—or writes—about his other climbing exploits. He writes a lot about *Genesis*, for instance, his futuristic 5.12c first free ascent in 1979, and his roped ascents of *The Naked Edge*, as examples of how to overcome fears and obstacles to create success in business and life.

Collins is the author or co-author of six books on business leadership that have sold in total more than ten million copies worldwide, including *Good to Great*, a bestseller, which examines why some companies make the leap to superior results. In 2017, *Forbes* selected Collins as one of the 100 Greatest Living Business Minds. But Collins also lists on his biography that he's been an avid rock climber for more than forty years and has made single-day ascents of both El Capitan and Half Dome. He may be a business genius, but he's still a climber, after all.

There's a story in one of his books about David Breashears, a young climber who in 1975 made the first ascent of a blank, unprotected face on the Mickey Maus Wall in Eldorado Canyon. There were no cracks to place chocks for protection, so climbing the face in the traditional style—from the ground up—would require great skill and boldness. Breashears gave the route a try, thinking the hardest moves would be lower down; from below it looked like there were some good holds higher up. He led upward and tied into a rope, but found no gear placements. Fifty feet up the wall, he realized what had looked like positive holds from below were actually sloping and polished. Although he was tied into a rope, he had no protection. If he fell, he'd hit the ground and probably die; he was effectively free soloing. Encouraged by what looked like good holds a few feet higher, he went for it. He found a ripple in the polished sandstone that he could hang onto, just barely. He committed to the move and pulled himself tenuously upward.

"Was this a risky situation?" Collins asked in an article titled "Hitting the Wall: Realizing That Vertical Limits Aren't." Not for Breashears, he answered. "Sure, the consequences of a fall were severe, but the probabilities of a fall were close to zero. David was such a gifted climber at his prime that—to him—the route formed a puzzle to solve, but not a particularly difficult one." Collins compared Breashears's situation to that of a crossword-puzzle expert facing death as a consequence for not finishing a puzzle correctly. "The consequences of failure are extreme," he wrote, "but the probabilities of failure are low."

The key for Breashears, according to Collins, was to keep his mind clear of distracting thoughts—thoughts of falling and dying—and climb with laser focus. He latched onto the ripple and pulled upward, found another hold, then another, and was soon at the top of the wall, having made the first ascent of *Perilous Journey*, a 5.11a to which the guidebook affixed an X-rating to signify that the route had basically no protection, and you'd probably die if you fell off.

Collins wrote about Breashears's first ascent of *Perilous Journey* as a life and business lesson on separating probability from consequence:

> *The people who choose to climb* [Perilous Journey] *are those for whom the odds of falling are close to zero, yet who understand that it doesn't matter how easy or hard the climbing, how high or low the probabilities of falling, if you fall hundreds or thousands of feet, the consequences are severe. They go at* Perilous Journey *with a mindfulness that respects not just the climb, but the potential fall.*

According to one report, before his 1978 free-solo ascent, Collins had climbed *The Naked Edge* only six times and had only climbed the final pitch once without falling. Given that Collins wrote or spoke prolifically about his other climbing exploits, especially his first free ascent of *Genesis*, I expected to find a story about it in one of Collins's books or articles. But I couldn't. It seemed odd that he would not talk about soloing *The Naked Edge*—about how to approach a challenge in spite of risk and the high consequences of failure, about being mindful, about overcoming and succeeding, and how that mindset could be used to succeed in business. But as Tommy Caldwell, who climbed the *Nose* in a day with Collins, wrote in *The Push*, "Apparently he wasn't proud of it . . . too much risk as he subsequently reflected—so he kept it quiet." (Through an intermediary, Collins politely declined my request for an interview.)

I was finally able to find an account of Collins's free solo ascent in *Creativity in Business*, a business book published in 1986, in which the authors wrote about the importance of "being ordinary" to be successful. "Being ordinary," they wrote, "is acknowledging, without thinking about it, that you possess the capacity to meet, gracefully and productively, whatever situation or challenge you find on your plate." They gave examples of people who, through the simple fact of being ordinary, had persevered and succeeded in achieving their goals. One of their examples of a person "being ordinary" was Jim Collins.

"Being ordinary has helped me to understand a number of very significant events in my life," Collins is quoted as saying. "The difference between making something happen and letting something happen is the centerpiece of these very meaningful (to me) experiences." And being ordinary, according to Collins, is what allowed him to free solo the route without falling to his death. "The consequence of a mistake while free soloing is instant death," he said. "Free soloing *The Naked Edge* would normally be deemed sheer lunacy, even in the climbing community."

As Collins described it, he had been arguing with his ex-girlfriend that morning and just wanted to get out and climb to clear his head. Why he chose to free solo such a difficult climb was unclear even to Collins. The way he described it, it almost sounded impulsive.

"I never told myself, 'I'm going to get up tomorrow morning and make a free solo of *The Naked Edge*,'" he said. "Instead, I just let it happen. This was taken to such an extreme that I didn't even think about doing the whole climb while I was actually on the climb."

THE MAY–JUNE ISSUE OF *Rock and Ice* came out a month before my trip to Colorado. It had an article by Dan Mannix about Derek Hersey free soloing *The Naked Edge* for a film he was making. Tied to Redgarden Wall 300 feet above the ground, Mannix waits with his cameras positioned to capture Hersey soloing the 5.11 first pitch, thinking about what he's doing and why he's there, and wondering why Hersey was late.

Hersey began climbing as a teenager in the late 1960s, without a rope or protection, on the quarries near Manchester and the gritstone of the Peak District in Derbyshire—there he once took a 35-foot ground fall while daydreaming about a cheese sandwich. He moved to Boulder, Colorado, in the mid-1980s, and almost immediately started attracting attention. His second climb in Eldorado Canyon, a free solo of the *Diving Board*, a 5.11a crack with hard climbing 600 feet off the ground, was followed closely by an unroped ascent of *The Naked Edge*, the most imposing line on the biggest wall. People knew Jim Collins had soloed the route in 1978 but didn't really believe it, but they weren't sure what to think of Hersey, who was relatively unknown, had just arrived in Colorado, and was already tearing up the place.

"People didn't know who he was," said his friend Mary Reidmiller in an interview with *Climbing* magazine. "He was supposed to be a rich Englishman who had lost his fortune, was profoundly depressed and had come to Boulder to lose his life." That was a plausible explanation; in fact, it made sense.

Hersey wasn't rich—far from it, unless you count having a lot of friends, free time, and all the rock you could ever wish to climb as being rich. But he was a character among characters in the climbing world, a free spirit who liked to party as much as he liked to climb, who was friendly toward everyone. As Alison Osius wrote in her 1993 obituary of Hersey, published in *Climbing* after he fell while free soloing the *Steck-Salathé* in Yosemite, "Hersey was . . . treasured for his exceedingly gregarious nature, his cheer, for his wildness and long hair, and amusingly ragamuffin ways." Known for his willingness to climb anything with anyone, Hersey didn't seem like a hard-core rock athlete. But his penchant for free soloing miles of rock, including routes near his technical limit—often on-sight—marked him as something of an outlier even among climbers.

"Watching Derek was like a breath of fresh air," his friend Steve Bartlett said after Hersey's 1990 free solos of *Yellow Wall* (5.10), down *Casual Route* (5.10a), and up *Pervertical Sanctuary* (5.11a) on the Diamond. "So fast and efficient."

Hersey was well known for his casual efficiency and almost cavalier approach to soloing. In his article, Mannix recalled an incident that occurred while he was filming Hersey soloing *Rosy Crucifixion*, a 5.10 on Redgarden Wall. "He was effortlessly connecting move after move," Mannix wrote, "when in the middle of the second pitch a large pigeon flew out of the crack and hit him dead on the face, causing him to lurch backward on one handhold over the 200-foot abyss." Hersey quickly regained his composure, then turned and looked directly into the camera: "Did you get that mate?" he asked in his dry Manchester accent, then continued calmly up the pitch as if nothing had happened.

Hersey eventually arrived, late, hungover from too many beers the night before, but insistent on going through with it. Watching Hersey free solo for the film, Mannix was all business, focusing the camera on his subject clinging to tiny holds hundreds of feet off the ground, but watching the video later, he had a different reaction: "My stomach would tighten up as I watched Derek struggle with those elusive finger locks." Mannix wondered how Hersey had survived to age thirty. "Not only was the lad bold," he decided, "but he had nerves of steel, and liquid helium in his veins."

"Soloing is kind of a selfish way of climbing but I enjoy meself," Hersey told Annie Whitehouse in an interview published in *Climbing* in 1992. "One of the reasons I want to solo is because I want to do it by meself. Not to be antisocial, but I just love climbing by meself. I know my talents and skills. I've got a very good temperament and you have to have a little bit of ego to go with it, for sure. Soloing's definitely kind of an ego thing."

"You've got to know yourself and keep your ego out of it," Hersey explained to Mannix. "When I'm up there, it's just me and my chalk bag: it's ballet 300 feet in the air. I never go up with the impression that I've got it wired. I go up as if I'm doing it for the first time: that way you stay alive."

THE MORNING AFTER CLIMBING *The Naked Edge* with Stickler, I was alone again, wandering along the base of the walls of Eldorado Canyon, soloing. I wasn't climbing anything specific, just whatever was easy or straightforward, mostly the same routes I'd soloed on earlier days. I had a sort of circuit going of easy routes—5.6s and 5.7s—but was thinking of something bigger.

Looking up at the great overhanging prow above me, the thought came back. *You could solo it.* I'd been climbing 5.11 consistently, mostly roped up but also unleashed. I'd cruised the route the day before. In fact, when I thought about it, I hadn't fallen off a 5.11 for longer than I could remember. I knew I could do it physically. The mental part was another story. Still, I started up the wall. I felt really good, in a flowy mood, still stoked from my flawless ascent of the route the day before. Pulling it off would be magical.

But by the time I reached the ledge, the magic had worn off. I'd started analyzing the route, thinking it through, and doubts had crept in. A lot of them. *The last moves of the first pitch are pretty thin,* I reminded myself. *It would be easy to fall there. And what about the bulge on the second pitch? Although only 5.10, it was sloping and greasy, kind of dicey, wasn't it? And even if the chimney didn't seem that hard, what about the 5.11 traverse at the top and the boulder problem right off the hanging belay?*

I couldn't hang at the belay and rest like yesterday. I'd go straight from a 5.11 chimney into a 5.11 face traverse capped by a 5.11 boulder problem crux and have to keep going up an overhanging 5.10 crack to the top of the wall, above 600 feet of raw exposure, without stopping. *And if I fell?* I shuddered to think of it.

Part of me still wanted to do it, but another part was screaming, *No!* I sat there for several minutes looking up at the route and down at the ground, having an internal debate.

You shouldn't let your fears stop you, a voice was telling me. *You need to control them, lock them away. You can do this. You know you can. You did it without falls. Without falls! If you pull it off, you'll be like a god. If you don't, you'll regret it forever.*

But another voice was saying, *Look down. See how far that is? A long fucking way. If you fall, you die. It isn't worth it. You need to get out of here before you fuck it up.*

I looked up at the route again and laughed at myself for even thinking about it. *What* was I doing there? I was out of my league and knew it. I turned around, climbed down, and walked away—a decision I still do not regret.

CHAPTER 29

A Very Fine Line

I was sitting in the shade of a cliff at Smith Rock State Park one July afternoon with Alan Watts. We were waiting for a group to finish climbing a route, which was taking longer than expected. Watts pointed up at a nearby route and said, "I'll bet that hasn't had a second ascent."

I looked up at a seemingly blank wall of flaky red-and-orange volcanic rock without bolts. "Is that a toprope?" I asked him.

"I guess you could toprope it," he said.

"Is there any protection?" I asked.

"No."

"You *led* it?"

"Well . . ."

I was surprised to learn Watts had free soloed the 5.10 face, trailing a rope only so he could rappel off when he got to a ledge 60 feet up the wall. He's the father of American sport climbing, a notorious hangdogger, the guy who popularized rappel bolting, who put Smith Rock on the map. I knew he had done some unroped climbs here and there. What surprised me was that he had been free soloing at Smith Rock. I would never have guessed that any rational person would climb in that area without a rope, but it turns out a few people have, including Peter Croft, Alex Honnold, and apparently Alan Watts. He attributes his willingness to solo at Smith Rock to a supreme sense of self-confidence, a belief that he was so good and so strong that even if a nubbin popped or a foot slipped, he could hang on and not fall. But mostly, his reason for free soloing was that he couldn't find a partner.

It's hard to imagine a time when someone climbing at Smith Rock could not find a partner. These days, the park is crowded with climbers from all over the world, so much so that you often have to wait your turn to climb. But if you visited in the early 1980s, you might find yourself alone, as I did the first time I stopped there in 1983. There was literally no one else in the entire park. If I had wanted to climb, I would have had to climb alone. After hiking around and evaluating the rock quality, I dismissed that idea as foolish.

In the summer of 1985, Watts lived in a big tent on a property literally a stone's throw from Smith Rock State Park. The area was still relatively unknown at the time; it wasn't discovered by the rest of the climbing world until the following spring when *Mountain* magazine published a feature article of mine. Back in 1985, Watts was often the only one at Smith Rock, and he rarely had anybody to climb with.

"I've never considered myself a free soloist," Watts says. "It was just part of what climbing was for me. I was never a John Bachar, a Peter Croft, or an Alex Honnold. I was just somebody who loved to climb and spent a lot of time alone at the crag."

Watts got into the habit of speed soloing two long 5.6s and recording his time, what he calls "low-stress solos." He'd climb the first 300-foot route, run to the top of the wall and down the trail, then dash up the second route and down the trail back to the base of the wall. He wasn't competing with any other climbers—just himself.

Fearing it would encourage someone to try to beat his time and put themselves at risk, Watts never told anyone about his circuit or reported his times. We all know how fast Dan Osman and Alex Honnold speed soloed *Bear's Reach*, how fast *The Naked Edge* has been climbed, and the current speed record for climbing the *Nose*. If Watts had publicized his times, he thinks, it's almost certain somebody would have tried to beat them. "Back then, nobody cared," he says. "These were before the days when speed ascents made news."

"I never soloed anything hard," Watts admits. "I recognized that the rock simply wasn't suited for that. I spent most of my time soloing routes under 5.11." He did solo two 5.11s, including a 5.11a called *I Almost Died*, but shrugs those off as insignificant. The fact that he was soloing on rock notorious for flakes and knobs breaking off didn't concern him at the time. He climbed carefully, avoiding anything that looked suspicious, only continuing if he had a grip on at least one good hold. But sometimes, he ventured into uncharted territory, free soloing up a section of rock that hadn't been climbed.

WATTS CONSIDERS ALEX HONNOLD'S FREE solo of *Freerider* the greatest athletic feat in the history of sport. "Not just climbing, but all sports," he says. He has an interesting perspective, as the chief instigator of the sport climbing revolution in the 1980s. He credits both the influence of Bachar and Croft, as well as the more liberal attitudes toward working routes, for providing the foundation that Honnold built on to achieve what he did. He especially credits Bachar, one of Watts's chief rivals during the 1980s. The pair eventually developed a relationship built on mutual admiration, but it was despite their ethical differences.

No doubt Watts admired Bachar more than the other way around. "Bachar had very strong convictions," Watts says. "He was not one to compromise his values. He developed free soloing into an art form. . . . He was very good at soloing—better than anyone else in the world, and he was well aware of this fact. And it gave him a firm leg to stand on as he preached his purity ethics."

Although he credits Bachar for laying a foundation for Honnold, he recognizes that Honnold has taken soloing to a new level. "In some ways, I think Alex accomplished both of his goals—being a superhero and being as close to perfect as a climber can be," he said. "I especially appreciate the thoroughness of his approach. He prepares more carefully than any soloist has ever prepared." But Watts also credits other styles of climbing, including sport climbing, as providing a foundation for what Honnold accomplished. "His approach blends the best of the different realms of rock climbing—trad, sport, bouldering, and soloing," he says. "He's shown what's possible when the conflicting styles from the old days (sport versus trad) merged into one."

It all came together, Watts believes, in Honnold's free solo of El Cap. "The only way to do what he's done is to execute a route flawlessly," he adds. "You can get by from time to time sketching through things soloing, but that'll catch up with you."

Like me, Watts knows that climbers can be tremendously obsessive and find it difficult to let go of a goal once it's in their heads. "I've always thought there is a very fine line between the safe and reckless pursuit of a goal," he says. "I would never say that those who push the limits 'have a screw loose.' But I think the very thing that fuels obsession can kill you in the end."

He also acknowledges that his thought patterns were obsessive and compulsive at times. "The only way to quiet my head was to get the goal done so I could move onto something else," he says. "It's one thing when your goal in climbing is to redpoint a 5.14, boulder a V12, or free climb El Cap, but sometimes, the stakes can become absurdly high" like free soloing El Capitan or something bigger. "Once the obsession shifts to soloing a new route on an 8000-meter peak, or free soloing the *Nose*, it can be very hard to put those dreams to rest without first taking the risks to make it happen," Watts says.

"High achievers in many walks of life are those who become obsessed with something that they simply can't let go. Stories abound of creative geniuses who are, at least to some degree, mentally ill," he adds. "It's a very fine line. There seems to be some connection between greatness and obsessiveness."

Watts is glad that he inspired climbers with the athleticism and difficulty of the sport climbs he developed, not his free soloing, although he doubts anybody would have taken up free soloing at Smith Rock as a serious pursuit. In retrospect, at age sixty-one, Watts thinks it was a bad idea to solo at Smith. In fact, he thinks it was a bad idea to solo at all. "What was I thinking?" he wonders. "That was so dumb. But with that said, free soloing was immensely satisfying. . . . Days at Smith when I free soloed a few thousand feet and never saw another person were some of the best memories of my life."

He recalls how absorbing those climbs felt, "I still vividly remember the feeling of being immersed in the moment, far off the ground, fully confident and in total control. Nothing in my life has ever matched the youthful exuberance of those experiences." Reflecting on how his relationship with climbing has changed, he says, "I'm glad I left soloing behind as I got older because I don't think I was good enough to survive a long soloing career. But I'm grateful I had those moments."

CHAPTER 30

Welcome Back, My Friend

It was my first time climbing with Morgan Balogh. Our goal was an 8000-foot peak in the central Cascades that neither of us had climbed before. We had made good time, but Morgan had fallen behind. At about 7000 feet I reached a rocky ridge with several small rock pinnacles. After several thousand feet of steep meadows and scree, the pinnacles provided something approximating real climbing; nothing difficult, just some athletic, exposed moves that added some spice to what had so far been a tedious slog. The guidebook had offered scant details, which was part of the attraction. We were going to discover the mountain's secrets as we climbed.

I looked out at the steep rocks we'd have to traverse to get to the top—we hadn't brought a rope—then down the ridge where Morgan was nowhere to be seen. Impatient, I continued toward the summit, heading rightward across a blocky ledge, hopping across a steep, narrow gully and then a wider gully. The ledge led around the first gendarme and soon I was facing the second, which had a longer, more pronounced arête. I looked for a way to skirt under it or pass it directly, but neither seemed appealing. The gully looked loose and steep, the arête difficult and exposed. I tried the direct route, but after a few tenuous moves, I encountered a blank slab above a 50-foot drop-off. I backed off and reconsidered the gully, but it seemed worse than the slab. Maybe there was a way to traverse around the east side. I backtracked and scrambled up a talus basin to a notch in the ridge to have a look.

The east face of the peak fell away several hundred feet to a glacier. My first impulse was *no way!* This option was even worse than the other two—steep and exposed, definitely too dangerous. But as I looked down the face, I saw a narrow ledge not far below that seemed to lead across the face toward the summit block. Even if that ledge was part of a route, it would be foolish to try it. Prudence dictated that the way to go was back down the gully and around the arête on the west side. It would be loose and might be unpleasant, but I wouldn't free fall hundreds of feet to my death if I slipped. Maybe the ledge led to a hidden gully; maybe, despite the obscene exposure, this was the easiest way. I stood there for some time having an internal debate about which way to go.

I was working on a climbing guide that summer and had been sorting out the details of dozens of climbing routes in the Cascade Range and Olympic Mountains. This fieldwork had involved the enviable task of climbing several mountains each week, usually alone, especially on weekdays when my regular partners had to work. It's a common hazard of guidebook writers, who often end up soloing routes, thinking they have to do all the routes to be able to write definitively about them. As their deadlines approach, they get desperate and start taking chances: like climbing multiple peaks in a day, soloing rock climbs to count the bolts, venturing alone into uncharted territory. Despite the dangers, when you solo exposed rock day after day, you get used to it.

As I stood there, I persuaded myself that I had an obligation to explore every option. It would be negligent of me to tell my readers to go down the rotten gully if the ledge provided an easier alternative. If it didn't, I could turn back and try the other way. I was lying to myself, of course, making up an excuse to go down there. I knew that it was a hot day, ninety-five degrees, that I was separated from my partner, and that I'd allowed myself to become dehydrated. And intuitively, I knew that this was the wrong way, that I would never recommend it to anyone because it looked and felt too dangerous, but I wanted to go down there. The ledge was calling me.

Climbing down to the ledge was not difficult. I traversed it carefully, making sure I had solid handholds before moving my feet across, mindful of the drop-off behind me. The ledge dead-ended after 60 feet; the summit pinnacle stood tantalizingly close, a dark point of rock just 50 feet above me. I scanned the wall for a possible route, which did not look promising. The easy gully I had hoped to find had not materialized; instead, there was only a steep, blank wall. Below me, the shaded face fell away sharply to the sunlit icefield below.

I should not be here, I knew instinctively. *If I fall from here, no one will find me.*

No, that wasn't going to happen. Not today. I turned around and traversed back across the ledge. Or started to, but after a couple of moves I took another look at the summit pinnacle and stopped.

From this angle, I could see a crack running up the wall to a higher ledge not far below the summit. *That might be a route*, I thought. *It would be real climbing though, up near-vertical rock with oppressive exposure. One slip, a loose hold, and I'd fall a long way.*

No, I told myself again. *It's a bad idea.*

It doesn't look that hard, a voice said. *You may as well try it.*

I moved back a few feet and gave it a closer look. The crack was deep and solid, so I jammed a hand in it and pulled myself up. The first moves were easy, with big footholds and solid edges. Several moves above the ledge, the crack widened to fist size. I jammed and laybacked my way upward and was soon manteling onto the higher ledge, which angled down to a stunningly exposed spot just below the summit pinnacle. But there was no gully, just a dihedral, dead vertical, leaving me seemingly stranded just a few feet below the summit. Seeing a crack in the corner, I stuck my fingers in as far as they'd go and gave a tug. Solid.

I looked down and considered my situation. The face fell away steeply, how far I could not tell. If I fell, I'd free fall a long way before I hit the next ledge. From there I would bounce out of control, hitting ledge after ledge before finally landing broken and bloody on the white snow far below.

Go for it, the voice implored. *The summit's right there.*

I knew I shouldn't do it; I had a wife and kids after all, people who loved me and relied on me. *Wasn't I being reckless, risking everything for—for what? To get to the summit of an obscure peak so I could write about it in a guidebook? There was an easier way. There had to be.* I should have turned back. I should have taken the gully. But I'd chosen the dangerous way; felt the twitch and followed it into the unknown.

It wasn't too late, though—I could still turn back. I could downclimb the crack, retrace my steps across the ledge, go back through the notch, and scramble down the gully, but I didn't want to. I felt a strange comfort here. I felt no fear. This was where I was meant to be, for better or for worse. I turned back toward the summit, jammed my fingers deep in the crack and pulled upward, stemming and edging carefully up the dihedral. It was joyous.

A loose block guarded the notch. If I had grabbed it, it would certainly have pulled loose and sent me flying. I had to do a few delicate stemming moves without handholds to get past it, but I didn't hesitate. Looking down at the open air beneath my feet, I smiled at the insane pleasure of it. There was nowhere I would have rather been at that moment.

Still after reaching the top, I felt slightly ill at ease standing on the edge of the small, fantastically exposed summit block and peering down the mountain. It was strange to feel so vulnerable there after feeling so confident on the exposed face, standing on narrow ledges, jamming up cracks, stemming through the final corner. I had felt more comfortable because there was something to hold onto, even if it was only a few fingers clinging to an inch-wide edge. Balancing on the narrow summit felt precarious. I was reminded of my first climb, when I looked down the east face of The Tooth and felt a sudden urge to jump into the void. But now, looking down and imagining what it would be like to fall that far, I didn't recoil in horror. The void and I were old friends. There was no reason to be afraid.

A few minutes later, I heard scuffing on the rock below me and looked down to see Morgan climbing up from the highest notch.

"How'd you get around the second gendarme?" I asked him.

"Down the gully and across a ledge," he said. "It was easy. Which way did you go?"

"The wrong way," I told him, smiling. "Definitely the wrong way."

AUTHOR'S NOTE

After two years of intensive research and writing on the subject, I don't disagree with John Long's opinion that "there is no objective truth to any judgment per soloing." I have not tried to make a definitive judgment about the merits of climbing without a rope; I have only explored what motivates people to pursue free soloing despite the risk and emotional toll. Is free soloing crazy? A death wish? Or a life-affirming activity that has positive emotional and psychological benefits? I think I know, but know others will disagree.

Because people have strong opinions about free soloing, some will inevitably criticize this book, possibly claiming that I am romanticizing free soloing or encouraging others to try it. Others may suggest that I wrote it for egotistical reasons, to let everyone know what a badass I once was. I wasn't. I was just one of many young men (and a few women) who were inspired to try it, got delusions of grandeur, pushed a little too far, and were lucky to have survived. If anything, I hope my story will inspire someone *not* to solo, or at least to more deeply examine their motivation and the risks involved. While free soloing can be life-affirming, it can also kill you.

This is not a comprehensive history of free soloing. I included characters and stories related to my narrative and the questions I sought to explore. The door is open to build on this foundation, and I look forward to seeing what direction other writers take this fascinating subject.

At times this book examines the lives and mental states of many highly regarded free soloists, including some who are deceased. While I do not speculate or make any personal judgments, the book does consider what they or others—including friends, family, and mental health experts—had already said. I don't necessarily agree with any psychological diagnoses offered by researchers. As Ernest Becker wrote, we're all crazy.

Peter Croft free soloing Clean Crack *(5.11b), Squamish, British Columbia* (Photo by Jeff Smoot)

ACKNOWLEDGMENTS

The idea for this book came from a social-media post expressing concern that the film *Free Solo* might inspire someone to imitate Alex Honnold. That got me thinking about what had inspired me to take up free soloing. After watching the film several times, I had more questions than answers, so I started writing. I initially thought it might make for an interesting article but soon realized that the subject was too deep and "messy" (as Sharon Wood put it) to be contained in the pages of a magazine. If I was going to write about it, to quote Alex Honnold, I "might as well go big."

Of course, the task of writing this book would have been impossible without the contributions of the many people who shared their experiences and views about free soloing or engaged me in a friendly debate that helped me reframe some of my thoughts. Some offered advice about books, articles, research papers, blogs, and films that might be useful; others helped me locate elusive interview subjects, or sat down with me for a few minutes to chat. Although not everyone's contribution was featured in the book, all those who talked to me or provided their support, whether they knew it or not, have my deep appreciation, including but certainly not limited to Peter Croft, Ron Fawcett, Barry Blanchard, Simon Carter, Alexander Huber, Mark Twight, John Long, Mark Hudon, Bob Horan, Kerwin Klein, Luke Mehall, Chris Weidner, Rolo Garabotti, Barb Clemes, Matthew Pain, David Roberts, Maria Coffey, Paul Diffley, Dave Barnes, Blue Hargreaves, Andrew Logerwell, Dave MacLeod, Claire MacLeod, Michael Meadows, John Middendorf, Andrew Waite, Brittany Goris, Michael Stanton, Ben Tibbetts, Doug Weaver, Shannon Sperry, Linda Ebberson, and Christine Fitzgerald.

I cannot express enough my gratitude to those who consented to be interviewed for this book or who provided detailed written responses to my persistent emails, many of whom shared personal stories about their own experiences and challenges, and to the many experts who took the time to speak or correspond with me about their research. While not everyone was willing to talk, and many climbers I contacted either declined an interview or simply did not respond, the contribution of those who did was invaluable: Rowena Fletcher-Wood, Geoff Powter, Eric Brymer, Jacob Sparks, Ed Mosshart, Arno Ilgner, Dierdre Wolownick, Sharon Wood, Hazel Findlay, Leslie Flood, Mike Flood, Joshua Ourada, Russ Clune, Scott Franklin, Henry Barber, Alan Watts, Michael Layton, Mark Radtke, Peter Mortimer, Dan Krauss, Ryan Jurkowski, Justin Martin, Drew Ruana, Rudy Ruana, Chris Ruana, Matt Robertson, Maren Nelson, August Welch, Archer Welch, and Don Smoot.

I am especially indebted to David Smart for introducing me to stories about the Bedouins of the Wadi Rum, bird snatchers of St. Kilda, birdmen of Rapanui, and the early Queensland mountaineers, and permitting generous reference to his excellent biographies of Paul Preuss and Emilio Comici. Also to Nick O'Connell for his guidance, encouragement, and critique and for permitting the generous use of the interviews in *Beyond Risk*; to Sarah Wolfe for her excellent transcription of many hours of interviews; to Paul Ross for letting me stay at his home and for sharing stories and photos of his climbing exploits; and to Joanna Croston and Kenna Ozbick for providing access to the Banff Centre's recorded programs.

My thanks to Alex Honnold, Jimmy Chin, and Elizabeth Chai Vasarhelyi for making *Free Solo*, and thus setting off the chain of events that led to this book. Thanks, too, to Mike Hoover for making *Solo* and to my fifth-grade teacher, Richard Barcott, for choosing to show it to us that afternoon so many years ago. I'm sure he did not know what a profound effect it would have on me.

Of course, thanks to my publisher and editors, Kate Rogers, Emily White, Laura Lancaster, and Laura Shauger, and everyone else at Mountaineers Books who contributed to making this book possible, including shepherding it through some rough early drafts.

I'm especially grateful to my wife, Beth Harman, for tolerating my bad habit of writing books about climbing, and for supporting me while I selfishly toil away at them. And, as always, I am thankful to my parents for letting me run wild in the mountains in my youth.

SELECT SOURCES

BOOKS

Achey, Jeff, Robert Godfrey, and Chelton Dudley. *Climb!: The History of Rock Climbing in Colorado*. Seattle: Mountaineers Books, 2002.

Agnafors, M. "The Ethics of Free-Soloing." In *Climbing: Philosophy for Everyone*, edited by S. E. Schmid, 158–68. Oxford: UK Wiley-Blackwell, 2010.

Allhoff, Fritz, ed. *Climbing: Philosophy for Everyone*. Chichester, UK: Blackwell, 2010.

Anderson, Ben. *Cities, Mountains and Being Modern in Fin-de-Siècle England and Germany*. London: Palgrave Macmillan, 2020.

Auer, Hansjörg. *Südwand: Vom Free-Solo-Kletterer zum Profibergsteiger*, Munich: Piper, 2017.

Bane, Michael. *Over the Edge: A Regular Guy's Odyssey in Extreme Sports*. New York: Macmillan, 1996.

Becker, Ernest. *The Denial of Death*. New York: Free Press, 1973.

Caldwell, Tommy. *The Push: A Climber's Journey of Endurance, Risk, and Going Beyond Limits*. New York: Viking, 2017.

Carr, Cynthia. *On Edge: Performance at the End of the Twentieth Century*. Rev. ed. Middletown, CT: Wesleyan University Press, 2008.

Coffey, Maria. *Where the Mountain Casts Its Shadow: The Dark Side of Extreme Adventure*. New York: St. Martin's, 2003.

Comici, Emilio. *Alpinismo Eroico*. Milan: Hoepli, 1942.

Csikszentmihalyi, Mihaly. *Flow: The Psychology of Optimal Experience*. New York: HarperPerennial, 1991.

Davis, Steph. *Learning to Fly: A Memoir of Hanging On and Letting Go*. New York: Touchstone, 2013.

Durkheim, Émile. *Suicide: A Study in Sociology*. 1897. London: Penguin, 2007.

Foster, Steven. *The Book of the Vision Quest: Personal Transformation in the Wilderness*. New York: Prentice Hall, 1988.

Gonzales, Laurence. *Deep Survival: Who Lives, Who Dies, and Why*. New York: Norton, 2017.

Grant, Richard. *God's Middle Finger: Into the Lawless Heart of the Sierra Madre*. New York: Free Press, 2008.

Hankinson, Alan. *The First Tigers: The Early History of Rock Climbing in the Lake District*. London: J. M. Dent & Sons, 1972.

Hill, Lynn. *Climbing Free: My Life in the Vertical World*. New York: W. W. Norton, 2002.

Holiday, Ryan. *Ego Is the Enemy*. New York: Portfolio/Penguin, 2016.

Honnold, Alex, and David Roberts. *Alone on the Wall*. New York: Norton, 2016.

Hunt, Tom. *Cliffs of Despair: A Journey to the Edge*. New York: Random House, 2006.

Ilgner, Arno. *The Rock Warrior's Way: Mental Training for Climbers*. La Vergne, TN: Desiderata Institute, 2006.

Jamison, Kay Redfield. *Night Falls Fast: Understanding Suicide*. New York: Vintage, 2000.

Jones, Robert Alun. *Emile Durkheim: An Introduction to Four Major Works*. Beverly Hills, CA: Sage Publications, Inc., 1986.

König, Erich, ed. *Empor! Georg Winklers Tagebuch in Memorium. Ein Riegen von Bergfahrten hervorragender Alpinisten von heute*. Leipzig, 1905.

Krakauer, Jon. *Eiger Dreams: Ventures among Men and Mountains*. New York: Anchor, 1990.

Kroeber, Theodora. *Ishi: Last of His Tribe*. New York: Bantam Starfire Books, 1973.

———. *Ishi in Two Worlds: A Biography of the Last Wild Indian in North America*. Berkeley: University of California Press, 2011.

Lammer, Eugen Guido. *Jungborn: Bergfahrten und Höhengedanken Eines Einsamen Pfadsuchers*. Munich: Austrian Alpine Club, 1935.

Lee, Bruce. *Tao of Jeet Kune Do*. Valencia, CA: Black Belt Communications, 2011.

Lee, Chip. *On Edge: The Life and Climbs of Henry Barber*. Boston: Appalachian Mountain Club, 1982.

Linden, David J. *The Compass of Pleasure: How Our Brains Make Fatty Foods, Orgasm, Exercise, Marijuana, Generosity, Vodka, Learning, and Gambling Feel So Good*. New York: Viking, 2011.

Long, John, ed. *The High Lonesome: Epic Solo Climbing Stories*. Helena, MT: Falcon, 1999.

Lyng, Stephen. *Edgework: The Sociology of Risk-Taking*. New York: Routledge, 2005.

Mallory, George Leigh. "The Mountaineer as Artist." In *The Armchair Mountaineer*, edited by David Reuter and John Thorn, 172–79. Birmingham, AL: Menasha Ridge Press, 1989.

Martin, Martin. *A Late Voyage to St. Kilda: The Remotest of All the Hebrides or Western Isles of Scotland. With a History of the Island, Natural Moral and Topographical. Wherein Is an Account of Their Customs Religion, Fish, Fowl, &c.: As Also a Relation of a Late Imposter There, Pretended to Be Sent by St. John Baptist*. London: D. Brown & T. Goodwin, 1689.

Maslow, Abraham H. *Religions, Values, and Peak Experiences*. Columbus: Ohio State University Press, 1964.

———. *Toward a Psychology of Being*. New York: D. Van Nostrand Company, 1968.

Matthiessen, Peter. *The Snow Leopard*. New York: Penguin, 2008.

Meadows, Michael. *The Living Rock: The Invention of Climbing in Eastern Australia*. Brisbane: Living Rock Press, 2015.

Mehall, Luke. *American Climber*. Durango, CO: Benighted Publications, 2016.

Messner, Reinhold. *Free Spirit: A Climber's Life*. Seattle: Mountaineers Books, 1998.

Messner, Reinhold, and Horst Höfler, eds. *Eugen Guido Lammer: Durst nach Todesgefahr*. Augsburg: Steiger, 1999.

Mitchell, Richard G., Jr. *Mountain Experience: The Psychology and Sociology of Adventure*. Chicago: University of Chicago Press, 1983.

Muir, John. *Mountaineering Essays*. Salt Lake City: Peregrine, 1989.

———. *My First Summer in the Sierra*. Boston: Houghton Mifflin, 1979. https://vault.sierraclub.org/john_muir_exhibit/writings/my_first_summer_in_the_sierra.

———. *A Thousand-Mile Walk to the Gulf*. Boston: Houghton Mifflin, 1981. https://vault.sierraclub.org/john_muir_exhibit/writings/a_thousand_mile_walk_to_the_gulf.

Murphy, Michael, and Rhea A. White. *In the Zone: Transcendent Experience in Sports*. New York: Penguin, 1995.

Nietzsche, Friedrich. *A Nietzsche Reader*. Translated by R. J. Hollingdale. New York: Penguin Classics, 1977.

O'Connell, Nick. *Beyond Risk: Conversations with Climbers*. Seattle: Mountaineers Books, 1993.

O'Grady, John P. *Pilgrims to the Wild*. Salt Lake City: University of Utah Press, 1993.

Parry, Jim, Simon Robinson, Nick J. Watson, and Mark Nesti. *Sport and Spirituality: An Introduction*. Abingdon, UK: Routledge, 2007.

Powter, Geoff. *Inner Ranges: An Anthology of Mountain Thoughts and Mountain People*. Victoria, BC: Rocky Mountain Books, 2018.

———. *Strange and Dangerous Dreams: The Fine Line Between Adventure and Madness*. Seattle: Mountaineers Books, 2006.

Radtke, Mark. *A Canvas of Rock*. Burton in Kendal: 2QT, 2012.

Ray, Michael, and Rochelle Myers. *Creativity in Business*. New York: Doubleday, 1986.

Robinson, Doug. *The Alchemy of Action*. Kirkwood, CA: Moving Over Stone, 2013.

Saint Sing, Susan. *Spirituality of Sport: Balancing Body and Soul*. Cincinnati: St. Anthony Messenger, 2004.

Sands, J. *Out of the World, or Life in St. Kilda*. Edinburgh: MacLachlan & Stewart, 1878.

Sartre, Jean-Paul. *Being and Nothingness*. New York: Washington Square Press, 2021.

Smart, David. *Emilio Comici: Angel of the Dolomites*. Victoria, BC: Rocky Mountain Books, 2020.

———. *Paul Preuss: Lord of the Abyss*. Victoria, BC: Rocky Mountain Books, 2019.

Smith, William Parry Haskett. *Climbing in the British Isles*. 3 vols. London, 1894.

Sōhō, Takuan. *The Unfettered Mind*. Translated by William Scott Wilson. Berkeley, CA: Shambhala, 2012. Originally pubished as *Fudōchi Shimmyō Roku*.

Synnott, Mark. *The Impossible Climb: Alex Honnold, El Capitan, and the Climbing Life*. New York: Dutton, 2018.

Talbot, Margo. *All That Glitters: A Climber's Journey through Addiction and Depression*. Victoria, BC: Rocky Mountain Books, 2020.

Tibbetts, Ben. *Alpenglow: The Finest Climbs on the 4000m Peaks of the Alps*. Self-published, 2019.

Twight, Mark. *Kiss or Kill: Confessions of a Serial Climber*. Seattle: Mountaineers Books, 2001.

———. *Refuge*. Non-Prophet, 2019.

Whitehouse, Annie. "An Interview with Derek Hersey." In *The High Lonesome*, edited by John Long, 73–85. Helena, MT: Falcon Publishing, 1999.

Whymper, Edward. *Scrambles amongst the Alps in the Years 1860–69*. Washington, DC: National Geographic Society, 2002.

Wolownick, Dierdre. *The Sharp End of Life: A Mother's Story*. Seattle: Mountaineers Books, 2018.

SCHOLARLY ARTICLES AND PRESENTATIONS

Balocchini, E., G. Chiamenti, and A. Lamborghini. "Adolescents: Which Risks for Their Life and Health?" *Journal of Preventive Medicine and Hygiene* 54, no. 4 (2013): 191–94.

Brymer, Eric, and Robert Schweitzer. "Extreme Sports Are Good for Your Health: A Phenomenological Understanding of Fear and Anxiety in Extreme Sport." *Journal of Health Psychology*, 18 (June 2012).

———. "Extreme Sports as a Facilitator of Ecocentricity and Positive Life Changes." *World Leisure Journal* 51, no. 1 (2009): 47–53.

———. "Risk Taking in Extreme Sports: A Phenomenological Perspective." *Annals of Leisure Research* 13, no. 1–2 (2010): 218–238.

Brymer, Eric, Robert Schweitzer, and L. G. Oades. "Extreme Sports: A Positive Transformation in Courage and Humility." *Journal of Humanistic Psychology* 49, no. 1 (2009): 114–26.

Casey, B. J., and Kristina Caudle. "The Teenage Brain: Self Control." *Sage Journals* 22, no. 2 (2013): 87.

Conroy, Christina, and Gina Gonzalez. "Off Belay! The Morality of Free-Soloing." *Sport, Ethics and Philosophy: Journal of the British Philosophy of Sport Association* 13, no. 1 (2019): 62–77.

Dayan, Jacque, Alix Bernard, Bertrand Olliac, Anne-Sophie Mailhes, and Solenn Kermarrec. "Adolescent Brain Development, Risk-Taking and Vulnerability to Addiction." *Journal of Physiology-Paris* 104, no. 5 (2010): 279–86.

Hames, Jennifer L. "An Urge to Jump Affirms the Urge to Live: An Empirical Examination of the High Place Phenomenon." *Journal of Affective Disorders* 136, no. 3 (2012): 114–20.

Heirene, Robert M., et al. "Addiction in Extreme Sports: An Exploration of Withdrawal States in Rock Climbers." *Journal of Behavior Addictions* 5, no. 2 (2016): 332–41.

Hoffmann, Edward. "Abraham Maslow's Life and Unfinished Legacy." *Japanese Journal of Administrative Science* 17, no. 3 (2004): 133–38. www.jstage.jst.go.jp/article/jaas1986/17/3/17_3_133/_pdf.

Knutson, Kari, and Frank Farley. "Type T Personality and Learning Strategies." Paper presented at annual meeting of American Educational Research Association, 1995.

Kringelbach, Morten L., and Kent C. Berridge. "The Neuroscience of Happiness and Pleasure." *Social Research* 77, no. 2 (Summer 2010): 659–78.

Krueger, D. W., and R. Hutcherson. "Suicide Attempts by Rock-Climbing Falls." *Journal of Suicide and Life-Threatening Behavior* 8, no. 1 (1978): 41–45. https://pubmed.ncbi.nlm.nih.gov/675771.

Levensen, Michael R. "Risk Taking and Personality." *Journal of Personality and Social Psychology* 58, no. 6 (1990): 1073–80.

Llewellyn, David J., Xavier Sanchez, Amanda Asghar, and Gareth Jones. "Self-Efficacy, Risk Taking and Performance in Rock Climbing." *Personality and Individual Differences* 45 (2008): 75–81.

Luna, Beatriz. "Adolescent Decision Maaking and Legal Responsibility: The State of the Adolescent Brain," Colloquium on Law, Neuroscience, and Criminal Justice, Stanford University, March 2013.

Lyng, Stephen. "Edgework: A Social Psychological Analysis of Voluntary Risk Taking," *American Journal of Sociology* 95, no. 4 (1990): 855–86.

Maslow, Abraham. "A Theory of Human Motivation." *Psychological Review* 50, no. 4: 370–96.

McDonald, Matthew, Stephen Wearing, and Jess Ponting. "The Nature of Peak Experience in Wilderness." *The Humanistic Psychologist* 37, no. 4 (2009): 370–85. https://opus.lib.uts.edu.au/bitstream/10453/11843/1/2008002447.pdf.

Meadows, Michael. "The Changing Role of Queensland Newspapers in Imagining Leisure and Recreation." *Ejournalist*, 2001. https://ejournalist.com.au/public_html/v1n2/MEADOWS.pdf.

Nicholson, Nigel, Emma Soane, Mark Fenton-O'Creevy, and Paul Willman. "Personality and Domain-Specific Risk Taking." *Journal of Risk Research* 8, no. 2 (March 2005): 157–76.

Pain, M. T. G., and M. A. Pain, "Essay: Risk Taking in Sport." *The Lancet* 336 (2005): 533–34.

Preuss, Paul. "The Piton Dispute." Translated by Randolph Burks. Issuu.com, 2011. Articles originally published in 1911.

Tofler, Ian R., Brandon M. Hyatt, and David S. Tofler. "Psychiatric Aspects of Extreme Sports: Three Case Studies." *National Center for Biotechnology Information* 22 (2018): 17–71.

Zilboorg, Gregory. "Fear of Death." *Psychoanalytic Quarterly* 12, no. 4 (1943): 464–75.

Zuckerman, Marvin, Kuhlman, D. Michael. "Personality and Risk-Taking: Common Biosocial Factors." *Journal of Personality* 68, no. 6 (2000): 999–1029.

NEWSPAPER AND MAGAZINE ARTICLES

"Adventurers of the Year 2005 – Michael Reardon: Free Soloist." *National Geographic*, 2005. www.nationalgeographic.com/adventure/article/michael-reardon-2005.

Ament, Pat. "Why Is Peter Croft Our Hero?" *Climbing Art*, 1991.

Bachar, John. "What I've Learned." *Rock and Ice*, 2016. www.rockandice.com/people /john-bachar-what-ive-learned.

Barrington, R. M. "Ascent of Stack-na-Biorrach-St. Kilda." *Alpine Journal*, 1913.

Bartlett, Steve. "Derek Hersey, 36, Climbs to the End." *Climbing*, August/September 1993, 54–56.

Bisharat, Andrew. "Almighty Dolomites." *Evening Sends*, 2014. https://eveningsends.com /almighty-dolomites.

Blowers, Cody. "Shenandoah Student Dies in Rock Climbing Accident." *St. George Utah News*, March 20, 2019. https://valleynewstoday.com/news/shenandoah -student-dies-in-rock-climbing-accident/article_4d59f61c-4b24-11e9-9e93 -8f99fe110ddb.html.

Calio, Jim. "True Grip." *People*, May 5, 1985.

Callanan, Tom. "High on Danger." *Chicago Tribune*, October 23, 1988.

Cassin, Riccardo. "Italian Climbing between the Wars." Translated by S. K. Armistead. *Alpine Journal*, 1972, 149–56. www.alpinejournal.org.uk/Contents/Contents_1972 _files/AJ%201972%20149-156%20Cassin%20Italy.pdf.

Cherry, Christopher. "China's Cliff-Climbing 'Spiderwoman.'" *BBC News*, September 15, 2017. www.bbc.com/worklife/article/20170915-chinas-cliff-climbing-spiderwoman.

Chotzinoff, Robin. "Life on the Edge." *Westword*, 1995. www.westword.com/news /life-on-the-edge-5055629.

Churcher, Al. "Two Is One Too Many." *Climbers Club Journal*, 1991.

Clune, Russ. "Fool's Goal: Shawangunk Solo Climbs." *Climbing*, 1986.

Copeland, Drew. "The Calculated Madness of Marc-André Leclerc." *Climbing*, December 9, 2021.

Dadio, Jess. "What's Keeping Austin Weird?" *Blue Ridge Outdoors*, 2016. www.blueridge outdoors.com/climbing/whats-keeping-austin-weird.

de Bernieres, Louis. "Legends of the Fall." *Harper's*, January 1996.

Douglas, Ed. "John Bachar: American Rock Climber and Leading Exponent of the Technique Known as Soloing." *The Guardian*, July 10, 2009. www.theguardian.com /world/2009/jul/10/john-bacher-rock-climber.

Fairlie, H. "Fear of Living: America's Morbid Aversion to Risk." *The New Republic*, 1989.

Fairley, Bruce. "Peter Croft and the Mountaineering Tradition of Manners." *Canadian Alpine Journal*, 1988.

Goldman, Erica. "Why Climb Mountains? John Muir and Clarence King at a Historical Crossroads of American Climbing." *Sierra Club*, 1995. https://vault.sierraclub.org /john_muir_exhibit/life/why_climb_mountains_by_erica_goldman.aspx.

Graham, Pat. "Rock Star: After 'Free Solo' Documentary, Climber Alex Honnold Unsure of Next Journey." *Associated Press*, May 27, 2019.

Hadas, Pamela. "Ringling Bros. Present: The Lucky Lucie Lamort." *Poetry*, August 1982.

"Hansjörg Auer Free Solo Attraverso il Pesce—Fish Route—in Marmolada." *Planet Mountain*, May 23, 2007. www.planetmountain.com/en/news/climbing/hansjarg -auer-free-solo-attraverso-il-pesce-in-marmolada.html.

Heller, Seth. "A View from the Top." *Rock and Ice*, February 2017, 32.

Hevesi, Dennis. "Michael J. Ybarra, Extreme-Sports Reporter, Dies at 45." *New York Times*, July 6, 2012. www.nytimes.com/2012/07/07/business/media/michael-j-ybarra -author-and-extreme-sports-reporter-is-dead-at-45.html.

Honnold, Alex. "Freerider: Free Solo on El Capitan." *AAC Publications*, 2018.

Jackson, Jeff. "Naked Soloist Is Saner Than I Am." *Rock and Ice* online, April 6, 2015. rockandice.com/tuesday_night_bouldering/tnb_naked_soloist_is_saner_than_me/.

Johnson, Kevin. "A Free Soloist Remembers His Yosemite Free Fall." *Ouside*, June 29, 2021. www.outsideonline.com/outdoor-adventure/climbing/yosemite-free-solo -fall-josh-ourada-nutcracker.

Keith, David. "Free-Soloing for Profit: A Professor's Take on Free Soloing Culture." *Gripped*, April 11, 2021.

Lack, Clem. "Mountain Climbers of Queensland." *Sunday Mail Magazine Section*, July 10, 1938, 1.

Leibovitch, Zoe. "Broken Holds and Lost Lives: How Loose Rock and Free Soloing Ended Two Climbers' Lives." *Climbing*, July 5, 2019. climbing.com/news/broken_holds_and _lost_lives_how_loose_rock.

Levy, Michael. "Climbing Free: The Ropeless Ascents of Matt Bush." *Outdoor Journal*. www.outdoorjournal.com/uncategorized/climbing-free-ropeless-ascents-matt-bush.

———. "Fallen Soloist: 'I'm Remorseful for What Happened.'" *Climbing*, April 29, 2021.

Linden, David J. "The Neuroscience of Pleasure." *HuffPost*, July 7, 2011. www.huffpost .com/entry/compass-pleasure_b_890342.

Long, John. "John Yablonsky, 1956–1991." *Climbing*, December 1991, 24.

———. "The Only Blasphemy." *Backpacker*, October–November 1981, 102.

Longstaff, T. G. "Mountains in the Desert." *Ladies Alpine Club Journal* (1953), 13–19.

Lowther, Alex. "Less and Less Alone: Alex Honnold." *Alpinist* Summer 2011.

Lucas, James. "The Fallen Soloist: The Impact of a 60-foot Free Soloing Fall on Boulder's Second Flatiron." *Climbing*, May 15, 2019. www.climbing.com/news/the-fallen-soloist.

MacKinnon, J. B. "The Strange Brain of the World's Greatest Solo Climber: Alex Honnold Doesn't Experience Fear Like the Rest of Us." *Nautilus*, August 11, 2016. https ://nautil.us/issue/39/sport/the-strange-brain-of-the-worlds-greatest-solo-climber.

McClellan, Dennis. "Michael Reardon, 42; Free Solo Rock Climber Is Swept Away by Rogue Wave." *Los Angeles Times*, July 19, 2007. www.latimes.com/archives/la-xpm -2007-jul-19-me-reardon19-story.html.

McMahon, Bucky. "I Am Birdman, Hear Me Roar." *Men's Journal*. www.mensjournal .com/health-fitness/i-am-birdman-hear-me-roar-19691231.

"No Rope, No Fear: Free Solo Climber Matt Bush Climbs Table Mountain without Ropes." Video. *Red Bulletin*, January 19, 2017.

O'Donovan, Barry. "Remembering the Extraordinary Life of Free Climber Michael Reardon." *Irish Examiner*, January 4, 2014. www.irishexaminer.com/lifestyle/arid- 20254208.html.

Osius, Alison. "Longtime SoCal Climber Critical Following Free Solo Fall, Air Rescue at Stoney Point." *Rock and Ice*, June 22, 2020. www.rockandice.com/climbing-accidents /longtime-socal-climber-critical-following-fall-and-air-rescue-at-stoney-point.

———. "On the Earl." *Rock and Ice*, January 2018.

Paumgarten, Nick. "We Are a Camera." *New Yorker*, September 15, 2014. www .newyorker.com/magazine/2014/09/22/camera.

Perlman, Eric. "Backcountry Samurai: In Defense of the Wilderness Lunatic." *Backpacker*, May 1986.

Peruzzi, Marc. "Stop the Progression Already." *Outside*, January 23, 2018. www.outsideonline.com/culture/opinion/stop-progression.

Perzner, Sonya. "On Fear, Climbing, and Depression." *Climbing Zine*, vol. 12.

Poe, Edgar Allan. "The Imp of the Perverse." *Graham's Magazine*, July 1845. https://poestories.com/read/imp.

Potter, Dean. "A Life Lived on the Edge." *Outside* online, May 2015. www.outsideonline.com/outdoor-adventure/climbing/dean-potter-lived-life-edge.

———. "What I've Learned." *Climbing*, May 17, 2021. www.climbing.com/people/dean-potter-shares-views-free-solo-rock-climbing-base-jumping.

Rapold, Nicholas. "'Up There, I Have No Fear': Philippe Petit on 'Man on Wire.'" *New York Sun*, July 21, 2008.

Renda, Matthew. "The Wizardry of Dan Osman: Tracing the Rise and Fall of One of Tahoe's Most Talented and Charismatic Athletes." *Tahoe Quarterly*, 2018. https://tahoequarterly.com/best-of-tahoe-2018/wizardry-dan-osman.

Robinson, Doug. "The Climber as Visionary." *Ascent*, 1969. Reprinted in issue 242 in 2017.

———. "Running Talus." *Chouinard Equipment Catalog*, 1975. Available at www.movingoverstone.com.

"Rock Climbers Rescale Heights of Satisfaction as Tourists Return." *China Daily*, updated July 2, 2020. www.chinadaily.com.cn/a/202007/02/WS5efd0afca31083481725693c.html.

Rowell, Galen. "Climbing Half Dome the Hard Way." *National Geographic*, June 1974, 782–791.

Ryan, Timothy. "Public Enemy." *Climbing*, April/May 1991, 66–133.

Salahi, Lara. "The Science Behind Why Some Seek Danger for Fun." Boston.com, May 27, 2015. www.boston.com/news/science/2015/05/27/the-science-behind-why-some-seek-danger-for-fun.

Samet, Matt. "Crusty Corner: Free Soloing Sucks (And Why We're Going to Cover It Anyway)." *Climbing*, September 21, 2017. climbing.com/people/crusty-corner-free-soloing-sucks.

———. "Meet Mr. Producer." *Rock and Ice*, June 2005.

Siddique, Natalie. "Climber Spotlight: An Interview with Free Soloist, Matt Bush." Moja Gear. https://mojagear.com/interview-free-soloist-matt-bush.

Smoot, Jeff. "Peter Croft (Profile)." *Climbing*, June 1986.

Todhunter, Andrew. "The Preciptious World of Dan Osman." *Atlantic*, February 1996.

Truong, Timmy. "Boy Who Fell to Death at Snow Canyon State Park May Have Been Trying to 'Free Solo.'" *ABC News*, March 18, 2019. www.abc15.com/national/boy-who-fell-to-death-at-snow-canyon-state-park-may-have-been-trying-to-free-solo.

Twight, Mark. "Words with Climbing Legend Mark Twight." *Gripped*, 2019. https://gripped.com/profiles/words-with-climbing-legend-mark-twight.

Van Leuven, Chris. "Savage Arena: Soloing in Yosemite." *Adventure Sports Journal*, March 20, 2019.

Vučković, Aleska. "Easter Island's Birdman Cult: A Story of Struggle and Survival." *Ancient Origins*, February 2020. www.ancient-origins.net/ancient-places-americas/birdman-cult-0013253.

Ward, Mick. "Anthracite Eyes: A Tribute to John Syrett." *UK Climbing*, 2016. www.ukclimbing.com/articles/features/anthracite_eyes_-_a_tribute_to_john_syrett-8199.

Watterson, Johnny. "Game Changers: Living Beyond Fear Puts Alex Honnold Above All Others." *Irish Times*, July 15, 2020. www.irishtimes.com/sport/other-sports/game-changers-living-beyond-fear-puts-alex-honnold-above-all-others-1.4304416.

Weidner, Chris. "Nina Williams Risks It All in New REEL ROCK film: 'The High Road.'" *Daily Camera*, October 1, 2019. www.dailycamera.com/2019/10/01 /chris-weidner-nina-williams-risks-it-all-in-new-reel-rock-film-the-high-road.

Willman, David. "Derek Hersey Was a Free-Soloist, Using No Ropes or Equipment." *Los Angeles Times*, May 31, 1993. www.latimes.com/archives/la-xpm-1993-05-31-mn -41958-story.html.

Ybarra, Michael. "Climbing Alone, Risking it All." *Wall Street Journal*, August 11, 2009. www.wsj.com/articles/SB10001424052970204619004574320703021843332.

Zaleski, Luke. "Meet the California Crew That Brought Sex, Drugs, and Free Jazz to Rock Climbing—and Made It the Most Stylish Sport of the 1970s." *GQ*, September 19, 2013. www.gq.com/story/stonemasters-rock-climbing-oral-history.

THESES AND DISSERTATIONS

Grady, Brandy D. "Advertising in the X Games: An Attempt to Reach Generation Y." Master's thesis, Texas Tech University Library, 2005. https://ttu-ir.tdl.org/handle/2346/20018.

Heitzman, L. "The Plateau Experience in Context: An Intensive In-Depth Psychobiographical Case Study of Abraham Maslow's 'Post-Mortem Life.'" PhD diss., Saybrook University, 2003.

Holt, Lee Wallace. "Mountains, Mountaineering, and Modernity: A Cultural History of German and Austrian Mountaineering, 1900–1945." PhD diss., University of Texas at Austin, 2008. https://citeseerx.ist.psu.edu/viewdoc/download?doi=10.1.1.390.1279 &rep=rep1&type=pdf.

Sparks, Jacob Ray. "Extreme Sports: A Study of Free-Solo Rock Climbers." Master's thesis, Brigham Young University, December 1, 2016. BYU Scholars Archive.

BLOGS AND PERSONAL WEBSITES

Appleby, John. "The Paul Ross Interview." *Footless Crow* (blog), July 20, 2012. http://footlesscrow.blogspot.com/2012/07/the-paul-ross-interviewpart-one.html.

Auer, Hansjörg. Personal website. http://web.hansjoerg-auer.at.

Collins, Jim. "Hitting the Wall: Realizing That Vertical Limits Aren't." Jim Collins (website), September 2003. www.jimcollins.com/article_topics/articles/hitting-the-wall .html.

Fletcher-Wood, Rowena. "Call of the Void." *Things We Don't Know* (blog), March 21, 2019. https://blog.thingswedontknow.com/2019/03/the-call-of-void.html.

Gill, John. Personal website. www.johngill.net.

Howard, Tony. "Climbing the Bedouin Routes of Wadi Rum." *Cicerone* (blog). www.cicerone.co.uk/climbing-the-bedouin-routes-of-wadi-rum.

Howell, Austin. Personal website. Accessed July 15, 2019. https://web.archive.org /web/20181122070022/https://www.thefreesoloist.com.

Huber, Alexander. "Our Milestones." Personal website. https://huberbuam.de/en /our-milestones.html.

Ilgner, Arno. "Should I Free Solo?" *Arno's Blog, Warrior's Way*, December 14, 2019. warriorsway.com/should-i-free-solo.

MacLeod, Claire. "To Spain and Back." *Velvet Antlers Blog*, March 12, 2008. https://web .archive.org/web/20090429015814/http://www.velvetantlers.co.uk/2008/03/to -spain-and-back.html.

MacLeod, Dave. "8b+ Free Solo." Dave MacLeod (website), September 26, 2019. www.davemacleod.com/blog/freesolo8c?rq=darwin%20dixit.

———. "Training Climbs for Ben Nevis – 8c Solo." Dave MacLeod (website), March 12, 2008. https://web.archive.org/web/20111120012013/http://davemacleod.blogspot .com/2008/03/training-climbs-for-ben-nevis-8c-solo.html.

McCullogh, Gill. "What I Learned from 'Doctor Death.'" *Medium* (blog), January 6, 2020. https://medium.com/the-ascent/what-i-learned-from-doctor-death-2df95e85ff62.

Meadows, Michael. "The Living Rock: The Origins of Climbing in Eastern Australia." *Australian Climbing History* (blog). http://climbinghistoryoz.blogspot.com.

Reardon, Michael. Personal website. https://web.archive.org/web/20070814003208 /http://www.freesoloist.com.

Simone, Jada. "The Plateau Experience: Beyond Flow States." *Medium* (blog), December 1, 2017. https://medium.com/@jaidasimone/plateau-experience-hack -consciosness-1149db103481.

FORUMS

"Alex Honnold Free Solos Moonlight Buttress." Climber's Discussion Forum, SuperTopo, April 4, 2008. www.supertopo.com/climbers-forum/570480 /Alex-Honnold-Free-Solos-Moonlight-Buttress.

"Amazing Solo Stories . . ." Climber's Discussion Forum, SuperTopo, March 28, 2008. www.supertopo.com/climbers-forum/566549/Amazing-solo-stories.

"'Big Jim' Jewell." UK Climbing Forum, September 16, 2003. www.ukclimbing.com /forums/rock_talk/big_jim_jewell-57398.

"Dean Potter Appreciation [sic] Thread." Climber's Discussion Forum, SuperTopo, December 11, 2010. www.supertopo.com/climbers-forum/1342542/Dean-Potter -Appreciation-Thread.

"Dean Potter Interview Outside Magazine 2002." Climber's Discussion Forum, SuperTopo, March 27, 2012. www.supertopo.com/climbers-forum/1785758 /Dean-Potter-Interview-Outside-Magazine-2002.

"Discussion Topic." Climber's Discussion Forum, SuperTopo, July 13, 2010. www.supertopo.com/climbers-forum/1216869/Michael-Reardon.

"Georg Winkler." Climber's Discussion Forum, SuperTopo, March 31, 2016. www.super-topo.com/climbers-forum/2790396/Georg-Winkler.

"Honnold Free Solos El Cap!" Climber's Discussion Forum, SuperTopo, June 3, 2017. www.supertopo.com/climbers-forum/2981562/Honnold-Free-Solos-El-Cap.

"John Bachar—In Memory of a Great Man 1957–2009." Climber's Discussion Forum, SuperTopo, July 5, 2009. www.supertopo.com/climbers-forum/896012 /John-Bachar-In-memory-of-a-great-man-1957-2009.

"John Syrett—Who Is He?" UK Hillwalking Forum, October 1, 2004. www.ukclimbing .com/forums/rock_talk/john_syrett_-_who_is_he-102218.

"Michael Reardon In Memoriam." Climber's Discussion Forum, SuperTopo, July 20, 2007. www.supertopo.com/climbers-forum/419804/MICHAEL-REARDON -IN-MEMORIAM.

"Remembering Dean Potter and Graham Hunt." Climber's Discussion Forum, SuperTopo, May 17, 2015. www.supertopo.com/climbers-forum/2626754 /Remembering-Dean-Potter-and-Graham-Hunt.

"Remembering John Bachar." Climber's Discussion Forum, SuperTopo, July 5, 2017. www.supertopo.com/climbers-forum/2991236/Remembering-John-Bachar.

"Why Do We Idolize John 'Yabo' Yablanski [sic]?" Climber's Discussion Forum, SuperTopo, January 18, 2011. www.supertopo.com/climbers-forum/1385246 /Why-do-we-idolize-John-Yabo-Yablanski.

"Why Is This Man Smiling?" Climber's Discussion Forum, SuperTopo, December 15, 2004. www.supertopo.com/climbers-forum/49087/Why-is-this-man-smiling.

ABOUT THE
AUTHOR

Jeff Smoot is an outdoor adventure writer, photographer, and lawyer. He is the author of several hiking and climbing guides, as well as articles published in *Alpinist*, *Climbing*, *Backpacker*, *Outside*, and *Western American Literature*. His memoir, *Hangdog Days: Conflict, Change, and the Race for 5.14*, chronicling the evolution of sport climbing in the 1980s was a finalist for the Boardman Tasker Award for Mountain Literature and the Banff Mountain Book Competition.

A Seattle native, he resides in Honolulu where he is learning to overcome his fear of deep water and sharks. Find out what he's up to on Instagram @smootopia.

MOUNTAINEERS BOOKS

recreation • lifestyle • conservation

MOUNTAINEERS BOOKS is a leading publisher of mountaineering literature and guides—including our flagship title, *Mountaineering: The Freedom of the Hills*—as well as adventure narratives, natural history, and general outdoor recreation. Through our two imprints, Skipstone and Braided River, we also publish titles on sustainability and conservation. We are committed to supporting the environmental and educational goals of our organization by providing expert information on human-powered adventure, sustainable practices at home and on the trail, and preservation of wilderness.

The Mountaineers, founded in 1906, is a 501(c)(3) nonprofit outdoor recreation and conservation organization whose mission is to enrich lives and communities by helping people "explore, conserve, learn about, and enjoy the lands and waters of the Pacific Northwest and beyond." One of the largest such organizations in the United States, it sponsors classes and year-round outdoor activities throughout the Pacific Northwest, including climbing, hiking, backcountry skiing, snowshoeing, camping, kayaking, sailing, and more. The Mountaineers also supports its mission through its publishing division, Mountaineers Books, and promotes environmental education and citizen engagement. For more information, visit The Mountaineers Program Center, 7700 Sand Point Way NE, Seattle, WA 98115-3996; phone 206-521-6001; www.mountaineers .org; or email info@mountaineers.org.

Our publications are made possible through the generosity of donors and through sales of 700 titles on outdoor recreation, sustainable lifestyle, and conservation. To donate, purchase books, or learn more, visit us online:

MOUNTAINEERS BOOKS
1001 SW Klickitat Way, Suite 201 • Seattle, WA 98134
800-553-4453 • mbooks@mountaineersbooks.org • www.mountaineersbooks.org

An independent nonprofit publisher since 1960

YOU MAY ALSO LIKE:

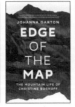